Game AI Pro 360

Game AI Pro 360

Guide to Movement and Pathfinding

Edited by
Steve Rabin

CRC Press
Taylor & Francis Group
Boca Raton London New York

CRC Press is an imprint of the
Taylor & Francis Group, an **informa** business

CRC Press
Taylor & Francis Group
6000 Broken Sound Parkway NW, Suite 300
Boca Raton, FL 33487-2742

© 2020 by Taylor & Francis Group, LLC
CRC Press is an imprint of Taylor & Francis Group, an Informa business

No claim to original U.S. Government works

Printed on acid-free paper

International Standard Book Number-13: 978-0-367-15111-9 (paperback)
International Standard Book Number-13: 978-0-367-15113-3 (hardback)

Visit the Taylor & Francis Web site at
http://www.taylorandfrancis.com

and the CRC Press Web site at
http://www.crcpress.com

Contents

About the Editor

Steve Rabin has been a key figure in the game AI community for more than a decade and is currently a principal software engineer at Nintendo Technology Development. After initially working as an AI engineer at several Seattle startups, he managed and edited seven game AI books in the "Game AI Pro" series and the "AI Game Programming Wisdom" series. He also edited the book *Introduction to Game Development* and has more than two dozen articles published in the "Game Programming Gems" series. He has been an invited keynote speaker at several AI conferences, founded the AI Game Programmers Guild in 2008, and founded the GDC AI Summit where he has been a summit adviser since 2009. Steve is a principal lecturer at the DigiPen Institute of Technology, Redmond, Washington, where he has taught game AI since 2006. He earned a BS in computer engineering and an MS in computer science, both at the University of Washington, Seattle, Washington.

About the Contributors

Bobby Anguelov is a South African expat currently working as a senior programmer at Ubisoft, Montreal, Canada, primarily in the field of animation. Prior to joining Ubisoft, he worked as an AI/animation programmer at IO-Interactive. Outside of the game industry, he has worked in a variety of roles ranging from computer graphics lecturer to enterprise software consultant. Bobby holds an MS in computer science from the University of Pretoria, South Africa, with a focus on computational intelligence and computer graphics.

Stephen Bjore graduated from Washington State University with a bachelor's degree in computer science, and later acquired a BS in real-time interactive simulation from DigiPen Institute of Technology. After graduating, he spent 2 years working at Wizards of the Coast, initially on various video game prototypes and later on the server side for *Magic the Gathering Online*. In 2008, he moved to Nintendo of America, where he became a part of its Software Development Support Group. After several years with SDSG, he switched over to an internal development group which has been working on 3DS and Wii-U projects.

Daniel Brewer graduated from University of Natal Durban, South Africa, in 2000 with a BSc (engineering) in electronic engineering focusing on artificial intelligence, control systems, and data communications. He worked at Cathexis Technologies for six years, as a software engineer writing software for digital surveillance systems, where he was responsible for operating system drivers for PCI video capture cards, image capture scheduling, video compression, and image processing algorithms such as motion detection, people counting, and visual camera tamper detection. He moved to Digital Extremes in 2007 where he is the lead AI programmer and has worked on several titles including *Dark Sector* (March 2008), *BioShock 2* multiplayer (February 2010), and *The Darkness II* (February 2012), *Halo 4* multiplayer DLC packages (2012), and *Warframe* (2013).

Jérémy Chanut has a master's degree in computer science. Passionate about development and AI, he has been working as a software engineer at MASA Group since 2013, in the MASA LIFE team. As an intern, he worked on Recast/Detour and group navigation under the supervision of Clodéric Mars. He now focuses on software architecture in MASA LIFE while maintaining and updating his work on Recast/Detour.

Jarosław Ciupiński knew what he wanted to do with his life when he turned 9 years old. While he was coding since then, he started to work professionally in game development in 2007 as an animation programmer. In 2012 he still sees many things that can be improved in the field of animation in game development.

Elijah Emerson started his lifelong dream of creating video games in his childhood, creating games on paper for friends and family to play. Since then, every step in his life was toward that singular goal of creating new and creative game experiences for others to enjoy. After obtaining a BS in real-time interactive simulation from Digipen Institute of Technology, he began work as a game programming teacher for Digipen. A year later he went to Amaze Entertainment to work on *Harry Potter 2*. After that he moved to Gas Powered Games to work on *Dungeon Siege 2*, *Supreme Commander 1* and *2*, *Age of Empires Online*, and other unannounced titles over the last 12 years. He currently works at Gas Powered Games as the lead engineer on an unannounced project.

Andrew Fray is a ten-year veteran of the video game industry. He has worked on AI in many genres, including FPS and racing games. Andrew was the lead AI programmer on Codemasters' *F1 2010* and *F1 2011*. He has spoken at the Game Developers Conference (GDC) multiple times, as well as at other conferences. Andrew currently works for Spry Fox, making original digital games. You should follow him on twitter at @tenpn and read his blog at http://andrewfray.wordpress.com.

Fabien Gravot made his debut in the game industry in 2011 as an AI researcher with Square Enix. He has worked on a navigation mesh solution for both *FINAL FANTASY XIV: A REALM REBORN* and *FINAL FANTASY XV*. Previously, he had been working on robot AI and autonomous driving. He thought that games were less risky than moving one ton of metal with his program. He received his PhD in computer science from the Paul Sabatier University, Toulouse, France, in 2004.

Ingimar Hólm Guðmundsson is an AI engineer at Square Enix and is focused on character motion, simulations, and workflow tools. His current project is *FINAL FANTASY XV*, a Japanese role-playing game that takes players on a journey of four friends, as their kingdom is threatened and potentially lost. Ingimar has worked on numerous titles in the video game industry, most notably the BAFTA award winning, *Total War: Shogun 2* (2011) by Creative Assembly, where he was the battle AI programmer responsible for the real-time battle strategies. Previously he worked on other *Total War* games, such as *Napoleon: Total War* (2010), and *Empire: Total War* (2009), which was his first foray into the game industry. Ingimar has a master's degree in applied artificial intelligence from the University of Exeter, Exeter, the United Kingdom, and an undergraduate degree in physics from the University of Iceland, Reykjavík, Iceland.

Stephen J. Guy is an assistant professor in the Department of Computer Science and Engineering at the University of Minnesota, Minneapolis, Minnesota. His research focuses on the areas of interactive computer graphics (real-time crowd simulation, path planning, intelligent virtual characters) and multirobot coordination (collision avoidance, sensor fusion, path planning under uncertainty). Stephen's work on motion planning has been licensed for use in games and virtual environments by Relic Entertainment, EA, and other companies; his work in crowd simulation has been recognized by best paper awards at international conferences. Prior to joining the University of Minnesota, he received his PhD in computer science in 2012 from the University of North Carolina at Chapel Hill with support from fellowships from Google, Intel, and the UNCF, and his BSc in computer engineering with honors from the University of Virginia in 2006.

D. Hunter Hale, PhD, completed his doctoral work at the University of North Carolina at Charlotte in 2011. He has been a research assistant in the Game Intelligence Group in the Games + Learning Lab for the last 4 years; prior to that he was a research assistant in the Visualization Lab at UNC–Charlotte while completing his master's degree. He received his bachelor's degree with honors from Western Carolina University in 2005.

Chris Jenner obtained his PhD in 1998 from the University of Newcastle upon Tyne, the United Kingdom. He has been working as a programmer in the game industry since 1999, in the studio that is now known as Ubisoft Reflections, and have worked on *Driver 2, Stuntman, Driver 3, Driver Parallel Lines, Driver San Francisco, Just Dance 3, Just Dance 4, The Crew, Assassins Creed: Syndicate*, and *The Division*.

Ioannis Karamouzas is a research associate in the department of computer science and engineering at the University of Minnesota, Minneapolis, Minnesota. His research focuses on the development of motion planning algorithms for autonomous virtual humans, robots, and crowds of virtual characters. Prior to joining the University of Minnesota, Ioannis received his PhD in computer science from Utrecht University in the Netherlands, with a thesis that focuses in the area of motion planning for human crowd simulations. His doctoral work has been integrated into commercial gaming applications including driving simulators and pedestrian simulation suites. He previously earned an MSc in computer science from the University of Manchester in the United Kingdom and a BSc in applied informatics with honors from the University of Macedonia in Greece.

Sven Koenig is a professor in computer science at the University of Southern California, Los Angeles, California. He received his PhD in computer science from Carnegie Mellon University and is a fellow of the Association for the Advancement of Artificial Intelligence. Most of his research centers on techniques for decision making (planning and learning) that enable single agents (such as robots or decision-support systems) and teams of agents to act intelligently in their environments and exhibit goal-directed behavior in real time, even if they have only incomplete knowledge of their environment, imperfect abilities to manipulate it, limited or noisy perception, or insufficient reasoning speed.

Mark Langerak is the principal software engineer at Microsoft, where he works on augmented reality applications and computer vision technologies for the HoloLens platform. Mark has been in the game industry since the early 1990s. Before joining Microsoft, he worked at Microprose, Sony/Psygnosis, Sega, DreamWorks Interactive, Maxis, Electronic

Arts, and Pandemic Studios, in graphics engineer, lead programmer, and technical director roles.

Clodéric Mars has tried to make simulated characters behave "autonomously *and* as they are told to" for more than 6 years. At Golaem, he worked on a navigation engine used, for example, in a train passengers' simulation and a crowd simulation tool for animation and vfx. Now leading the developments of MASA LIFE, he is dedicated to make behavior authoring easy, fun, and accessible to game designers and field experts. Clodéric has a master's degree in computer science, with a specialization in AI. He spoke at the Paris Game/AI Conference 2011 and at the Game Developers Conference (GDC) 2014 AI Summit.

Eric Martel has been developing games for more than 15 years. He has worked on numerous franchises such as *Far Cry*, *Assassin's Creed*, and *Thief*. He is the published author of "An Analysis of *Far Cry: Instincts'* Anchor System" in AI Game Programming Wisdom 3 and "Tips and Tricks for a Robust Third Person Camera System" in *Game AI Pro*. He is currently a lead AI programmer at Ubisoft Québec studio where he recently worked on *Assassin's Creed Syndicate*.

Youichiro Miyake is the lead AI researcher at Square Enix, working as the leader of the AI unit for the next-generation game engine Luminous Studio. He is the chairman of the IGDA JAPAN SIG-AI and a board member of DiGRA JAPAN. He has been developing and researching game AI since 2004. He developed the technical design of AI for the following game titles: *Chromehounds* (2006, Xbox 360), *Demon's Souls* (2009, PlayStation 3), and *Armored Core V* (2012, Xbox 360, PlayStation 3), developed by FromSoftware. At Square Enix, he was engaged in the AI development of *FINAL FANTASY XIV: A Realm Reborn*. At present, he is developing AI in *FINAL FANTASY XV* as the lead AI technical architect. He has published papers and books about game AI technologies and has given many lectures at universities and conferences. He was a keynote speaker of GAMEON ASIA 2012 and a game AI course speaker in SIGGRAPH ASIA 2015. His paper "Current Status of Applying Artificial Intelligence in Digital Games" will be published in the *Handbook of Digital Games and Entertainment Technologies* by Springer.

Jan Müller studied computational visualistics at the University of Koblenz-Landau, Germany. During his master's thesis, he worked for the Fraunhofer Institute for Applied Information Technology near Bonn, Germany. The focus of his research was augmented and virtual reality as well as early prototypes of VR smart phone games. Among others, he published a research poster about image space constructive solid geometry at the Visualization 2005 conference. After graduating in 2005, he joined Crytek to work as a game and network programmer on *Crysis 1* and *Crysis 2*. In 2009, he joined the Fachhochschule Darmstadt as a guest lecturer teaching game development with CRYENGINE 2. In September 2010, he moved to Los Angeles, California, to work for Insomniac Games. There he was involved with the *Ratchet & Clank* franchise, *Fuse*, and *Sunset Overdrive* as a senior game programmer.

Alex Nash received his BSc in computer science from Yale University, New Haven, Connecticut, in 2004, his MS in computer science from the University of Southern

California in 2006, and his PhD in computer science from the University of Southern California, Los Angeles, California, in 2012 for his dissertation on "Any-angle path planning." Since 2005, he has been performing mission-planning research and development for the Information systems sector of the Northrop Grumman Systems Corporation. His research has been used on ground-based and embedded mission-planning systems for both manned and unmanned aerial vehicles.

Sergio Ocio Barriales has been working in the game industry since 2005. He received his PhD in 2010 from the University of Oviedo, Asturias, Spain, with his thesis about hinted-execution behavior trees. He has worked on the AI for numerous major titles, such as *Driver San Francisco*, *Splinter Cell: Blacklist*, *DOOM*, and *Watch_Dogs 2*. He joined the team at Hangar 13 as a lead AI engineer in 2016, where he continues pushing character AI forward.

Graham Pentheny is an independent game developer from Cambridge, Massachusetts. He currently runs the local Boston Unity3D user group and does engineering work and consultation with various local studios. Previously, he worked with Dr. Jeff Orkin on conversational AI systems at Giant Otter, led AI and engine development at Subatomic Studios, and is credited on the *Fieldrunners* tower defense games. He received a BS in both computer science and interactive media and game development from Worcester Polytechnic Institute, Worcester, Massachusetts. (grahamboree.com)

Fernando Silva is a software engineer at Nintendo of America, providing engineering support to licensed game developers and internal groups, specializing on the Nintendo Wii U platform. He completed an undergraduate degree in computer science in real-time interactive simulation at DigiPen Institute of Technology, where he minored in mathematics. He also develops tools for current and next-gen Nintendo platforms. In his free time, Fernando enjoys working on electronic projects with a focus on the Arduino platform, reverse engineering processes or devices, studying biological processes that can be applied to computer science, and most importantly, dining.

Hendrik Skubch joined Square Enix in Japan in 2013 as an AI researcher, where he develops generic AI technologies for all aspects of game AI. In 2014, he joined a focused effort on *FINAL FANTASY XV* as a senior AI engineer. Before entering the game industry, he researched cooperative robotics and led a robotic soccer team within the RoboCup initiative. He received his PhD for work on robotic teams in 2012 from the University of Kassel, Kassel, Germany.

Nathan R. Sturtevant is an associate professor of computer science at the University of Denver, Denver, Colorado, where he works on AI and games. He began his games career working on shareware games as a college student in the mid-1990s, and returned to the game industry to write the pathfinding engine for *Dragon Age: Origins*. In addition to his work collaborating with the game industry (through work on "Game AI Pro" books, speaking at GDC, and other projects), Nathan guides capstone game projects at the University of Denver and develops games in his free time.

Ben Sunshine-Hill is the lead developer of Havok AI. He holds a PhD in computer science from the University of Pennsylvania, Philadelphia, Pennsylvania, for his work in perceptually driven simulation. He once saw a really cool-looking cow.

Tansel Uras is a PhD student in computer science at the University of Southern California, Los Angeles, California, working with Sven Koenig. Tansel received his BSc in computer science (with a minor in mathematics) in 2009 and his MSc in computer science in 2011 from Sabanci University, Istanbul, Turkey. Tansel is interested in incremental heuristic search, path planning, and game theory, among other topics. He developed a novel optimal path-planning approach (based on subgoal graphs) that was nondominated in the Grid-Based Path Planning Competitions in 2012 and 2013 and won a Best Research Assistant Award from the Computer Science Department at USC in 2014 for this achievement.

Takanori Yokoyama has worked as a game programmer in the game industry since 2004. He has been especially interested in game AI and implemented it for many game titles including *ENCHANT ARMS* (2006, Xbox360), *CHROME HOUNDS* (2006, Xbox360), and *Demon's Souls* (2009, PlayStation3) developed by FROM SOFTWARE. He is now working as an AI engineer at SQUARE ENIX.

G. Michael Youngblood, PhD, is an associate professor of computer science at the University of North Carolina at Charlotte. He is codirector of the Games + Learning Lab and head of the Game Intelligence Group, which conducts research on and builds systems involving interactive artificial intelligence in the games and simulation domains, focusing on character behaviors, creation, and analysis. He has published over 60 scholarly papers on topics of interactive artificial intelligence and support technologies. More information about him can be seen on his website at gmichaelyoungblood.com.

Introduction

Steve Rabin's *Game AI Pro 360: Guide to Movement and Pathfinding* gathers all the cutting-edge information from his previous three Game AI Pro volumes into a convenient single source anthology covering movement and pathfinding in game AI. This volume is complete with articles by leading game AI programmers that explores better ways to smooth paths, avoid obstacles, and navigate 3D space with cutting-edge techniques.

This book, as well as each volume in the *Game AI Pro* series, is a testament to the generous community of game AI developers as well as the larger game development community. Everyone involved in this effort believes that sharing information is the single best way to rapidly innovate, grow and develop. Right now, the game AI community is larger than ever and we invite you to discover all the wonderful resources that are available.

In addition to reading about new game AI techniques in the *Game AI Pro* series, there are annual conferences, which are academic and developer-centric, all over the globe. Organized by developers, there is the Game AI summit at GDC in San Francisco each year and the game/AI conference in Europe. Organized by academia, there is the AAAI conference on Artificial Intelligence and Interactive Digital Entertainment (AIIDE) and the IEEE Conference on Computational Intelligence and Games. Outside of events, there are two communities that have also sprung up to help developers. The game AI Programmers Guild is a free professional group with more than 500 worldwide members (www.gameai.com) and there is a wonderful community of hobbyists and professionals at www.AIgameDev.com. We warmly welcome you to come and hang out with us at any one of these conferences or participate in one of the online communities.

Web Materials

Example programs and source code to accompany some of the chapters are available at http://www.gameaipro.com.

General System Requirements

The following is required to compile and execute the example programs:

- The DirectX August 2009 SDK
- DirectX 9.0 compatible or newer graphics card
- Windows 7 or newer
- Visual C++ .NET 2008 or newer

Updates of the example programs and source code will be updated as needed.

1

Pathfinding Architecture Optimizations

Steve Rabin and Nathan R. Sturtevant

1.1 Introduction

Agent path requests are notorious for devouring huge proportions of the AI's CPU cycles in many genres of games, such as real-time strategy games and first-person shooters. Therefore, there is a large need for AI programmers to all be on the same page when it comes to optimizing pathfinding architectures. This chapter will cover in a priority order the most significant steps you can take to get the fastest pathfinding engine possible.

All game developers understand that A* is the pathfinding search algorithm of choice, but surprisingly, or not so surprisingly, it is not a panacea. There is a huge realm of knowledge that is crucial to crafting the fastest engine. In fact, even if a large number of pathfinding design choices have already been made, there is still much you can do.

1.2 Orders of Magnitude Difference in Performance

What is the difference between the fastest and slowest A* implementations?

At the DigiPen Institute of Technology video game university, the introductory AI course has students program a simple A* implementation on fixed regular grid as one of the first assignments. As extra credit for the assignment, there is a contest held to see who can write the fastest A* implementation. So if you were to guess the difference between the fastest and slowest solutions, what would you guess? Would you guess that the best solution is several times faster than the slowest?

The true answer is quite surprising. Given hundreds of students who have taken the course over the years, the fastest implementations are 2 orders of magnitude faster than the slowest implementations (a 100× difference). The fastest implementations are also 1 order of magnitude faster than the average implementation (a 10× difference). To put concrete numbers behind this example, on a given map, the fastest implementation finds a path in ~200 us, the average takes ~2500 us, and the slowest implementations take upwards of 20,000 us. Given that these are junior, senior, and master's students, how do you think you would rank if given the same task? It's a strange question, since as a professional game programmer you would never be put in such a position. Wherever you might rank, it is a scary thought that you might be 1 to 2 orders of magnitude slower than the best solution.

Although with fewer students, the second author has had similar experiences with his students in both regular assignments and competitions. The insights of both authors have been distilled here. Thus, you might want to scour this chapter for the nuggets of wisdom that will keep you within spitting distance of the best implementations.

1.3 Optimization #1: Build High-Quality Heuristics

This first optimization is the epitome of the classic programming trade-off between memory and speed. There are many ways that heuristics can be built; we will go through several useful approaches here.

1.3.1 Precompute Every Single Path (Roy–Floyd–Warshall)

While at first glance it seems ridiculous, it is possible to precompute every single path in a search space and store it in a look-up table. The memory implications are severe, but there are ways to temper the memory requirements and make it work for games.

The algorithm is known in English-speaking circles as the Floyd–Warshall algorithm, while in Europe it is better known as Roy–Floyd. Since the algorithm was independently discovered by three different mathematicians, we'll give credit to each and refer to it as the Roy–Floyd–Warshall algorithm [Millington 09].

While we won't explain the algorithm in enough detail to implement it, you should be aware of its basic advantages and properties so that you can make an informed choice whether to pursue implementing it for your game. Here are the facts:

- Roy–Floyd–Warshall is the absolute fastest way to generate a path at runtime. It should routinely be an order of magnitude faster than the best A* implementation.
- The look-up table is calculated offline before the game ships.
- The look-up table requires $O(n^2)$ entries, where n is the number of nodes. For example, for a 100 by 100 grid search space, there are 10,000 nodes. Therefore, the memory required for the look-up table would be 100,000,000 entries (with 2 bytes per entry, this would be ~200 MB).
- Path generation is as simple as looking up the answer. The time complexity is $O(p)$, where p is the number of nodes in the final path.

Figure 1.1 shows a search space graph and the resulting tables generated by the Roy–Floyd–Warshall algorithm. A full path is found by consecutively looking up the next step in the path (left table in Figure 1.1). For example, if you want to find a final path from B to A, you would first look up the entry for (B, A), which is node D. You would travel to node D, then look up the next step of the path (D, A), which would be node E. By repeating this all the way to node A, you will travel the optimal path with an absolute minimum amount of CPU work. If there are dynamic obstacles in the map which must be avoided, this approach can be used as a very accurate heuristic estimate, provided that distances are stored in the look-up table instead of the next node to travel to (right table in Figure 1.1).

As we mentioned earlier, in games you can make the memory requirement more reasonable by creating minimum node networks that are connected to each other [Waveren 01, van der Sterren 04]. For example if you have 1000 total nodes in your level, this would normally require $1000^2 = 1,000,000$ entries in a table. But if you can create 50 node zones of 20 nodes each, then the total number of entries required is $50 \times 20^2 = 20,000$ (which is 50 times fewer entries).

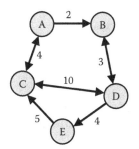

Next Node Look-Up Table

	A	B	C	D	E
A	A	B	C	B	B
B	D	B	D	D	D
C	A	A	C	A	A
D	E	B	E	D	E
E	C	C	C	C	E

Cost to Goal Look-Up Table

	A	B	C	D	E
A	0	2	4	5	9
B	16	0	12	3	7
C	4	6	0	9	13
D	13	3	9	0	4
E	9	11	5	14	0

Figure 1.1

A search space with its corresponding Roy–Floyd–Warshall path look-up table on the left and a very accurate heuristic cost look-up table on the right.

1.3.2 Lossless Compression of Roy–Floyd–Warshall

Another approach to reducing the memory requirement is to compress the Roy–Floyd–Warshall data. Published work [Botea 11] has shown the effectiveness of compressing the data, and this approach fared very well in the 2012 Grid-Based Path Planning competition (http://www.movingai.com/GPPC/), when sufficient memory was available.

An alternate way to compress the Roy–Floyd–Warshall data is to take advantage of the structure of the environment. In many maps, but not all maps, there are relatively few optimal paths of significant length through the state space, and most of these paths overlap. Thus, it is possible to find a sparse number of "transit nodes" through which optimal paths cross [Bast et al. 07]. If, for every state in the state space, we store the path to all transit nodes for that state, as well as the optimal paths between all transit nodes, we can easily reconstruct the shortest path information between any two states, using much less space than when storing the shortest path between all pairs of states. This is one of several methods which have been shown to be highly effective on highway road maps [Abraham et al. 10].

1.3.3 Lossy Compression of Roy–Floyd–Warshall

The full Roy–Floyd–Warshall data results in very fast pathfinding queries, at the cost of memory overhead. In many cases you might want to use less memory and more CPU, which suggests building strong, but not perfect heuristics.

Imagine if we store just a few rows/columns of the Roy–Floyd–Warshall data. This corresponds to keeping the shortest paths from a few select nodes. Fortunately, improved distance estimates between all nodes can be inferred from this data. If $d(x, y)$ is the distance between node x and y, and we know $d(p, z)$ for all z, then the estimated distance between x and y is $h(x, y) = | d(p, x) - d(p, y) |$, where p is a pivot node that corresponds to a single row/column in the Roy–Floyd–Warshall data. With multiple pivot nodes, we can perform multiple heuristic lookups and take the maximum. The improved estimates will reduce the cost of A* search.

This approach has been developed in many contexts and been given many different names [Ng and Zhang 01, Goldberg and Harrelson 05, Goldenberg et al. 11, Rayner et al. 11]. We prefer the name *Euclidean embedding*, which we will justify shortly. First, we summarize the facts about this approach:

- Euclidean embeddings can be far more accurate than the default heuristics for a map, and in some maps are nearly as fast as Roy-Floyd-Warshall.
- The look-up table can be calculated before the game ships or at runtime, depending on the size and dynamic nature of the maps.
- The heuristic requires O(kn) entries, where n is the number of nodes and k is the number of pivots.
- Euclidean embeddings provide a heuristic for guiding A* search. Given multiple heuristics, A* should usually take the maximum of all available heuristics.

Why do we call this a Euclidean embedding? Consider a map that is wrapped into a spiral, such as in Figure 1.2. Points A and B are quite close in the coordinates of the map, but quite far when considering the minimal travel distance between A and B. If we could just unroll the map into a straight line, the distance estimates would be more accurate. Thus, the central problem is that the coordinates used for aesthetic and gameplay

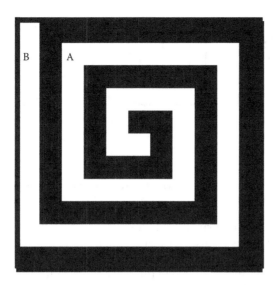

Figure 1.2

A map where straight-line distances are inaccurate.

purposes are not the best for A* search purposes. That is, they do not provide accurate heuristic estimates. If we could provide a different set of coordinates optimized for A* search, we could use these coordinates to estimate distances between nodes and have a higher quality heuristic. This process of transforming a map into a new state space where distance estimates are (hopefully) more accurate is called an *embedding*. A single-source shortest-path search from a pivot node is equivalent to performing a one-dimensional embedding, as each node gets a single coordinate, and the heuristic in this embedding is the distance between the embedded points. Other types of embeddings are possible, just not yet well understood.

The key question of this approach is how the pivots should be selected. In general, a pivot should not be at the center of the map, but near the edges. The heuristic from pivot p between nodes x and y will be most accurate when the optimal path from p to x goes through y. In many games, there are locations where characters will commonly travel, which suggests good locations for pivots. In a RPG, for instance, entrance and exit points to an area are good locations. In a RTS, player bases would be most useful. In a capture-the-flag FPS, the location of the flag would probably work well.

1.4 Optimization #2: Using an Optimal Search Space Representation

If you have to search for a path at runtime, then the number one optimization you can make is to use an efficient search space representation. The reason is that the time spent looking for a path is directly proportional to the number of nodes that must be considered. Fewer nodes equates to less time searching. A more in-depth discussion on choosing a search space representation can be found within this book [Sturtevant 13].

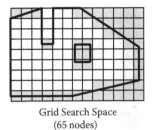 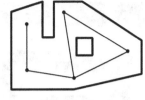 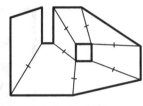

Grid Search Space
(65 nodes)

Waypoint Graph
(5 nodes)

Navigation Mesh
(7 nodes)

Figure 1.3

Three search space representations. Note the number of nodes in each representation, which affects search speed.

Figure 1.3 shows the three primary search space representations available. As you can plainly see, the most nodes are used by a grid search space, with an order of magnitude fewer nodes in the waypoint graph and the navigation mesh (navmesh).

If you have a large world, none of the three search space representations will be sufficient to keep CPU load to a minimum. Instead, you need to resort to subdividing the search space with a hierarchical representation. *Hierarchical pathfinding* is the concept that the search space can be subdivided into at least two levels: a high-level zone-to-zone representation and a low-level step-by-step representation [Rabin 00]. In this scheme, a path is first found in the high-level representation from the starting zone to the goal zone (think of rooms in a castle, starting in the foyer and finding a room-to-room path to the balcony). Then, to begin moving, the low-level path is found from within the starting zone to the next zone on the path (for example, from the standing place in the foyer to the next room on the path). Once the second zone is entered, a step-by-step path is then found from the second zone to the third zone, and so on.

Two concrete examples of hierarchical pathfinding in shipped games include *Dragon Age: Origins* [Sturtevant 08] and *Company of Heroes* [Jurney et al. 07]. The final architecture in *Dragon Age: Origins* used two levels of grid-based abstraction above the low-level grid. In *Company of Heroes*, the high-level search space representation was a hex-grid and the low-level representation was a regular square grid. If there isn't enough memory to store the Roy–Floyd–Warshall solution in memory for the low-level state space, there is usually enough memory to store this information in an abstract state space.

1.5 Optimization #3: Preallocate All Necessary Memory

Once you have optimized the search space, the next step is to ensure that absolutely no memory is allocated during the search. Although this knowledge should be ingrained among all game programmers, it can't be stressed enough. Memory allocation during a search can increase search times by at least an order of magnitude.

How do you avoid memory allocations? Simply preallocate a pool of memory at start time and reuse it. Since nodes are all the same memory size, they can easily be pulled out of a pre-allocated buffer without any fragmentation issues.

The memory needed for A* can also be part of the map representation. This avoids the need to explicitly store a separate closed list, as each node in the map can have a flag indicating whether it is on closed or not. If an id is used instead of a Boolean flag, the search can avoid having to reset the nodes in the closed list between most searches.

1.6 Optimization #4: Overestimating the Heuristic

In order for A* to guarantee an optimal path, the heuristic must be admissible, meaning that the heuristic guess of the cost from the current node to the goal node must never overestimate the true cost. However, by using an overestimating heuristic, you can get a tremendous speed-up at the possible expense of a slightly nonoptimal path. While this sounds like a terrible trade-off initially, it turns out that a small amount of overestimating has large benefits with very little noticeable nonoptimality. In the world of search algorithms this once might have been seen as heresy, but in the video game industry it's a shrewd and worthwhile optimization.

In order to understand how to overestimate the heuristic, let's first look at Equation 1.1, which is the classic A* cost formula. As you can see, the final cost, $f(x)$, is the sum of the given cost, $g(x)$, and the heuristic cost, $h(x)$. Each node added to the Open List gets this final cost assigned to it and this is how the Open List is sorted.

$$f(x) = g(x) + h(x) \qquad (1.1)$$

Equation 1.2 shows the addition of a weight on the heuristic portion of the formula.

$$f(x) = g(x) + \big(h(x) \times weight\big) \qquad (1.2)$$

By altering the weight, we can tune how A* behaves. If the weight is zero, then the formula reduces down to just $g(x)$, which is identical to the Dijkstra search algorithm. This approach is guaranteed to find an optimal path, but is not a "smart" search because it explores uniformly outward in all directions. If the weight is 1.0, then the equation is the classic A* formula, guaranteed to expand the minimal number of nodes needed to find an optimal path given the current heuristic estimate, modulo tie-breaking. If the weight is larger than 1.0, then we are tilting the algorithm toward the behavior of Greedy Best-First search, which is not optimal but focuses the search on finding the goal as quickly as possible.

Thus, we can tune A* with the weight to lean it toward Dijkstra or Greedy Best-First. By using weights in the neighborhood of 1.1 to 1.5 or higher, we can progressively force the search to more aggressively push toward the goal node, at the increasing expense of a possible sub-optimal path. When the terrain is filled with random obstacles that resemble columns or trees, then a larger weight makes a lot of sense and the path is not noticeably suboptimal. However, if significant backtracking away from the goal is required for the final path, then a lower weight is advisable.

The correct weight for your game or parts of your game must be discovered experimentally. There is also the possibility of adaptively discovering the ideal weight for an area given a particular error tolerance on how suboptimal the path is allowed to be. See [Thayer and Ruml 08] for one such algorithm. At any rate, overestimating the heuristic is a tried and true optimization for games that you will want to explore.

1.7 Optimization #5: Better Heuristics

There are two ways to use better heuristics. First, some heuristics are more suited to solve certain problems, and so selecting the correct heuristic can significantly reduce the work required to solve a problem. The second approach is to build and store improved heuristics, of which the Roy–Floyd–Warshall algorithm is just one example. Building a new heuristic is most useful when the map topology is relatively static, as changing the world can invalidate a heuristic.

As for heuristic selection, consider pathfinding on a grid, with 8-directional movement. Three possible heuristics are straight-line (Euclidean) distance, octile distance, which assumes that only 45° and 90° angles are allowed, and Manhattan (city-block) distance. Manhattan distance is a poor heuristic, because it will overestimate distances, not taking diagonal movement into account. A straight-line heuristic is also poor, because it will underestimate distances, assuming that paths can take any angle. The octile heuristic, which corresponds exactly to movement in the world, is the most accurate and best heuristic to use on a grid. The octile heuristic between two points can be computed as $max(\Delta x, \Delta y) + 0.41 \cdot min(\Delta x, \Delta y)$, assuming that diagonal movement has cost 1.41.

1.8 Optimization #6: Open List Sorting

A textbook description of A* states that the node with the lowest f-cost should be expanded at each step. A more efficient implementation will break ties between nodes with equal f-costs towards those with largest g-cost, as these nodes are expected to be closer to the goal. This results in better tie-breaking, which can be quite significant in some maps. The sorting for the Open list can be done in a priority queue structure such as a heap, although researchers have spent significant effort improving these data structures, so if full sorting is required, a weak-heap [Edelkamp et al., 12] is just one option for speeding up A*. It is very often the case that the last node inserted into priority queue is immediately removed again for the next expansion. Caching an inserted node before inserting it into the Open List can reduce this overhead.

An even more efficient approach is to avoid explicitly sorting states. In state spaces where the number of unique f-costs will be small, a list can be maintained for each unique f-cost; finding the best node on the Open List is as simple as taking the first node off the list with the smallest f-cost. It would seem that this would preclude tie-breaking by higher g-costs, but treating each f-cost list as a LIFO stack will produce similar tie-breaking.

In some searches, the number of nodes considered is limited, such that the Open List typically has under 10 or so nodes with a max of 20 or 30. In such a case, an unordered Open List represented as an array might actually be the best choice, although this should always be verified experimentally. Inserting new nodes is essentially free, O(1), and finding the cheapest node is a matter of simply walking the short list. Without the overhead of even a trivial scheme, an unordered Open List can be extremely fast since it simply doesn't execute that many instructions. To offer a little more detail, the unordered Open List is held as an array, with inserted nodes placed at the end of the array. When a node must be removed, it is replaced with the node at the end, in order to stay packed. With this data structure, the overhead in maintaining the data structure is almost nonexistent and its minimalist size (one pointer per node) means that it is very cache-friendly, thus resulting in even more speed.

1.9 Optimization #7: Don't Backtrack during the Search

It might seem obvious, but no path ever backtracks along the same nodes it's already visited, so similarly an A* search should also not consider nodes that backtrack. In practice, this is as simple as not considering a neighboring node if it is the same as the parent node. This simple optimization will speed up a search by roughly one over the branching factor. For a grid search space this is 1/8, but for a navmesh search space it's about 1/3.

In grids there are many short cycles, meaning that there is overhead from redundantly looking up a given state from many different neighbors. An inexpensive scan through the state space can allow the search to skip many intermediate nodes to avoid these redundant lookups. The full details of this approach are part of the Jump-Point Search algorithm [Harabor and Grastien 11].

1.10 Optimization #8: Caching Successors

One of the most common operations in an A* search is to look up the neighbors of a node. Thus, it follows that this operation should be as cheap as possible. Storing the neighbors of each node explicitly, rather than traversing more expensive data structures, can result in significant improvements in speed, at the cost of additional memory.

1.11 Bad Ideas for Pathfinding

The following are a list of bad ideas that usually result in slower pathfinding searches.

1.11.1 Bad Idea #1: Simultaneous Searches

When many pathfinding search requests are required all at once, an architectural decision must be made as to how many simultaneous search requests should be processed at the same time. For example, if 10 requests are all needed, it's a tempting thought to time-slice between all of the requests so that one very slow search doesn't hold the others up.

Unfortunately, supporting many simultaneous searches at the same time is fraught with disaster. The primary problem is that you'll need to support separate Open Lists for each request. The implications are severe as to the amount of memory required, and the subsequent thrashing in the cache can be devastating.

But what is to be done about a single search that holds up all other searches? On one hand, this might be a false concern because your pathfinding engine should be blindingly fast for all searches. If it isn't, then that's an indication that you chose the wrong search space representation or should be using hierarchical pathfinding.

However, if we concede that a single search might take a very long time to calculate, then one solution is to learn from supermarkets. The way supermarkets deal with this problem is to create two types of check-out lanes. One is for customers with very few items (10 items or less) and one for the customers with their cart overflowing with groceries. We can do a similar thing with pathfinding by allowing up to two searches at a time.

One queue is for requests deemed to be relatively fast (based on distance between the start and goal) and one queue for requests deemed to take a long time (again based on distance between the start and goal).

1.11.2 Bad Idea #2: Bidirectional Pathfinding

One innovative approach for a search algorithm is to search the path from both directions and complete the path when the searches meet each other. This bidirectional pathfinding reduces the amount of nodes visited with breadth-first and depth-first searches [Pohl 71], but what about A*?

One brilliant reason to consider this approach is the continent and island problem. Consider a search that begins on the continent and the goal is on an island, but we are unable to cross water. With a traditional A* search starting on the continent, the entire continent must be explored before the search concludes that no path exists, which is very, very time consuming. With bidirectional pathfinding, the search starts at both ends, the island side quickly runs out of nodes, and the search concludes that there is no path (with a minimal amount of work).

The continent-island argument however is better solved using a hierarchical approach. At a minimum, the continent would be considered one zone and the island another zone. For a hierarchical architecture, the top-level search would almost instantly discover that no path connects the two zones and the search would fail quickly.

But even without considering the continent-island argument, the truth is that bidirectional pathfinding for A* often requires twice the amount of work. This can be seen when the two searches are separated by a barrier and both searches back up behind the barrier until one spills over and connects. Since we care more about the worst case than best case, this is an important case to avoid. For these reasons, bidirectional pathfinding for A* is usually a poor choice.

1.11.3 Bad Idea #3: Cache Successful or Failed Paths

While caching results for expensive operations is generally good optimization advice, it is not a good idea for paths. The reason is that there are simply too many unique paths. The memory requirements would be very large (similar to Roy–Floyd–Warshall), and the chance that you'll request exactly the same path again is very small.

1.12 Conclusion

This article has covered the techniques for improving the speed of your A* implementation. Using these ideas can ensure that your code is on par with the best possible implementations, and several orders of magnitude faster than more naïve implementations.

References

[Abraham et al. 10] I. Abraham, A. Fiat, A. V. Goldberg, and R. F. F. Werneck. "Highway Dimension, Shortest Paths, and Provably Efficient Algorithms." *ACM-SIAM Symposium on Discrete Algorithms*, pp. 782–793, 2010. Available online (http://research.microsoft. com/pubs/115272/soda10.pdf).

[Bast et al. 07] H. Bast, S. Funke, P. Sanders, and D. Schultes. "In Transit to Constant Time Shortest-Path Queries in Road Networks." Workshop on Algorithm Engineering and Experiments, 2007. Available online (http://www.siam.org/proceedings/alenex/2007/alx07_transit.pdf).

[Botea 11] A. Botea. "Ultra-fast optimal pathfinding without runtime search." *AAAI Conference on Artificial Intelligence and Interactive Digital Entertainment*, pp. 122–127, 2011. Available online (http://www.aaai.org/ocs/index.php/AIIDE/AIIDE11/paper/view/4050).

[Edelkamp et al., 12] S. Edelkamp, A. Elmasry, and J. Katajainen. "The weak-heap family of priority queues in theory and praxis." *Proceedings of the 18th Computing: The Australasian Theory Symposium, Conferences in Research and Practice in Information Technology*, pp. 103–112, 2012. Available online (http://www.cphstl.dk/Paper/CATS12/cats12.pdf).

[Goldberg and Harrelson 05] A. V. Goldberg and C. Harrelson. "Computing the shortest path: A search meets graph theory." *ACM-SIAM Symposium on Discrete Algorithms*, pp. 156–165, 2005.

[Goldenberg et al. 11] M. Goldenberg, N. R. Sturtevant, A. Felner, and J. Schaeffer. "The compressed differential heuristic." *AAAI Conference on Artificial Intelligence*, pp. 24–29, 2011. Available online (http://www.aaai.org/ocs/index.php/AAAI/AAAI11/paper/view/3723).

[Harabor and Grastien 11] D. Harabor and A. Grastein. Online Graph Pruning for Pathfinding On Grid Maps, *Proceedings of the AAAI Conference on Artificial Intelligence (2011)*, pp. 1114–1119. Available online (http://www.aaai.org/ocs/index.php/AAAI/AAAI11/paper/view/3761).

[Jurney et al. 07] C. Jurney and S. Hubick. "Dealing with destruction: AI from the trenches of company of heroes." *Game Developers Conference*, 2007. Available online (https://store.cmpgame.com/product.php?cat=24&id=2089).

[Millington 09] I. Millington. "Constant Time Game Pathfinding with the Roy–Floyd–WarshallAlgorithm." http://idm.me.uk/ai/wfi.pdf, 2009.

[Ng and Zhang 01] T. S. Eugene Ng and H. Zhang. "Predicting Internet network distance with coordinates-based approaches." *IEEE International Conference on Computer Communications (INFOCOM)*, pp. 170–179, 2001.

[Pohl 71] I. Pohl. "Bi-directional search." In *Machine Intelligence 6*, edited by Meltzer and D. Michie. American Elsevier, 1971, pp. 127–140.

[Rabin 00] S. Rabin. "A* Speed optimizations." In *Game Programming Gems*, edited by Mark DeLoura. Hingham, MA: Charles River Media, 2000, pp. 272–287.

[Rayner et al. 11] C. Rayner, M. Bowling, and N. Sturtevant. "Euclidean Heuristic Optimization." *AAAI Conference on Artificial Intelligence*, pp. 81–86, 2011. Available online (http://www.aaai.org/ocs/index.php/AAAI/AAAI11/paper/view/3594).

[Sturtevant 08] N. Sturtevant. "Memory-efficient pathfinding abstractions." In *AI Game Programming Wisdom 4*, edited by Steve Rabin. Hingham, MA: Charles River Media, 2008, pp. 203–217.

[Sturtevant 13] N. Sturtevant. "Choosing a search space representation." In *Game AI Pro*, edited by Steve Rabin. Boca Raton, FL: CRC Press, 2013.

[Thayer and Ruml 08] J. T. Thayer and W. Ruml. "Faster Than Weighted A*: An Optimistic Approach to Bounded Suboptimal Search," *Proceedings of the Eighteenth International Conference on Automated Planning and Scheduling (ICAPS-08)*, pp. 355–362, 2008. Available online (http://www.cs.unh.edu/~ruml/papers/optimistic-icaps-08.pdf).

[van der Sterren 04] W. van der Sterren. "Path look-up tables—small is beautiful." In *AI Game Programming Wisdom 2*, edited by Steve Rabin. Hingham, MA: Charles River Media, 2004, pp. 115–129.

[Waveren 01] J. P. van Waveren. "The Quake III Arena Bot," pp. 40–45, 2001. Available online (http://www.kbs.twi.tudelft.nl/docs/MSc/2001/Waveren_Jean-Paul_van/thesis.pdf).

2

Choosing a Search Space Representation

Nathan R. Sturtevant

2.1 Introduction

The choice of a path planning architecture for a game will help determine what features the game can support easily, and what features will require significant effort to implement. There are good articles describing different types of path planning architectures [Tozour 04], and there have been debates in different forums [Tozour 08, Champandard 10] about the correct choice for a path planning architecture. Each choice comes with its own set of benefits and drawbacks, the strength of which will depend on the type of game being developed and the time allotted to developing the architecture. The goal of this article is to summarize and extend some of the arguments made for different architectures.

It is important to know that, for most games, all feasible path planning architectures are abstractions of the space through which characters can walk in the game. This is because the physics that are used to simulate the world are not directly used as the path planning representation. So, in some sense, much of the debate here is related to what representation most closely matches the underlying physics of the game world.

This article focuses on the primary representations: grids, waypoint graphs, and navigation meshes. We assume that most readers are familiar with these representations, as they are probably the most common architectures used today. Furthermore, examples of several of these architectures can be found in this book. But, for reference, an example map is shown in Figure 2.1(a). Figure 2.1(b) shows the grid decomposition of the map, Figure 2.1(c) shows a waypoint graph on the map, and Figure 2.1(d) shows a triangle decomposition, which is a type of navigation mesh. This article is primarily directed

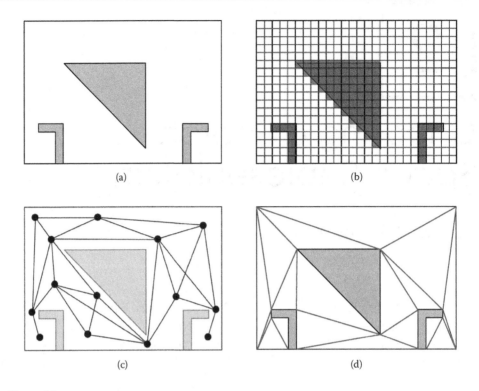

Figure 2.1

Three common world representations. (a) Original map, (b) grid decomposition, (c) waypoint graph, (d) nav mesh.

towards independent or small developers, as they are more likely to have a choice in the architecture they use.

2.2 Tasks

To begin, we briefly highlight the characteristics that we will consider when comparing path planning representations. These include memory usage, the ease of localization, planning, smoothing, path following, and dynamic modification of the representation. We also discuss the time required for implementation.

Memory usage is measured simply by the overhead of building and storing the representation of the map in memory. *Localization* is the process of moving from a spatial coordinate to a representation that is native to the path planning representation. When a user clicks the mouse, for instance, the coordinates of the click are recorded. This must then be converted into a grid cell or polygon in a navigation mesh. *Planning* is the cost of finding a valid path between two locations. *Smoothing* and *path following* is the process of taking a planned path and removing sharp turns or discontinuities to improve the overall quality. This can be done as part of planning, postplanning, or while the path is being followed by a character. *Dynamic modification* is the cost of performing changes to the representation on the fly, while the game is being played.

Note that the exact combination of each of these tasks depends on the game being created, and so the weight of each argument below depends on the importance of each task in your game. Grids, for instance, are a suitable representation for tower-defense games, but large open worlds in a MMORPG are usually too large for grids.

In addition to representing space for path planning, the representation can often be used for more generic queries to facilitate AI behavior. These may include positioning in battle, the best location for new buildings to be constructed, or the most protected location during battle. These queries are game-dependent, and so we will not directly consider them here.

2.3 Grids

The simplest implementation of a grid represents the world via an array of blocked and unblocked cells. More sophisticated implementations can include information on slope, terrain type, or other meta-information which is useful for planning. Grids traditionally represent only two-dimensional worlds, but can be used to represent three-dimensional worlds as well [Sturtevant 11].

The pros are:

- Grids are one of the simplest possible representations and are easy to implement. A working implementation can be completed in a few hours.
- A grid representation can be easily edited externally with a text editor. This can save significant tool-building efforts [Van Dongen 10].
- Terrain costs in grids are easy to dynamically update. For example, player-detected traps in Dragon Age: Origins are easily marked with a few bits in the relevant grid cells. It is easy for A* to account for these costs when planning, although the cost of planning will be increased if too many cells are re-weighted.
- Passable cells can be quickly modified in a grid in a similar way to terrain costs being updated.
- Localization in a grid is easy, simply requiring the coordinates to be divided by the grid resolution to return the localized grid cell.

The cons are:

- Grids are memory-intensive in large worlds. Note that a sparse representation can be used when the world is large, but the walkable space is relatively small [Sturtevant 11].
- Path smoothing usually must be performed to remove the characteristic 45° and 90° angles that are found in grid-based movement, although any-angle planning approaches can also be used [Nash et al. 07].
- Path planning in grids can be expensive due to the fine-grain representation of the world. This can be addressed using some form of abstraction [Rabin 00, Sturtevant 07].
- Grid worlds often contain many symmetric paths, which can increase the cost of path planning. Some techniques can be used to avoid this (e.g., [Harabor and Grastien 11]), but this can also be avoided with different state representations.

2.4 Waypoint Graphs

Waypoint graphs represent the world as an abstract graph. Importantly, waypoint graphs do not have an explicit mapping between nodes in the graph and walkable space. Waypoint graphs were widely used before the popularity of navigation meshes grew. While they have been criticized for their shortcomings [Tozour 08], they have also been praised for their strengths [Champandard 10].

The pros are:

- Waypoint graphs are relatively easy to implement.
- Waypoint graphs are easy to modify if the changes are known ahead of time. For instance, if a door in the world closes and is locked, it is easy for the developer to mark the edges in the graph that cross the opening of the door and block them when the door is shut.
- Waypoint graphs represent only a small fraction of the points found in a grid. This sparse representation of walkable space is both cheap to store and leads to inexpensive path planning requests.

The cons are:

- Path quality can suffer if there are not enough walkable edges in the graph, but too many walkable edges will impact storage and planning complexity.
- Waypoint graphs may require manual placement of nodes to get good path quality.
- Localization on waypoint graphs requires mapping between game space and the graph. If a character is knocked off of the graph, it may be unclear where the character should actually be within the waypoint graph.
- Because there is no explicit representation of the underlying state space, smoothing off the waypoint graph can result in characters getting stuck on physics or other objects.
- Dynamic changes are difficult when they aren't known ahead of time. If a character can create an unexpected hole in a wall, new connections on the waypoint graph are needed. However, it can be expensive to check all nearby connections to verify if they have become passable due to the changes in the map.

2.5 Navigation Meshes

Navigation meshes represent the world using convex polygons [Tozour 04]. A special case of navigation meshes are constrained Delaunay triangulations [Chen 09], for which the world is only represented by triangles. Note that grids can also be seen as a special case of navigation meshes, as both representations use convex polygons, but their usage is significantly different in practice.

The pros are:

- Polygons can represent worlds more accurately than grids, as they can represent non-grid-aligned worlds.

- With the accurate representation of a polygon it is easier to correctly perform smoothing both before and during movement. This accuracy can also be used for tighter animation constraints.
- Path planning on navigation meshes is usually fast, as the representation of the world is fairly coarse. But, this does not impact path quality, as characters are free to walk at any angle.
- Navigation meshes are not as memory-intensive as grids as they can represent large spaces with just a few polygons.

The cons are:

- The time required to implement a navigation mesh is significant, although good open-source implementations are available [Mononen 11].
- Navigation meshes often require geometric algorithms, which may fail in special cases such as parallel lines, meaning that implementation is much more difficult [Chen 09].
- Changes to navigation meshes can be difficult or expensive to implement, especially when contrasted with changes to grid worlds.
- Localization on navigation meshes can be expensive if poorly implemented. Good implementations will use additional data structures like grids to speed up the process [Demyen 06].

2.6 Conclusion

To conclude, each path planning architecture has its own strengths and weaknesses. The choice of an architecture should depend on the type of game being developed, the tools already available, and the time available for implementation and debugging. Many game engines ship with their own path planning representation, but for the cases where a new implementation must be performed, we summarize the pros and cons as follows:

Grids are most useful when the terrain is fundamentally 2D, when implementation time is limited, when the world is dynamic, and when sufficient memory is available. They are not well suited for very large open-world games, or for games where the exact bounds of walkable spaces are required for high-quality animation.

Waypoint graphs are most useful when implementation time is limited, when fast path planning is needed, and when an accurate representation of the world is not necessary.

Navigation meshes are best when there is adequate time for testing and implementation. They are the most flexible of the possible implementations when implemented well, but can be overkill for smaller projects.

Ultimately, the best representation is the one that minimizes developer effort and helps make the game-playing experience as compelling as possible. This may be different in any game, but being aware of the trade-offs between each architecture will help you make the best decisions on any new project.

References

[Champandard 10] A. Champandard. "Are Waypoint Graphs Outnumbered? Not in AlienSwarm." http://aigamedev.com/open/review/alienswarm-node-graph/, 2010.

[Chen 09] K. Chen. "Robust Dynamic Constrained Delaunay Triangulation for Pathfinding." Master Thesis, 2009.

[Demyen 06] D. Demyen. "Efficient Triangulation-Based Pathfinding." Master Thesis, 2006. Available online (https://skatgame.net/mburo/ps/tra.pdf).

[Harabor and Grastien 11] D. Harabor and A. Grastein. Online graph pruning for pathfinding on grid maps, *Proceedings of the AAAI Conference on Artificial Intelligence (2011)*, pp. 1114–1119. Available online (http://www.aaai.org/ocs/index.php/AAAI/AAAI11/paper/view/3761).

[Mononen 11] Mikko Mononen. "Recast." http://code.google.com/p/recastnavigation/, 2011.

[Nash et al. 07] A. Nash, K. Daniel, S. Koenig, and A. Felner "Theta*: Any-angle path planning on grids." *Proceedings of the AAAI Conference on Artificial Intelligence (2007)*, pp. 1177–1183. Available online (http://idm-lab.org/bib/abstracts/papers/aaai07a.pdf).

[Rabin 00] S. Rabin. "A* Speed Optimizations." In *Game Programming Gems*, edited by Mark DeLoura, Hingham, MA: Charles River Media, 2000, pp. 272–287.

[Sturtevant 07] N. R. Sturtevant, "Memory-efficient abstractions for pathfinding." *Artificial Intelligence and Interactive Digital Entertainment*, pp. 31–36, 2007. Available online (http://web.cs.du.edu/~sturtevant/papers/mmabstraction.pdf).

[Sturtevant 11] N. R. Sturtevant. "A sparse grid representation for dynamic three-dimensional worlds." *Artificial Intelligence and Interactive Digital Entertainment, 2011.* Available online (http://web.cs.du.edu/~sturtevant/papers/3dgrids.pdf).

[Tozour 04] P. Tozour. "Search space representations." In *AI Game Programming Wisdom 2*, edited by Steve Rabin. Hingham, MA: Charles River Media, 2004, pp. 85–102.

[Tozour 08] P. Tozour. "Fixing Pathfinding Once and For All." http://www.ai-blog.net/archives/000152.html, 2008.

[Van Dongen 10] J. Van Dongen. "Designing Levels without Tools." http://joostdevblog.blogspot.com/2010/12/designing-levels-without-tools.html, 2010.

3

Creating High-Order Navigation Meshes through Iterative Wavefront Edge Expansions

D. Hunter Hale and G. Michael Youngblood

3.1 Introduction

When placing AI-driven characters into your immersive game world, one large problem needs to be addressed, and that is the issue of a meaningful representation of the environment. The only source for information about the layout of the environment available to these characters is that which is provided to them by the game designers usually in the form of the geometric models that are assembled spatially to create the world. In all but the simplest of games, the level of detail in those model files is often too complex, too detailed, and organized more for display than spatial reasoning. Instead, some form of spatial abstraction is needed to group similar areas in single regions of space for the character to consider.

Historically, this representation was generally presented in the form of a waypoint map (i.e., valid points of known open points in a space with a collection of known good routes between them). Searching such a structure allowed AI characters to make paths through traversable space that appeared reasonable [Tozour 04]. The usage of waypoint graphs has been in decline as the navigation mesh spatial representation has risen in usage [McAnils 08]. A navigation mesh (often referred to as a *navmesh*) is composed of a listing of regions, which are well-defined convex groupings of traversable space (usually defined by polygons or polyhedrons) and an additional listing describing connectivity (as a topological graph). This collection of regions organized as a graph can be rapidly searched to generate a path and characters can walk from region to region knowing they will remain in traversable areas.

Traditionally, navigation meshes have been created either by hand or using some form of automated spatial decomposition algorithm that examines the obstructions present in the environment and then breaks down the area between them into as few regions as possible. Reducing the number of regions present in a world yields a smaller search space and is generally considered to be highly important to a spatial decomposition. Unfortunately, creating a decomposition for a game environment with an optimal (absolute minimum) number of regions is NP-Hard [Lingas 82]. This means that there is no *best* technique. Instead there are many techniques that attempt to approach the optimal one. These approaches generally start with some form of triangulation of the environment [Delaunay 34] and then attempt to minimize the number of regions present in the environment through combining these triangles [Hertel 83].

The problem with this approach is that the triangles that remain in the navigation mesh cause problems for character navigation in areas where many triangles come together at a single point. It is all but impossible for a character to say which region they are standing in at the confluence points. These confluence points unfortunately show up all too often in complex environments. This leads to localization and pathfinding issues (i.e., if the character does not know where it is, then how can it find a path to its destination) [Hale 11].

The alternative to the triangular decomposition approaches, and one that will help minimize the character localization problem, is a growth-based approach. In our previous work we have presented 2D (PASFV) and 3D (VASFV) growth-based spatial decomposition algorithms [Hale 08, Hale 09], which were inspired by the Space-Filling Volumes algorithm [Tozour 04]. While these approaches do generate quality navigation meshes they can be slow when executed on large environments (the runtime of the algorithm increases based on the area to be decomposed). This is due to the fact these algorithms perform many unnecessary collision tests since they have to verify that every growing region has not intruded into another region or obstruction on every growth step. The vast majority of the time this is not the case, and this test will return a negative result. This unnecessary testing is a consequence of the sequential iterative expansion in traditional growth-based algorithms.

We have developed the Iterative Wavefront Edge Expansion Cell Decomposition (referred to as *Wavefront* for brevity) algorithm to address the problems of previous techniques by reducing collision tests and iterative growth. This algorithm works by scanning the world geometry visible from each region we place in the world and determines where possible collisions might occur (i.e., interesting places to expand toward). By forcing our regions to expand directly to these locations, we eliminate all but a handful of collision tests. This alters the runtime of the growth-based algorithm such that it increases with the complexity of the world (number of obstructions) instead of the area of the world. Not only is this technique faster than existing growth-based techniques, but the resulting navigation meshes produced using the Wavefront algorithm retain the high mesh quality exhibited by the PASFV and VASFV algorithms by providing regions of higher-order polygonal/polyhedron geometry [Hale 11].

3.2 Wavefront Spatial Decomposition

The Wavefront Edge Expansion Cell Decomposition (Wavefront) algorithm is derived from the PASFV and VASFV algorithms [Hale 08, Hale 09] and shares several implementation steps with them. The algorithm generates decompositions via a four-step process. First, unit-sized potential regions (seeds) are placed into the world. Next, one of these regions is selected at random and obstructions present in the world are analyzed from this region's perspective. In the third step of the algorithm the selected region enters a phase of accelerated expansion. This expansion is towards the obstructions found by the analysis in the second step of the algorithm. Steps two and three of the algorithm repeat for each region; this expands each region to their maximum possible size. Finally, in the fourth step of the algorithm new seeds are placed into any traversable space (a.k.a., empty space, unconfigured space, negative space) adjacent to the regions just created and the algorithm returns to step two, allowing these new regions to expand. If no new seeds are placed the algorithm terminates.

3.2.1 Initial Seeding

Traditionally, growth-based algorithms start using a grid-based pattern to place the initial unit-sized regions into the world. These approaches then iteratively give every region the chance to grow and expand outward in the direction of the normal of each edge (or face in 3D—we will use edge for simplicity here since they are both effectively boundaries for occupied space) of that region.

When using the Wavefront algorithm on our initial entry into the seeding phase we generate a list of *potential* seed points using a seeding algorithm that places a potential seed next to every exposed obstruction edge. This results in better overall coverage of the environment with fewer unit-sized quad (or cube in 3D) regions placed into the world over simple grid seeding [Hale 11]. Then one of these seed points is randomly selected to use as our initial region. The other potential seed points will be retained for later seeding passes, but will only be used if they are still in areas of traversable space that are as yet unclaimed by any regions. If on later passes through the seeding phase this list is empty, we will attempt to refill it by looking for areas of unclaimed traversable space adjacent to the regions we have placed. If this list remains empty after that point then the Wavefront algorithm will terminate.

3.2.2 Edge Classification

After a seed region has been generated, we proceed to the edge classification step of the Wavefront algorithm. These next two steps are the most computationally intensive steps of this algorithm, and we only wish to perform them on valid regions that we know are going to expand. Therefore, we only expand one region at a time and discard region seeds that are covered by earlier expansion. During this step, we iterate through each of the edges of obstructions present in the world as well as any edges present in regions that we have already placed into the environment. We then discard any edges whose normal faces away from the target seed point of the region as these edges are back facing and they cannot interact with the region. We then sort these edges into categories based on their relative spatial position when compared to the target seed location ($+x$, $-x$, $+y$, $-y$, $+z$, $-z$). Note that this technique creates axis-aligned edges between decomposed regions (obviously not guaranteed between regions to obstructions), which makes it easier for AI characters to reason and traverse regions. Edges that span multiple categories are placed in the first applicable one, depending on the evaluation order used in the implementation of the algorithm. Our reference implementation uses the following ordering +y, −y, +x, −x, +z, and −z. Any ordering will work as long as it is consistently followed.

Once the edges have been sorted, we locate all potential event points. Our region will have an edge that is perpendicular to each of the sorting classifications and whose normal matches the sorting classification (we will refer to this as the classification edge). By comparing the slope of each of our sorted obstruction edges to the appropriate classification edge, we can determine in advance how the expanding region would interact with the obstruction. This can be visualized by thinking of a radial half-plane sweep drawn from the initial seed point and then rotated in 90 degree arcs along each edge as shown in Figures 3.1 and 3.2. This sweep line will report the orientation of the edges it finds as well as the closest point on the edge to the initial seed point. The interactions between these edges of occupied space and the edge of the region we just placed can be reduced down to a series of cases.

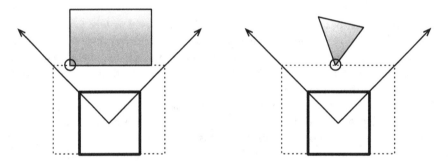

Figure 3.1

Two simple cases for event-based spatial decompositions: the case on the left shows expansion towards a parallel element and the case on the right shows the discovery of an intruding vertex.

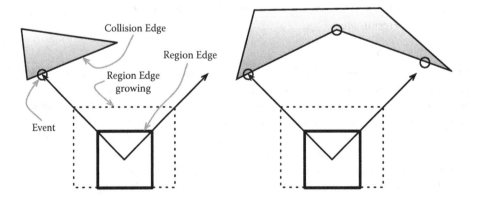

Figure 3.2

Two complex cases for the Wavefront decomposition involving splitting events.

         3. Creating High-Order Navigation Meshes through Iterative Wavefront Edge Expansions

The first of these cases occurs if the tested edge is found to be parallel to the classification edge as shown on the left side of Figure 3.1. In this case, we will wish to move the classification edge such that it is adjacent and co-planar to the target edge. We accomplish this by calculating the closest point on the edge to the initial seed point of the region we are evaluating. We then log this point and the distance from it to the region's initial seed point as an event. Incidentally, since all of our placed regions only expose axis-aligned edges and our expanding regions also only expose axis-aligned edges, any events involving other regions of traversable space will fall into this category.

A slightly more complicated case occurs when the edge is examined and found to be sloping inward towards the classification edge (i.e., region edge under evaluation) as shown in the right side of Figure 3.1. In this case, we will only be able to expand such that the closest vertex of that edge lies on the classification edge without changing the slope of the classification edge. We cannot change this slope as this would result in previously claimed areas of traversable space being relinquished, which would violate one of our invariants (claimed region space must always remain claimed by that region). This case is also resolved by storing the location of the closest vertex on the edge under evaluation along with the distance to that vertex from the initial seed point of the region.

Finally, we come to the most complicated case, which might result in the potential addition of new edges to the expanding region. In this case, as shown on the left side of Figure 3.2, the closest obstruction edge is sloping away from the midpoint of the classification edge, and it would be possible to move the classification edge such that one of its vertices could intersect the edge under consideration. This is an edge splitting case, and in order to calculate where this split should occur, the closest point on the edge under evaluation to the initial seed point of the region is found. This point is then stored as an event point along with the distance between this point and initial seed point of the region. Additionally, we wish to store the two end points of the edge under consideration (assuming the closest point was not an end point) so that we will be able to increase the order (order indicates the relative number of sides of a polygon/polyhedron, so a triangle has order three, an octagon order eight, and so forth) of this region such that it adds a new edge that is adjacent to the entire length of the edge under consideration. However, instead of calculating the distance between each of these end points and the initial seed point, we will treat them as a special case that looks at them as if they are only slightly further away from the initial point than the point we are using to split. This will prevent those points from interfering with other calculations in the process.

A more complex case with multiple splitting events can be seen on the right side of Figure 3.2. The events should be processed in order based on the distance from the initial seed point of the expanding region, and by altering the distance of these two end points we will ensure that the region tries to fully encompass all of the space that is adjacent to the edge it splits on as that point is processed.

At this point we have a collection of potential events for our new region to expand towards; however, we need to do two things before we can begin the expansion. First, if the edges of the world are defined as some boundary conditions rather than nontraversable space, events will need to be inserted to allow each region to expand outward to the edges of the world. Then this list will need to be sorted based on the distance between each event and the initial seed point of the region. This results in the processing of closer events first as we are more likely to reach them as further events are oftentimes unreachable due to the presence of more immediate obstructions.

3.2.3 Edge Expansion

With the completed event list for this region we are able to proceed to the expansion phase of the Wavefront algorithm. First, the expansion rates of all of the edges of the region are reset to zero. Then, the first (closest) unprocessed expansion event is selected and removed from the list of potential events. The distances that the edges of the region would have to move such that they reach this expansion event are then calculated. This is done by calculating the distance between the current location of the two (three in 3D) closest edges and the target expansion location. This result is then broken down into its principal components (x, y, z) and if these values are positive they are set as expansion rates for the edge or edges that have a normal that points toward the target event. The use of rates is a legacy from stepwise growth, but here the rates indicate jumps directly to event points. Expansion should then occur with each edge iteratively moving outward. Once all the edges have moved, then the check for any collisions or invalid expansion conditions can be executed. This happens because there are splitting events that may result in invalid configurations if only half of the event (i.e., one rather than two edges are allowed to expand) is executed.

Once the region has finished expanding, any collisions with other regions or obstructions must be resolved. Any vertices of the expanded region that collided with an obstruction must be split, and the region must be converted to a higher-order polygon/polyhedron by inserting a new edge. To construct this new edge take the opposite normal of the obstruction edge and constrain this new edge to the extents of the obstruction edge. Since expansion events are calculated in isolation with no consideration for other regions or potential obstructions, it is possible that a collision will occur and that the region will have to contract from a potential expansion event. If this happens, then the edge involved in the collision should cease further attempts to expand. The algorithm will then select another expansion event, repeating this process until there are no more events or all of its edges have ceased attempting to expand due to collisions.

3.2.4 Reseeding

After all regions have finished expanding, additional regions will be placed as per the seeding process discussion earlier. If the algorithm enters the seeding phase, and is unable to place any new regions, it terminates. This results in a collection of regions that is ready to serve as a navigation mesh. Additionally, if desired, this collection of regions can be cleaned up by combining adjacent regions such that the result would still be convex.

3.3 Postdecomposition

Existing growth-based spatial decomposition algorithms (e.g., PASFV, VASFV, and SFV) took advantage of a postprocessing step to improve the quality of the resulting navigation mesh. Occasionally, two or more region seeds will grow into an area of the environment that could be filled by a single convex region. This is a natural consequence of placing and growing multiple seeds at the same time, and is generally corrected by combining the regions. However, this combining takes time and effort, and it would be nice if it was not required. A strength of the Wavefront algorithm is that it avoids most of this form of cleanup due to the fact it only grows one region at a time. Since two regions are never growing at the same time, they cannot both attempt to subdivide the same convex area of traversable space, thus yielding a cleaner decomposition.

3.4 Wavefront Runtime

The Wavefront algorithm enjoys a worst case runtime, bounded by the complexity of the environment it is executed on of $O(n*m)$. In this case n is the number of obstructions present in the world, each of which will have to be evaluated by m regions that will be seeded by the algorithm. This runtime might seem to be worse than existing growth-based spatial decomposition algorithms (they generally increase fractionally, $O(n^{1/x})$ where n is the number of square units in the world, and x is the number of regions), but remember that the runtimes of these increase based on the size of the world (due to the additional growth steps that have to be performed to fill the world).

The runtime of the Wavefront algorithm only increases with the actual complexity of the environment and not due to the introduction of additional unoccupied space. In general, across a variety of game environments of different sizes and complexities, our reference implementations of these two algorithms average runtimes in the milliseconds to seconds range for Wavefront in comparison to a range of seconds to minutes for our growth-based implementations. The memory footprint of the Wavefront algorithm grows linearly as each newly generated region only needs to interact and know about existing regions and obstructions at any given point in time.

3.5 Comparisons to Existing Techniques

The Wavefront algorithm has been compared to existing methods of generating spatial decompositions with particular focus on those currently in use in industry, namely Delaunay Triangulation, Hertel–Melhlorn Decompositions, and Trapezoidal Cellular Decompositions. We only targeted algorithms for comparison that also generate full coverage decompositions in order to ensure the comparisons were valid. Evaluations were conducted on 25 procedurally generated worlds composed of randomly generated and placed obstructions with no axis-aligned restrictions and a basic set of rules that generated test worlds similar in geometry to those found in many games (the generation rules were influenced from public *Quake 3* levels, which were used in initial testing).

We generated decompositions for the worlds using each algorithm under consideration (one of these levels and the Wavefront Decomposition for it is shown in Figure 3.3). We then evaluated the decompositions based on the number of regions present, and the quality of the decomposition (using navigation mesh evaluation metrics [Hale 11] to determine the number and shape of any degenerate or low quality regions). We found that the decompositions generated with the Wavefront algorithm contained both fewer total regions and fewer near-degenerate regions than the Trapezoidal Decompositions or Delaunay Triangulation Decompositions. We define a near-degenerate region to be one that an AI character would have difficulty moving into or out of. Such regions are characterized as oddly or bizarrely shaped areas (e.g., fans of triangles all coming together at a single point, long thin slivers of quad-based regions spanning an environment, regions

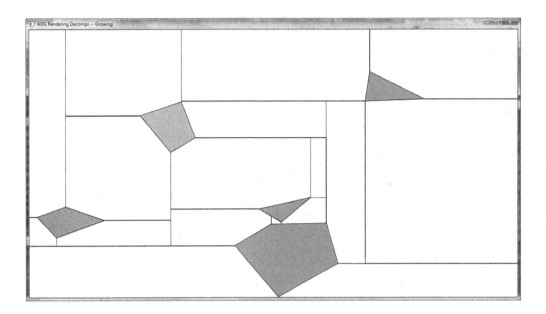

Figure 3.3

A decomposition produced by the Wavefront algorithm. Obstructions are shown in gray, while the decomposition regions are shown with black outlines.

with very narrow adjacencies to other regions, or disjoint/poorly connected regions), which we are able to test for and detect.

The number of regions was consistent between the Wavefront algorithm and the Hertel–Melhlorn decomposition; however, the Wavefront decompositions had fewer near-degenerate regions than the Hertel–Melhlorn decompositions [Hale 11]. It is not surprising that the Wavefront algorithm has fewer of these near-degenerate regions as it possesses a unique property not shared by the other decomposition techniques we tested against. Namely, there is an upper limit on the number of regions that come together at a single point of traversable space of five (10 in 3D); mathematical proof in [Hale 11]. The other commonly used techniques have no upper bound on how many regions can converge at a single point of traversable space. This convergence of many regions onto a single point is what often leads to the creation of near-degenerate regions and should be avoided if possible.

It is worth noting that the Wavefront algorithm generates decompositions that appear to be similar to those generated by the Trapezoidal cell decomposition algorithm. However, they are distinct decompositions, due to the fact the Wavefront algorithm will consistently produce decompositions with fewer regions. This is due to Trapezoidal Decomposition being restricted in only decomposing the world in a single direction (vertical or horizontal) while the Wavefront algorithm is in effect a multidirectional decomposition (both vertical and horizontal wavefronts originate from the initial region seeds).

For detailed information on the evaluation of the Wavefront technique, quantitative numbers, and navmesh quality metrics, please refer to Hale's *A Growth-Based Approach to the Automatic Generation of Navigation Meshes* [Hale 11].

3.6 Conclusion

Overall, the Wavefront algorithm generates fast, high-quality decompositions for use as navigation meshes via a quad-based expansion algorithm. Such decompositions have fewer small and degenerate regions (generally triangles) that can interfere with character navigation. This algorithm improves on previous growth-based approaches by performing fewer expansion steps, which reduces the number of collision tests that must be performed. This yields an algorithm whose runtime scales with the complexity of the world rather than the size of the world as existing growth-based approaches do. Additionally, since this algorithm only grows one region at a time, there is less post processing that would normally be caused by multiple regions competing to fill the same convex area. The decompositions generated by this algorithm compare favorably with those produced by existing popular algorithms (e.g., Hertel–Melhlorn or Trapezoidal Cell Decomposition).

References

[Delaunay 34] B. Delaunay. "Sur la sphere vide" *Classe des Sciences Mathematiques et Naturelle* 7. 1934.

[Hale 08] D. Hunter Hale, G. Michael Youngblood, and P. Dixit. "Automatically-generated convex region decomposition for real-time spatial agent navigation in virtual worlds." *Artificial Intelligence and Interactive Digital Entertainment (AIIDE).* 2008.

[Hale 09] D. Hunter Hale and G. Michael Youngblood. "Full 3D spatial decomposition for the generation of navigation meshes." *Artificial Intelligence and Interactive Digital Entertainment (AIIDE).* 2009.

[Hale 11] D. Hunter Hale. A Growth-Based Approach to the Automatic Generation of Navigation Meshes. Doctoral Dissertation. University of North Carolina at Charlotte, December 2011.

[Hertel 83] S. Hertel and K. Mehlhorn. " Fast triangulation of the plane with respect to simple polygons." *International Conference on Foundations of Computation Theory.* 1983.

[Lingas 82] A. Lingas. "The power of non-rectilinear holes." *Proceedings 9th International Colloquium on Automata, Language, and Programming.* 1982.

[McAnils 08] C. McAnils and J. Stewart. "Intrinsic detail in navigation mesh generation." In *AI Game Programming Wisdom 4*. Hingham, MA: Charles River Media, 2008, pp. 95–112.

[Tozour 04] P. Tozour. "Search space representations." In *AI Game Programming Wisdom 2*. Hingham, MA: Charles River Media, 2004, pp. 85–102.

4

Precomputed Pathfinding for Large and Detailed Worlds on MMO Servers

Fabien Gravot, Takanori Yokoyama, and Youichiro Miyake

4.1 Introduction

Precomputed solutions for pathfinding were common on old generation consoles, but have rarely been used on current hardware. These solutions give the best results in terms of computation cost, as all path request results are precomputed in a lookup table. However, they have two drawbacks: memory cost and loss of flexibility. Currently most games use dynamic algorithms like A* for navigation.

In the context of MMO games, however, precomputed solutions are still used. While the corresponding servers are typically equipped with ample memory, they have very few CPU cycles available for each request. This article will show how precomputed pathfinding has been implemented for *FINAL FANTASY XIV: A Realm Reborn*.

This game has very large and detailed maps (about 4 km² each), with cliffs from which the agent can fall (unidirectional path). We will present an accurate navigation system with navigation mesh autogeneration and a component based hierarchical lookup table. We define a component to be a group of connected polygons (at the lowest layer) or connected sublayer components (at other layers). We will first give an overview of the whole navigation system, followed by a brief explanation of the navigation mesh autogeneration, finally focusing on the precomputed data generation.

4.2 System Overview

The navigation system presented in this article has been developed for *FINAL FANTASY XIV: A Realm Reborn*, "a Massively Multiplayer Online Game," developed by SQUARE ENIX. The choices made for this system are mostly driven by this game's needs; however, the techniques presented here can also be used in other environments.

The game performs all the navigation path computations on the servers. One server can simulate several maps. One map can be as large as 4 square kilometers with several thousand NPCs and players. Figure 4.1 shows an in-game screenshot of part of the world to explore. Because the pathfinding system must be very fast, meaning A* was not an option, a precomputed path lookup table was chosen.

Another important requirement was to have the pathfinding system be mostly automatic. It has to be able to generate accurate navigation for hundreds of maps without expert or manual input, but if necessary, it must be possible to edit the data directly. As a game rule, any NPC can go where the player can go (except when specified by the level designer). The navigation system must be as close as possible to the collision system used by the player. Since players can jump or fall off (from almost anywhere) the navigation system must support those features. It also means that large NPCs can go through narrow passages if the player can use them. The NPC size is not used to find a path, but it is still used to smooth it at run-time. To fill the role of world navigation representation, a navigation mesh was chosen.

The precomputed navigation data is generated from the navigation mesh, and this generation is the core concept of this article. The precomputed data is stored in a hierarchical lookup table. This approach was chosen to reduce the memory footprint while maintaining very fast computation time. These tables are used on the server to perform all the navigation system tasks.

Figure 4.1

FINAL FANTASY XIV: A Realm Reborn screenshot.

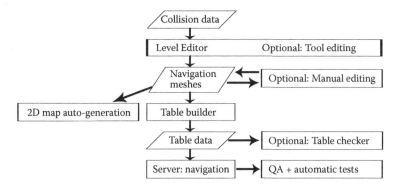

Figure 4.2

Tools flow chart from the collision data to the table data used by the server navigation system.

4.3 Tool Chain

The main tools used to generate the navigation table data are the Level Editor and the Table Builder (Figure 4.2). The Level Editor gathers all the collision data to generate the navigation mesh. The navigation mesh auto generation is done by Recast, an open source software library developed by Mikko Mononen [Mononen 12], released under the MIT license. The mesh is generated after a voxelization phase to identify the walkable areas [Miles 06, Axelrod 08]. The main modification made to Recast was the addition of the game-specific "falling mesh" into the generation process.

The level editor also allows editing the navigation mesh through various tools. For example, it is possible to remove the mesh generation inside a box or mark an area as only accessible by the player. Doors can also split and tag the mesh underneath, thus forbidding motion when closed. The most important feature is the navigation mesh seed point. It allows designers to remove all the polygons that are not connected to this point. Falling polygons are kept only if they allow the connection between two valid walkable polygons.

The navigation mesh by itself is simply a 3D polygon mesh model that can be edited or manipulated by other appropriate tools. For instance, it can be used by the 2D map auto-generation tool (Section 4.9.4).

Figure 4.3 shows a screenshot of a navigation mesh generated by this system, viewed in Maya. It is possible to edit it manually, but doing so invalidates further autogeneration. This option, if used, must be done in the final stages of the project.

The main purpose of the navigation mesh is to be used to compute table data through the Table Builder. This data is used in the server navigation system, which is checked by QA and other automatic tests (Figure 4.2). It is also possible to analyze the table data directly with the Table Checker tool. All of these quality checks expose problems in either the input data (collision data) or the algorithm. Quality checking is one of our main concerns in creating a system as robust as possible for autogeneration of navigation data.

4.4 Mesh Generation

Early in the project, navigation meshes were chosen for the navigation system. They describe a free moving space usable for steering.

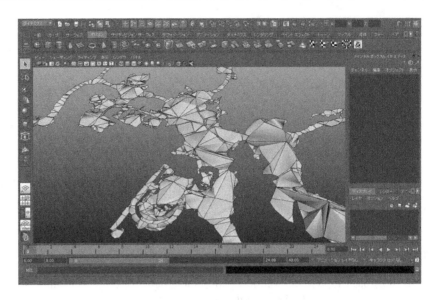

Figure 4.3

Navigation mesh of walkable areas generated for a town-like environment, viewed inside Autodesk® Maya®.

Since the world is very large, the navigation mesh generation splits it into a regular grid. Each tile generates a navigation mesh independently. We have chosen to keep this grid information in the precomputed data using small tiles of 32×32 meters.

Figure 4.4 shows a more detailed view of the navigation mesh. At its borders, the mesh is shrunk by the player radius, so that NPCs, or more precisely their centers, can move freely on the entire mesh surface. The generation process must try to minimize the number of polygons and match the collision data as much as possible.

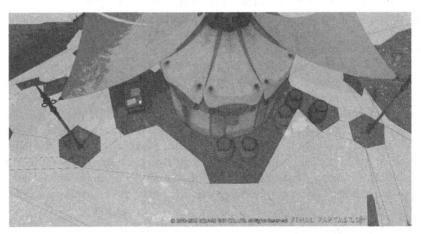

Figure 4.4

Navigation mesh autogenerated around a tent.

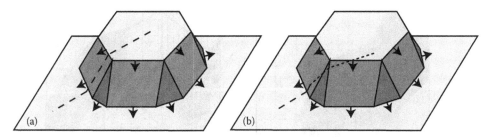

Figure 4.5

The falling mesh, in dark gray, and the desired output direction; (a) shows the unidirectional edges and how pathfinding is done; (b) shows how knock-back motion can cross falling polygon boundaries (dotted line).

As mentioned, we added falling meshes to the mesh generation algorithm. The generation of these is outside the scope of this article but some details are useful as it strongly influenced the Table Builder algorithm. The player can fall from anywhere from any height without taking damage. NPCs must be able to follow the player and avoid long detours. Designers can add an invisible wall to prevent the player from falling.

Moreover we added support for NPC knock-back, giving the player the ability to knock an NPC off a cliff. Figures 4.5a,b show how the falling mesh is used to support knock-back functionality, covering all possible falling directions. Figure 4.6 shows a falling mesh generated from a game map.

It is possible to use the mesh connectivity for the knock-back length (dotted line in Figure 4.5b). If the knock-back path stops in the middle of a falling mesh, a falling motion is appended to it.

The advantages of using falling meshes for knock-back in place of collision checks are computation speed and the guarantee that the NPC will always end up in a valid pathfinding position on the navigation mesh. The main drawback is the complexity of the autogeneration process.

Figure 4.6

Falling mesh generated for a game world. The falling polygons are darker. In those areas the slope of the collision data is too steep to allow walking.

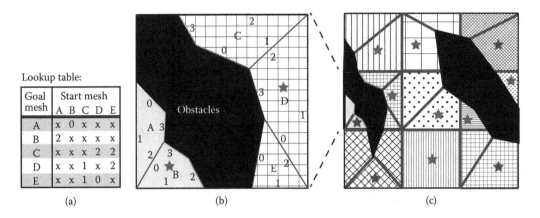

Lookup table:

Goal mesh	Start mesh A	B	C	D	E
A	x	0	x	x	x
B	2	x	x	x	x
C	x	x	x	2	2
D	x	x	1	x	2
E	x	x	1	0	x

(a)   (b)   (c)

Figure 4.7

Black shapes represent obstacles, while polygons within the same component have the same pattern. The gray stars show the polygons that are used as component centers. Figure (b) shows the detail of one tile of the whole navigation mesh (c). Figure (a) shows the lookup table of (b) with the polygon letter and the output edge number, or 'x' when there is no path.

4.5 Table Generation Overview

The precomputed navigation data is generated from the navigation mesh. For this purpose, lookup tables are built. Figure 4.7a shows such a lookup table. For instance, it indicates that traversing from C to E implies using Edge 1 of Polygon C. The lookup tables give the correct output edge to use when moving from one polygon to another. However, with the number of polygons generated (N) the table size will quickly become prohibitive ($N \times N$). A hierarchical approach is used to avoid the memory explosion [Dickheiser 03, Sterren 03]. With a hierarchical approach, we can split the N polygons into K groups and have K tables of size (N/K) × (N/K) and one portal table of size $P \times P$ where P is the number of portals connecting the polygon groups.

Instead of using portals to divide the regions, a connected component approach is used. This method is derived from the work done on *Dragon Age: Origins* (Bioware, 2009) [Sturtevant et al. 10]. A component is defined as a set of fully connected polygons. This component will be a node for the upper hierarchical level table. Since we use a hierarchical approach, we will use the term "node" in place of polygon when the description can be generalized to an upper hierarchical layer.

4.5.1 Component Approach

Figure 4.7b shows how 5 nodes are gathered into two components inside one tile. Since there is connectivity between the nodes C, D, and E, it is possible to gather them as one component. The stars show the nodes that are used as component centers. The component centers represent the upper layer nodes. They replace portals in describing component connectivity in our implementation. In general, the component center is the node which minimizes the distance to the other nodes inside this component.

Due to the size of the world, the navigation mesh autogeneration splits it into a regular grid and generates the mesh for each tile. The lowest level of the lookup tables is based on these tiles (Figure 4.7c). We define the following elements:

- *Node*: a polygon or a sublayer component.
- *Component*: a group of connected nodes. There is always a path between any two nodes in a component.
- *Tile*: a cell in the grid partitioned layer. It can have any number of components or nodes.

4.5.2 Table Connectivity

Each tile has a lookup table describing connectivity between all of its nodes. To avoid discontinuities at its borders, each tile also has a lookup table describing connectivity between its nodes to all its neighbor tiles' nodes (Figure 4.8b, left table). This ensures that when moving from tile to tile, there is always a detailed table showing which edge to choose.

Each tile also has a lookup table that describes connectivity between each of its nodes and the component centers two tiles away (Figure 4.8b, right table). As we will see in the next subsection, having this last table increases the quality of the pathfinding heuristic given by the upper layer. Figure 4.8a shows 25 tiles with the navigation mesh. The central tile (vertical line pattern) has a lookup table describing connectivity between its two nodes with each other, with all the 15 nodes of its eight neighbor tiles (horizontal line pattern) and with the component centers (14 nodes with gray star) of its 12 next neighbor tiles (grid pattern). In summation, the central tile has a lookup table from its two nodes to 31 (2 + 15 + 14) nodes.

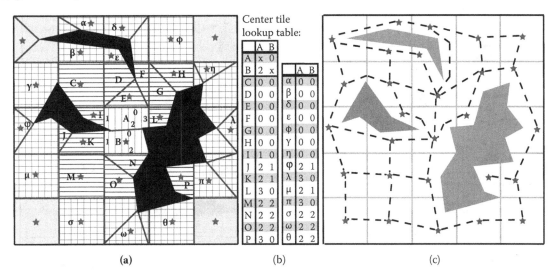

Figure 4.8

Figure (a) shows the local table connection levels. Latin letters represent polygons. Stars or Greek letters represent component center. The edge index of the polygons A and B is also shown. Figure (b) shows the center tile lookup table. It has a node-to-node table (left side) for the nine center tiles (line pattern) and node-to-component center table (right side) for the 12 border tiles (grid pattern). Figure (c) shows the top level node graph corresponding to Figure (a). Component centers of the lower layer, shown as gray stars, are the nodes of the top layer. The connections are shown with dashed lines.

4.5.3 Falling Meshes Outside the Table

When falling, the player loses control. In the same way, moving through a falling mesh changes the NPC's motion. We decided that for the purpose of simulating an agent falling, the falling mesh's polygons would each have only one output edge. The Table Builder uses this property to optimize the lookup table size. It first reorders the falling polygon edges so that the output edge is the first one. Thus, the output edge of any falling polygon will be Edge 0 for any goal in the lookup table (i.e., the lookup table column of a falling polygon is a null column). Moreover, we decided that any goal on the falling mesh will be changed to its ending fall point. This allows predictive motion and removes the need to have the falling polygon as a goal in the lookup table (i.e., the lookup table rows). This means that the falling mesh doesn't need to be stored in the lookup table. This method reduces the size of the lookup table by up to 20%.

4.5.4 Pathfinding Requests

Figure 4.9 shows an example of the pathfinding process. The path subgoals are in fact the component centers. The choice of which component center to use is made by the upper layer. In this simple example, there is only one upper layer with one lookup table in which to find the next node link to use. If a solution cannot be found at the lowest level,

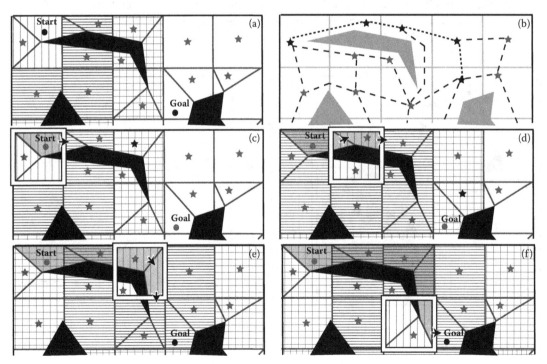

Figure 4.9

Example of pathfinding using precomputed data. Figure (a) shows the query start and goal point. Figure (b) shows the top level with the top level path. Figures (c,d,e,f) show the path planning process for the current tile (vertical line pattern) in each pathfinding iteration, as well as the edges chosen (black arrow). The resulting mesh path is shown in gray.

it is searched for in the upper level (b). Figures 4.9c,d show how the subgoal is chosen. It is the furthest component center on the upper layer path that is still inside the local lookup table (patterned tiles). The current tile's lookup table contains the next edge to use. The Figures 4.9e,f show that once the goal is inside the neighbor tiles, the direct node–node table is used. This example shows the complete pathfinding process, but if the goal is sufficiently far, it is not necessary to compute the complete path for every hierarchical layer. This allows for very fast path computation.

4.5.5 Hierarchy

In order to further reduce memory usage, we use not just two, but three hierarchical levels on the largest maps. For instance, with one of our tested maps, the table size is 16.5 mega octets with 2 levels, 8.8 with 3 levels, 8.7 with 4 levels, and more than 400 without any hierarchy.

We use the same process as previously described to create the upper level. Figure 4.10 shows the second level added to the example of Figure 4.8. In Figure 4.10, the second level has a tile size of 2 by 2 sublevel tiles. For the upper level tiles, the nodes (dots or stars in Figure 4.10a) are the component centers of the lower layer (stars in Figure 4.8a). For each tile it is possible to compute its component centers (stars in Figure 4.10a), which become the nodes of the highest layer graph (Figure 4.10c).

In our test, the mean and maximum number of components for the lowest layer (mesh) are 1.5 and 15, respectively, and for the middle layer, 3.2 and 19, respectively. This approach gives a good compression, minimizing the table size.

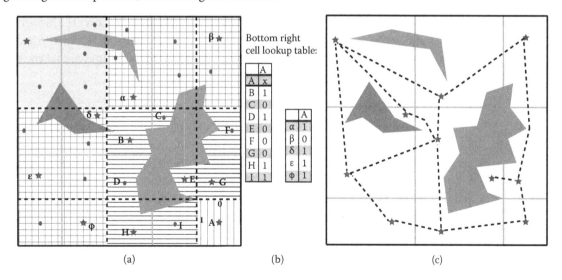

(a) (b) (c)

Figure 4.10

Figure (a) shows the second layer tile (dashed line) with dots for nodes and stars for component centers. The edge index of Node A is also shown. Figure (b) shows the bottom right tile lookup table. It has a node-to-node table (left side) for the center tiles (line pattern) and node-to-component center table (right side) for the border tiles (grid pattern). Figure (c) shows the top level node graph corresponding to Figure (a). Component centers of the lower layer, shown as gray stars, are the nodes of the top layer. The connections are shown with dashed lines.

Listing 4.1. Pseudocode of the table building process, showing the main steps of the algorithm.

```
ComputeConnectivity();
FallingMeshSetup();
BuildMeshTable();
for(int i = 0; i<max_level; ++i) {
    ComponentComputation(i);
    SplitProblematicComponents(i);
    ComputeComponentCenter(i);
    if (i+1 != max_level) {
        AddHierarchy(i);
        BuildHierarchicalTable(i);
    }
}
for(int i = max_level-1; i>0; --i) {
    RemoveInvalidSubLink(i);
}
```

4.6 Table Generation Algorithm

The previous section explained the main ideas behind the hierarchical table data used for navigation. In this section we will explain the algorithm computing this data in more detail and discuss some pitfalls that need to be avoided in order to obtain reliable data.

Listing 4.1 shows the table builder algorithm pseudocode. It iterates over the hierarchy of levels and applies specific functions to the lowest level (mesh data). In order to avoid several inconsistencies in the generated tables, some additional measures are taken. We will detail all those steps in this and the following sections.

4.6.1 Compute Connectivity

The ComputeConnectivity() function is probably the simplest one. Since the navigation mesh generation algorithm produces a 3D mesh file, it is necessary to compute the connectivity between its polygons. Our code is based on the "building an edge list for an arbitrary mesh" algorithm [Lengyel 05]. The only modifications made were to add support for falling polygons. Since these can overlap, additional rules were added based on the falling polygon's material (i.e., falling output, falling portal between tiles, falling path from edge, etc.).

4.6.2 Falling Mesh Setup

To simplify manual editing of falling meshes, the only requirement imposed on them is that a special output marker is placed at the end of a fall (a special triangle denoting the output edge). Because it is possible to have an output edge connected to several walkable polygons, the table must split falling edges to match the underlying polygon boundaries. FallingMeshSetup() is also in charge of computing the falling path and setting up the falling output edge.

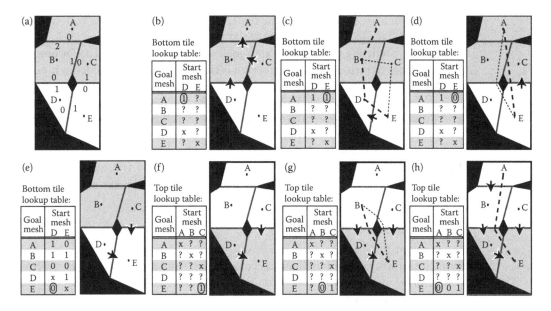

Figure 4.11

Figure (a) shows the two tiles used with the dots at the polygon center and the edge number. Figures (b), (c), and (d) show the table building process for the goal A and the bottom tile. Figure (b) shows the edge selection of D. Figure (c) and (d) show the edge selection of E, respectively, for the additional and smoothed distances. Figure (e) shows the table update for the last goal: E. Figures (f), (g), and (h) show the table building process for the top tile with the goal E for the starting polygons C, B, and A, respectively.

4.6.3 Distances Between Polygons

To build the lookup table, we tried to minimize the distance between the polygons' centers. We experimented with two ways of computing this distance: additional and smoothed.

The additional distance is the sum of the intermediate distances. Going from Polygon A to Polygon E through Polygon D, we have the distance AE equal to the sum of the distances AD and DE (Figure 4.11c).

The smoothed distance uses the smoothed path between centers as distance. In that case the distance from Polygon A to Polygon E through Polygon C is smaller or equal to the sum of the distances AC and CE (Figure 4.11d). Note that we will discuss the pros and cons of both distances in Section 4.9.

4.6.4 Table Builder

To decrease the computation time and memory usage, we decided to build the complete map lookup table data only for the highest layer (which has only one tile). For lower layers, the lookup tables take only the 21 neighboring tiles into account. In Figure 4.8a, these neighbor tiles are shown with line or grid patterns. Because we have not yet determined the component centers, a node–node table is computed instead of the node–component table.

The algorithm builds a lookup table for each tile independently (in fact, this process is multithreaded). Note that the shortest path result may change with the neighborhood; it is not possible to reuse it from tile to tile. For instance, in Figure 4.8a the path between π and θ makes a long detour inside the center cell neighborhood. In the bottom right tile neighborhood, the path from π to θ is the shortest one.

To avoid conflicting paths to one fixed goal, we compute the table data for one goal to all other nodes (reversed search). The search is stopped when all the nodes in the current tile are updated (Figure 4.11e).

Figure 4.11 shows the table building process for the Dijkstra algorithm at the mesh level (function `BuildMeshTable()`). As shown in Figure 4.11c,d, the smoothed-path distance can give a better result than the additional distance. However, this approach does not necessarily yield the shortest path (as for example in Figure 4.11h). Since it has been decided that going from B to E is done through D (Figure 4.11g), the path from A to E must go through D. Note also that with smoothed distance, paths are not symmetric (Figure 4.11d,h).

4.6.5 Hierarchical Table Builder

The function `BuildHierarchicalTable()` is in charge of the upper hierarchical levels. It is similar to the function `BuildMeshTable()`, explained previously. For this algorithm we also tried the smoothed and additional distances. The smoothed distance uses the distance computed in the lower layer between nonadjacent nodes (Figure 4.12a). This is valid only if the lower layer is not using additional distance. The smoothed distance significantly increased the quality of long paths.

Note that with smoothed distance, paths are not required to go through the component center as shown in Figure 4.12a. The shortest path from B to J is B, A, F, G, I, J. The shortest upper layer path, α, γ, δ, traverses through Component γ: {F, G, H, I}, but not through its center, Node H.

The function `BuildHierarchicalTable()` includes an additional constraint we refer to as the "subnode path" constraint. Its purpose is to ensure the validity of the algorithm responsible for solving the table inconsistencies presented in Section 4.7.2.

This constraint applies when the subnode center and one other subnode have different next components for the same goal. The Figure 4.12b shows such a situation. Imagine that the start point is B and the next subgoal is H. For the upper layer node there is a direct

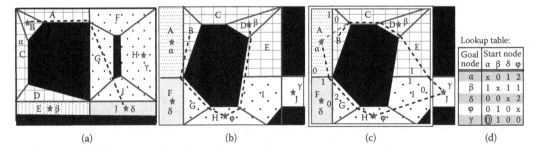

(a)   (b)   (c)   (d)

Figure 4.12

Problematic cases to take into account during the hierarchical table building process. The Greek letters represent the upper layer nodes (i.e., the polygon components). Mesh layer tiles have different patterns. Figure (d) shows the lookup table generated for the upper layer tile, which is a group of 2-by-2 mesh layer tiles shown inside the white border rectangle of Figure (c).

link β-φ, that is, the subnode path goes from D to H with only one change of component. However, for B, the shortest subnode path to H is B, A, F, G, H, which goes through α (A). Since the path β, φ can imply going through α, the upper layer path α, β, φ can yield a table inconsistency α, β, α (i.e., the subnode path A, B, A).

The algorithm detects all the cases where the component subnodes have a path not going directly to the adjacent components. These result in forbidden 3-node paths (e.g., α, β, φ) that are added as rule-based constraints. For instance, β cannot have α as previous node if its next node is φ. During the Dijkstra search process from goal to start, if one of these rules applies, the previous possible node is rejected. Figure 4.12c shows the table building process from the goal γ. The paths from β (β, φ, γ), δ (δ, φ, γ), and φ (φ, γ) have already been decided; α cannot be chosen as the previous node of β even if it is the shortest distance. Instead, the output of α must be δ (Figure 4.12d). Note, however, that in this example, the mesh tables have no inconsistencies between each other. The path from A to J will use the mesh table resulting in the shortest path A, B, C, D, E, I, J.

4.6.6 Add Hierarchy

The `AddHierarchy()` function is responsible for building a higher hierarchical level from the lower level component centers. The links between the upper layer nodes are defined as the paths between their subnode centers, as explained in Section 4.5.5.

4.6.7 Component Computation

Component computation is done in two phases. The first phase, performed by the function `ComputeComponent()`, calculates components using the node connectivity information see (Section 4.5.1). The only thing to keep in mind for the first phase is the use of unidirectional connections. For instance, with 3 nodes N_1, N_2, N_3, with the unidirectional connections N_1 to N_2, N_2 to N_3, and N_3 to N_1, we have N_1, N_2, N_3 in the same component.

The second phase splits those components, and will be explained in the following section.

4.7 Table Inconsistencies

If used as described previously, the table generation will produce inconsistencies. These are defined as infinite loops within the node path that ultimately prevents reaching the goal. Without unidirectional links, inconsistencies always occur between two bordering nodes (i.e., linked nodes in different tiles). With unidirectional links, the loop can include an indefinite number of nodes but at least two border nodes. These inconsistencies are due to both the local nature of the lookup table generation and the hierarchical approach, and are solved during the table building process.

4.7.1 Split Problematic Components and Compute Component Center

`SplitProblematicComponents()` is responsible for solving two possible inconsistency scenarios within the tables: the opposite path inconsistency and another one we refer to as the convexity problem. The methods of solving each of these are similar. For each node in a component, determine whether it is compatible with the other component node(s). This implies computing paths within the tile neighborhood. These paths are based on the 21 neighbor tiles in the lookup table computed in Section 4.6.

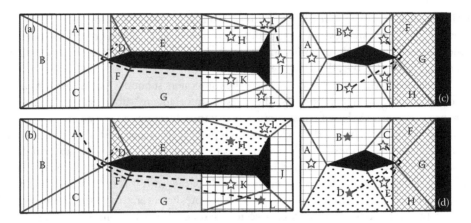

Figure 4.13

This figure shows how grid tile components are split. Areas with the same pattern correspond to the same component, while empty stars indicate potential component centers. Figures (a) and (b) show the opposite path inconsistency, while figures (c) and (d) show the convexity problem. Figures (a) and (c) show the components before and figures (b) and (d) show them after the split.

4.7.1.1 Opposite Path Inconsistency

The opposite path inconsistency is shown in Figures 4.13a,b. Going from D to K using the node–node table yields a shortest path of D, A, B, C, F, G, K. However, going from A to K is done through the node–component center table. If the center of the component including K is H, I, or J, the shortest path is A, D, E, H, I, J. This creates an inconsistency. In the same way K, L, J cannot be the center of the component including H or I. This shows that the pairs H, I, and K, L cannot be in the same component, and therefore we must split them.

This problem occurs only on the edge border of neighbor tiles (nodes D and F).

4.7.1.2 Convexity Problem

All paths inside a component are supposed to stay inside the component. An upper level node should not have a link to itself through another node. Figures 4.13c,d show such a case where the shortest path from C to D is C, F, G, H, E, D, and goes outside the component. This implies that C and D cannot be in the same component and should be split.

4.7.1.3 Component Center

Once the splitting constraints have been found the component is computed again. This time there are several possible choices of components. For instance, in Figure 4.13b we can have the components {H, I, J} and {K, L} or the components {H, I} and {J, K, L}. The algorithm selects the components with the smallest surface area first.

Afterwards, the component centers can be calculated. However, due to problems such as the opposite path inconsistency, some component centers may be illegal. For instance "J" cannot be a component center in Figure 4.13b.

Currently, the component center is chosen from within the set of allowed centers to be the barycenter of the component. It is possible to optimize center selection by, for instance, decreasing the distances between linked centers.

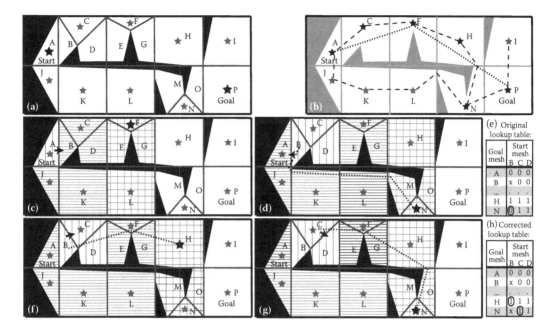

Figure 4.14

Invalid sublink. The pattern shows the table access method (line for node–node, grid for node-component). Dotted lines represent the shortest distances. Figure (a) shows the problem arising when the start point is within A, and the goal within P. Figure (b) shows the top layer nodes with links shown as a dashed line, the shortest path with black stars, and the smoothed distance is shown as a dotted line. Figure (c) shows how the subgoal F is used to go from A to B. Figure (d) shows that if the subgoal N is used from B, there is an inconsistency. Figure (f) shows that the inconsistency is solved if the subgoal H is used instead. Figure (g) shows that the path from C to N is valid. Figures (e) and (h) show the lookup table used in figures (d) and (e), respectively, before and after the sublink removal.

4.7.2 Remove Invalid Sublink

The function `RemoveInvalidSubLink()` is responsible for removing table inconsistencies due to both the local nature of the table building process and the path heuristic, which chooses the farthest component center as a subgoal. Depending on the tile neighborhood, the subgoal selection may produce a path that doubles back on itself. This is solved by disallowing the selection of the farthest subgoal by removing its link in the lookup table. Figures 4.14e,h show how the subgoal is changed by removing the output edge in the lookup table for the path B to N.

Since the hierarchical building process ensures that the upper layer tables are consistent for adjacent nodes (constraints in Section 4.6.5), removing the farthest subgoals will still result in a valid path.

This type of inconsistency can only occur on tile borders when the subgoal is changing, and is mainly a problem with long paths. In these cases, the upper layer data is more accurate than the lower layer and for this reason, the algorithm validates the layers from top to bottom.

Figure 4.14 shows a problem arising from the dynamic nature of the subgoal selection. In some cases, selecting the farthest possible subgoal can lead to doubling back. In the example shown in Figure 4.14d, the node-component table access from B to N is removed. The last valid subgoal to go to P will be H, removing the inconsistency in Figure 4.14f.

4.8 Table Use on Server

In Section 4.5.4, we saw how a path request is handled. As previously mentioned, it is not necessary to compute the polygons or the upper layer nodes path until the goal. Since no searching is required, the request is very fast.

However, this only yields a polygon sequence rather than the actual path to follow. An optimized version of the Funnel algorithm [Douglas 06] is used to calculate a smoothed path. Even if the NPC radius is not taken into account when finding the mesh path, it is used by the Funnel algorithm to push the path away from the border polygons.

The use of the agent radius for path smoothing leads to better looking paths but does not prevent large NPCs from intersecting with a collision boundary. It is possible to create a new table (not necessarily a new mesh) to avoid narrow passages, but this can result in long detours.

To further improve the path quality for small distances, a straight path search is done to the goal. If obstacles are found, the pathfinding algorithm is used.

4.9 Results

The presented navigation system provides very fast query speed at the cost of a loss of flexibility. One query takes about 4 micro seconds. The main problem with precomputed data is that any dynamic change requires a new table; therefore, this approach is best suited to static worlds. However, some dynamic changes such as opening/closing doors are supported by allowing/forbidding to cross the door polygons. This check is done at runtime.

This disadvantage is outweighed by the dramatic reduction in processing power needed at run-time by the navigation system. The most costly task is the relatively simple query for the nearest polygon, which is also facilitated by the regular grid partitioning. Even the smoothed path computation is less expensive.

4.9.1 Smoothed Distances

Using smoothed rather than additive distances for computing the lookup table (Section 4.6.3) improved the path quality.

Benchmarking with random trajectories showed that the length of more than 70% of the paths was unchanged. Of the remaining paths there were both increases and decreases in length. However, the number of trajectories reduced by more than 5% was 10 times greater than those that had increased by the same proportion.

The smoothed distance technique came at a cost: asymmetric paths, increased complexity of the algorithm, and twice the table computation time. However, the computational time is still within an acceptable range with less than 80 seconds for the largest maps tested.

4.9.2 Table Builder Algorithm

We experimented with three algorithms to compute the lookup table: Floyd–Warshall, Dijkstra, and A*. The best result in terms of path quality was given by Dijkstra using the smoothed distance. The fastest algorithm was given by the combination of A* using the additional distance. The heuristic used by A* was the distance to the tile being processed.

The Floyd–Warshall algorithm was slower, and it was difficult to add new constraints or to use the smoothed distance. It calculates all the shortest paths between all the nodes of all the 21 neighbor tiles. In the example in Figure 4.8a, this means that 42×42 paths were needed instead of 2×42 (Figure 4.8b).

The heuristic for A* with smoothed distance is the Euclidean distance to the nearest border of the currently processed tile. Even if this algorithm returned the shortest possible path for all the polygons in the processed tile, its global result would be worse than the Dijkstra version. The tiles tables' inconsistencies increased and, to resolve them, longer paths were used.

It is worth noting that all three algorithms yielded similar results when used in conjunction with the additional distance metric.

4.9.3 Table Size

The biggest table size is about 4 mega octets (Mo) for a 1.5 km^2 forest. Dungeon and town sizes are under 500 kilo octets. Note that this data is not based on the final maps, and that during the map design process, table sizes sometimes reached up to 10 Mo.

4.9.4 Alternative Uses

Other than navigation, the mesh was also used for checking the collision data, but its most interesting secondary application is the in-game 2D map autogeneration. The player has access to a 2D map of the world that must represent the areas accessible by the player. This map is basically a projection of the navigation mesh. Unfortunately, the details of its generation process are out of the scope of this article. However, it is worth showing in Figure 4.15 one of the maps that this cool feature enabled us to generate.

4.10 Conclusion

This article has described the steps taken for automatic generation of a precomputed navigation system. We have underlined ways to handle unidirectional paths and evaluated different methods of performing distance measurements. The resulting system allows very fast navigation requests for large and detailed worlds. It is a good solution for all server-based applications where there are strong constraints on security or client hardware limitations.

The whole generation system is completely automatic, freeing up the rest of the team to concentrate on more creative work. We hope that this article will be useful to others creating a precomputed navigation system and help them avoid potential pitfalls.

Acknowledgments

We would like to thank all the FFXIV team, and especially Shinpei Sakata who worked on the 2D map autogeneration, allowing us to share this unexpected use of the navigation mesh.

Figure 4.15

2D Game world map autogenerated from the navigation mesh.

References

[Axelrod 08] R. Axelrod. "Navigation graph generation in highly dynamic worlds." In *AI Game Programming Wisdom 4*, edited by Steve Rabin. Reading, MA: Charles River Media, 2008, pp. 124–141.

[Dickheiser 03] M. Dickheiser. "Inexpensive precomputed pathfinding using a navigation set hierarchy." In *AI Game Programming Wisdom 2*, edited by Steve Rabin, Reading, MA: Charles River Media, 2003, pp. 103–113.

[Douglas 06] D. Jon Demyen. "Efficient Triangulation-Based Pathfinding." Master Thesis, 2006. Available online (https://skatgame.net/mburo/ps/tra.pdf).

[Lengyel 05] Eric Lengyel, "Building an Edge List for an Arbitrary Mesh." Terathon Software 3D Graphics Library, 2005. http://www.terathon.com/code/edges.html.

[Miles 06] D. Miles. "Crowds in a polygon soup: Next-Gen path planning." Presentation on *Game Developers Conference (GDC)*, 2006.

[Mononen 12] M. Mononen, "Recast." http://code.google.com/p/recastnavigation/

[Sterren 03] W. van der Sterren. "Path look-up tables—small is beautiful." In *AI Game Programming Wisdom 2*, edited by Steve Rabin. Reading, MA: Charles River Media, 2003, pp. 115–129.

[Sturtevant et al. 10] N. Sturtevant and R. Geisberger. "A comparison of high-level approaches for speeding up pathfinding." *In Artificial Intelligence and Interactive Digital Entertainment (AIIDE), 2010.* Available online (http://web.cs.du.edu/~sturtevant/papers.html).

5

Techniques for Formation Movement Using Steering Circles

Stephen Bjore

5.1 Introduction

Moving formations around open terrain is fairly easy. However, it becomes more difficult to generate a path such that the formation ends at a specific point in a specified orientation, given the limitation that formations can only turn so quickly. A solution to this problem is presented in this chapter, and is an extension of the idea of using steering circles from Chris Jurney's GDC presentation [Jurney et al. 07]. The solution can be broken into two parts:

1. Generate the path to follow.
2. Navigate the formation along the path.

It's worth noting here that the first part of generating the path isn't limited to formations. It can be used for individual characters, vehicles, or any other moving object for which a steering circle can be defined. The second part is specific to formations and describes two different techniques for moving the formation along the path.

5.2 Generate the Path

Using two steering circles, one based on the current position of the formation and one based on the target position, we can calculate the path the formation needs to take.

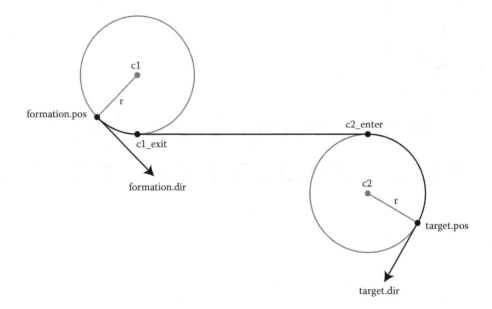

Figure 5.1

The final path starts at *formation.pos,* facing *formation.dir,* and ends at *target.pos,* facing *target.dir. c1* and *c2* show the centers of the steering circles. *c1_exit* is where the path breaks away from the starting circle and *c2_enter* is where the path joins the ending steering circle.

Figure 5.1 shows the most important information, as well as an example of what our final path could look like.

When we first begin generating the path, we start with five pieces of information: the current position of the formation (*formation.pos*), the current orientation (*formation.dir*), the target position (*target.pos*), the target orientation (*target.dir*), and the radius of the steering circles (or the turn radius of the formation, *r*). Based on this data, we need to calculate four additional values:

- *c1*, the center point of the starting steering circle.
- *c1_exit*, the point where the formation will break away from the starting circle.
- *c2*, the center point of the ending steering circle.
- *c2_enter*, the point where the formation will join the ending circle.

5.2.1 Calculating c1 and c2

The first step towards calculating the path is to generate the steering circles that will be used at the start and end points. To do this, we need to calculate the vector *target.pos–formation.pos,* which we will refer to as *dirVec*.

Next, we will calculate the center point of starting circle, *c1*. For this, we need the perpendicular vector of *formation.dir* in the same direction as *dirVec*. We can calculate this by taking the dot product of both perpendiculars of *formation.dir* with *dirVec*. We will use the perpendicular with the positive result, labeling it *formation.perp*. Scale *formation.perp* to have length equal to *r*, and then add it to *formation.pos* to get *c1*. The center point for the ending circle, *c2*, is calculated in the same way, using –*dirVec* (instead of *dirVec*) and the perpendicular vectors of *target.dir*. The vector with the positive dot product will be referred to as *target.perp*.

The only exception is when the distance between *c1* and *c2* is less than *2r* (i.e., the steering circles are overlapping). The solution in this case is to invert both *formation.perp* and *target.perp*. This will cause the formation to steer in the opposite direction, thereby giving it enough space to turn. For example, if we originally used the right-hand perpendicular of *formation.dir*, we will use the left-hand perpendicular instead, essentially flipping the steering circle to the other side of *formation.dir*.

5.2.2 Calculating c1_exit and c2_enter

The goal of this section, finding *c1_exit* and *c2_enter*, has two different cases that we need to consider. In order to determine which case we have, we first need to look at whether *position.perp* and *target.perp* are the left or right perpendiculars of *position.dir* and *target.dir*. For brevity, we will say *formation.perp* is equal to "Left" if it is the left-hand perpendicular of *formation.dir*; otherwise it is "Right." Likewise, *target.perp* is equal to "Left" if it is the left-hand perpendicular of *target.dir*; otherwise it is "Right."

The first case is for when *formation.perp* and *target.perp* fall on opposite sides (e.g., *formation.perp* equals *Right* and *target.perp* equals *Left*). In this instance, our goal is to calculate the angles where the points *c1_exit* and *c2_enter* are on the circumference of the two circles, relative to the x-axis (these angles are *a3* and *b3* in Figure 5.2). Once we have those angles, we can then calculate the two points.

The second case is when *formation.perp* and *target.perp* are on the same side. This case doesn't require us to calculate any angles, but instead relies on the observation that the important angles involved are all 90 degrees.

5.2.2.1 Calculation if Formation.Perp and Target.Perp Are on Opposite Sides

In the case where *formation.perp* is not on the same side as *target.perp*, our goal is to calculate the angles *a3* and *b3*. We will get into the details momentarily, but it should be noted that the calculation for *a3* and *b3* will change slightly, depending on which sides *formation.perp* and *target.perp* are on, which is why there are two diagrams in Figure 5.2.

Before we start the calculations, we will make several observations. First, the line from *c1* to *c1_exit* and the line from *c2* to *c2_enter* are both perpendicular to the line between *c1_exit* and *c2_enter*. Second, the lines *c1* to *c2* and *c1_exit* to *c2_enter* intersect each other at the midpoint of both lines. Third, we know the radius of the steering circles, *r*. And fourth, we are able to calculate the distance between *c1* and *c2*, which is labeled *d*. Looking at Figure 5.2, we can see that we now have two right-hand triangles, and that we know two sides of the triangles (one side is *r*, the other is ½*d*). This means that we can calculate the angle *a1*: `a1 = acos(r/(1/2 * d))`. We can also calculate *a2* by finding the angle of the vector *c2-c1* relative to the x-axis.

For *a3*, the calculation we need to use will depend on the values of *formation.perp* and *target.perp*. If *formation.perp* is Right, then we can refer to Diagram A, and *a3* is calculated by adding *a1* to *a2*. Else, if *formation.perp* is Left, we refer to Diagram B, and *a3* can be calculated by subtracting *a1* from *a2*.

The calculation for *c2_enter* is very similar to the calculation for *c1_exit*. The angle *b1* is calculated using the exact same equation and values that we used to find *a1*. The angle *b2*

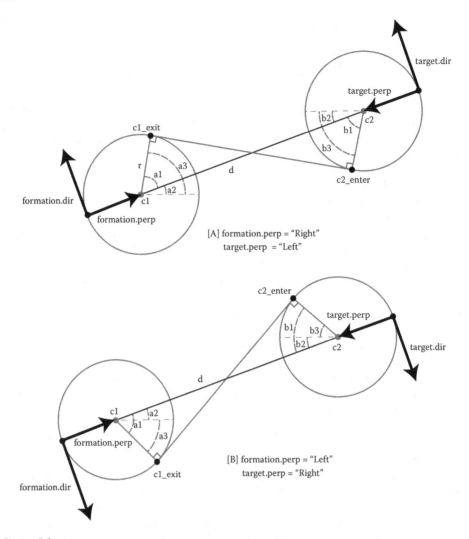

Figure 5.2

This diagram shows everything necessary to calculate the angles *a3* and *b3* when *formation.perp* and *target.perp* are on opposite sides. [A] shows the angles to be calculated when *formation.perp* is Right and *target.perp* is Left. [B] shows the angles for when *formation.perp* is Left and *target.perp* is Right.

is the angle of the vector *c1-c2* relative to the x-axis (unlike *a2*, which is the angle of *c2-c1* relative to the x-axis). The calculation for *b3* is also the same as the one we used for *a3*, and is simply *b2-b1* or *b2+b1*, depending on the values of *formation.perp* and *target.perp*.

Finally, now that we've calculated *a3* and *b3*, we can generate the points on the circles, *c1_exit* and *c2_enter*:

- $c1\_exit(x,y) = (c1.x + r * \cos(a3), c1.y + r * \sin(a3))$
- $c2\_enter(x,y) = (c2.x + r * \sin(b3), c2.y + r * \sin(b3))$

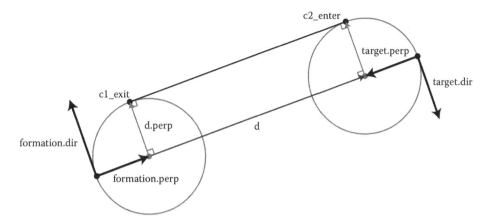

Figure 5.3

This shows what needs to be calculated when *formation.perp* and *target.perp* fall on the same side; in this case, they are both "Right."

5.2.2.2 Calculation if Formation.Perp and Target.Perp Are on the Same Side

In the case where *formation.perp* and *target.perp* both fall on the same side (meaning that they are both Right or Left), the calculation is a bit simpler. Here, we start by calculating the vector *c2-c1,* which we called *d*. As seen in Figure 5.3, if *formation.perp* is equal to Right, then we will use the left-hand perpendicular of *d*, labeled *d.perp*. Similarly, if *formation.perp* is equal to Left, then *d.perp* will be the right-hand perpendicular of *d*. In either case, once we have *d.perp*, add it to *c1* and *c2* to get *c1_exit* and *c2_enter*.

5.2.3 Generate the Points Along the Path

Finally, we can generate the points along the path for the formation to navigate by. The points will start at *formation.pos*, and move around the circle *c1* to *c1_exit*, move on to *c2_enter*, and finally around the circle *c2* until we arrive at *target.pos*.

The direction of travel around the circles is determined by *formation.perp* and *target.perp*. When they are equal to "Right," then we will generate points on the corresponding circle going around in the clockwise direction, and when they are "Left," we will generate points going around in the counter-clockwise direction.

5.3 Navigate the Formation

Moving a formation around in a way that looks reasonable requires the positions within the formation to be fluid. The following examples will keep the first row of the formation static, and the rows behind will follow in a couple of different ways. Here, we will look at two styles: the first style involves moving each unit within the formation towards the unit ahead of it, and the second style requires each unit to preserve its row by staying next to the units to its left and right.

Note that the points within the formation described here are intended to be pathfinding targets, not necessarily the actual locations of the units within the formation. This flexibility could allow units to go off and do other things, such as dealing with attacking enemies, gathering nearby resources, or navigate around smaller obstacles. Once the unit has completed whatever subtask it had, it can then resume pathfinding to its target position within the formation.

5.3.1 "Column" Formation

This technique involves moving each unit within the formation towards the unit in front of it, while maintaining a set distance. While this will result in a fairly fluid look, and maintain a connection between each unit in a column, it does not preserve the rows.

The first step is to update the position and direction of the formation, based on the velocity of the formation and the next point in the path. To keep the units of the first row in a straight line, their positions are calculated such that the line they form is perpendicular to the formation's updated direction, and is centered at the formation's position. Starting on the second row, calculate the direction between each target, and the target ahead of it in the same column. We then move the target in that direction until it's touching the unit ahead of it, repeating this process for the units in all of remaining rows in the formation.

5.3.2 "Band" Formation

For this movement style, the formation preserves the rows as it steers around corners. The first row is calculated in the same manner that was used for the *Column Formation* style.

Next, we need to determine whether the second row is turning left or right, based on the direction that the first row moved in. To do this, first calculate the direction from any unit in the second row to the unit in the same column of the first row, and then take the right-hand perpendicular, which we will call *rPerpendicular*. Next, take the dot product of the direction that the first row moved in with *rPerpendicular*. If that result is positive, the second row will be turning right, or else it will be turning left.

For the moment, let's assume that the second row is turning left. The next step will be to move the leftmost unit in the second row towards the unit ahead of it in the same column until they are touching. Next, starting with the second unit in the row, set each unit's position to be touching the unit to its left, moving in the direction of *rPerpendicular*.

If the row is turning right, there are only two minor differences. The main one is that we will want to calculate the position of the rightmost unit first, moving it towards the unit in front of it until they are touching. The other difference is that you will start with the second unit from the right, and will set each unit's position to be touching the unit to its right, moving in the direction of *-1*rPerpendicular*.

In either case, once we have the positions for all of the units in the second row, we can repeat this process for the remaining rows in the formation.

5.4 The Demo

A demo provided on the book's website (http://www.gameaipro.com) was created to be used as a proof-of-concept for the ideas presented in this paper. It was written in HTML5 and Javascript, with the intention of being as portable as possible. Nearly all of the logic for generating the path can be found within "main.js," while the logic for drawing, updating, and moving the formation and the units within the formation can be found in "formation.js."

5.5 Conclusion

This article has shown that steering a formation to end in a specific place and direction, with the use of some simple linear algebra, is not difficult. By calculating two steering circles based on the formation's current position and the destination position, it's possible to generate a path for the formation to follow that will ensure that the formation will never need to make turns sharper than it is capable of.

Further development of this concept could include the ability for the formation to take obstacles into account, on both a large and small scale. For smaller obstacles, the intention is that the formation can largely ignore them. This is because it is intended that the pathfinding targets within the formation will deal with finding a way around anything small. Large-scale obstacles would need to be dealt with separately, but could potentially be handled by taking into account the size of the entire formation, and then perform pathfinding for the formation as a whole.

Reference

[Jurney et al. 07] C. Jurney and S. Hubick. "Dealing with destruction: AI from the trenches of company of heroes." *Game Developers Conference, 2007*. Available online (https://store.cmpgame.com/product.php?cat=24&id=2089).

6

Collision Avoidance for Preplanned Locomotion

Bobby Anguelov

6.1 Introduction

Collision avoidance for NPCs is a critical component of any character locomotion system. To date, the majority of collision avoidance approaches are based either on Reynold's seminal steering articles [Reynolds 99] or one of the many reciprocal velocity obstacle techniques (RVO) [Guy et al. 10, v.d. Berg et al. 08]. In trying to increase the visual fidelity of our character locomotion by reducing artifacts such as foot sliding, some developers are moving away from traditional steering-based locomotion in favor of *animation-driven locomotion* (ADL) systems in combination with preplanned motion. This article discusses the implications of moving your locomotion system to a preplanned ADL system with regards to avoidance and why traditional collision avoidance systems may be overkill for preplanned motion. We present the collision avoidance approach used in *Hitman: Absolution* (HMA) and discuss how this system can be adapted for use with any preplanned locomotion system.

In traditional steering systems, characters are usually simulated as moving spheres and character trajectories are calculated based on the current velocities of these spheres. Appropriate character animations are then layered on top of this simulation to give the illusion that the character is actually moving. Since there exists a disconnect between the animation and the simulation, the animation is not guaranteed to exactly match the simulation and results in noticeable artifacts like foot sliding. ADL takes the opposite approach wherein a character's trajectory updates are read directly from the animation, meaning that the character's position updates and animations are in-sync, completely eliminating foot sliding. Unfortunately, in using ADL, we constrain character motion to the set of animations available, thereby potentially sacrificing the wide range of motion offered by steering systems. Furthermore, ADL systems have an inherent latency associated with them resulting from the fact that we can only change our motion whenever a foot is planted on the ground, meaning that we often have to wait for a footstep to complete before we can adjust our movement. A detailed discussion of these systems is beyond the scope of this article and interested readers are referred to [Anguelov et al. 12] for more information.

Once we have our characters moving around, we would ideally like to have them navigate from one location to another in our game world. The key difference, at least with regards to collision avoidance, is due to the path-following behavior in the locomotion system. In most cases, path points are simply treated as rough goals, and the steering system is tasked with navigating between them. In steering-based systems, the path resulting from the steering actions can deviate significantly from the original path found. Unfortunately, depending on the ADL motion constraints as well as the ADL latency, we could end up in problematic situations where characters clip corners or potentially leave the navigation mesh (navmesh).

This can occur when the steering desires are too fine grained for the locomotion system to satisfy or the locomotion system doesn't take the ADL latency into account, which is extremely problematic at high movement speeds. These problems can be ameliorated through complex adjustments to the steering system taking the ADL constraints into account as well as other measures such as constraining characters to the navmesh. Unfortunately, the complexity of such adjustments rapidly increases to the point where our locomotion system is significantly complex, without even taking collision avoidance into account. Now this is not to say such an approach will not work, since many developers use exactly this approach with great success, but we feel there is a simpler solution.

We think the important thing is to not look at the ADL reduced motion set as a disadvantage, but rather as a benefit, since the reduction in options makes it feasible for us to preplan our motion for the entire path. What we mean by preplanning is to plan the exact path, and potentially the set of animations needed, to reach our end goal prior to starting locomotion. This means that we can, for any given point in time, predict both the exact position and velocity of an agent. There are various ways to achieve this preplanning, and readers are referred to [Champandard 09] and [Anguelov 12] for more information.

It is with these preplanned systems that traditional avoidance techniques start to lose their applicability due to the exact precomputation of our locomotion. Standard RVO systems resolve collision by trying to find a local, collision-free velocity for a character, relative to other characters in the scene. The character's velocity is then adjusted to match the collision-free velocity. This is all done within a local neighborhood and only returns the immediate collision-free velocity, not taking anything else into account; this can potentially result in anomalous behavior such as agent oscillation. Discussing the potential problems with RVO is beyond the scope of this article and we simply wish to point out that RVO is a local avoidance system, which, given our global knowledge of our agents' locomotion, may not be the best approach to solving the avoidance problem.

6. Collision Avoidance for Preplanned Locomotion

6.2 Collision Avoidance for Preplanned Locomotion

We built a very simple yet robust avoidance system that allows us to detect collision on a more global scale than what RVO would have allowed. Our solution also allows us to resolve collision in a high fidelity manner entirely within the constraints of our ADL system. *Hitman: Absolution's* locomotion is a preplanned ADL-based system, with each character following a smoothed path precisely. These smoothed paths are created by postprocessing an existing navmesh path, and then converting this path into a set of continuous quadratic Bézier curves. Interested readers are referred to Anguelov [12] for information on the path postprocessing used in HMA.

Our characters will then follow these smoothed paths precisely, with the distance traveled per frame being read from the currently selected animation. Simply put, you could think of our characters as being on rails. These paths serve as the primary input to our avoidance system with the secondary input being the characters' current state and motion data, which is populated by the locomotion system.

Our avoidance system consists of three distinct stages: collision detection, trivial collision resolution, and nontrivial collision resolution. Our avoidance system is run once per agent per frame, and each agent is checked for a collision with every other agent (now termed *colliders*) in the scene sequentially. The result of this collision check is either a speed modification/stop order or a request for path replanning.

The first stage and the core of our avoidance approach is the collision detection mechanism. Our characters (now termed *agents*) are modeled as collision spheres with a fixed collision radius, and the premise behind the collision detection system is to simply slide our spheres along our paths and check whether they make it to the end of their paths without colliding with any other spheres.

During the frame update of each agent's animation/locomotion programs, the agent will query the avoidance system to see whether its current path is collision-free. The avoidance system will perform a collision detection pass as well as attempt to trivially resolve a detected collision. The details of this system are too complex to discuss here, since it is built around our locomotion system, so we will not attempt to do so but rather we will try to describe the higher level concepts the best we can to try to inspire you to build similar systems.

6.3 Collision Detection and Trivial Collision Resolution

Our collision detection works as follows: We first calculate a collision detection range for our agent. In our case, we know exactly how much time and distance is necessary for our agent to stop if we had to immediately issue a stop command. This stopping distance is then added to a specified time horizon length (in seconds) multiplied by our current velocity, the result being the collision detection range for our agent (refer to Figure 6.1a).

Stopping distance is important as we don't want to trigger a "stop" command which will result in our agent stopping in the path of another agent or, even worse, end up stopping inside another agent. The time horizon window allows us to detect collisions much further in advance than an RVO system could. In our testing, we've found it sufficient to only check two seconds ahead for a good balance of performance and fidelity.

Before we actually check the agent's path, we perform two exclusion checks on the collider. We first run a simple dot product check to determine whether the collider is in

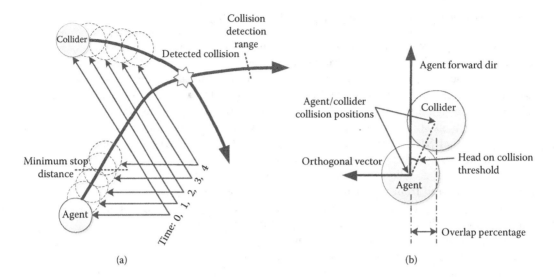

Figure 6.1

(a) Collision detection along an agent's path. (b) The stored collision data for a given collision.

front of the agent relative to the movement direction. In ignoring any colliders behind the agent, we implicitly delegate the responsibility for any potential collisions that may occur to those colliders. If the collider is determined to be in the direction of our movement, we perform a simple sphere–sphere intersection test [Ericson 05a] using the agent and collider positions for the sphere origins and the agent and collider's calculated collision detection ranges as the sphere radii. If both tests succeed, we then proceed to check the agent's path for a collision with the collider.

The path checking is performed by moving the agent along its path by the *agent's collision radius* (ACR). By moving the agent along its path in discrete intervals, we are discretizing our continuous path into ACR length pieces. The time needed for the agent to complete one ACR length movement (i.e., the *time per movement* or TPM) is determined by the agent's current velocity and is used to calculate the average velocity vector for the move. We then proceed to move the collider along its path by calculating the collider's position at the end of the TPM interval to ensure temporal consistency; this position and time is used to calculate a collider velocity vector.

In our case, our agents always move with a fixed velocity so this calculation is trivial, but it will be more complex if you have varying velocities per animation clip. This process of moving an agent's collision sphere along the path is visualized for 4 TPM intervals in Figure 6.1a. Once we have the agent and collider final positions and the average velocity vectors, we perform a moving-sphere–moving-sphere check [Ericson 05b].

If we detected an intersection between the spheres, we need to record some data regarding the collision for later use. This data initially contains the positions of the agent and collider at the point of collision. We also store whether the collision was head-on by checking whether the angle between the agent's forward direction and the vector to the center of the collider is within some threshold (in our case ~10 degrees). A rough estimate of the potential overlap percentage between the two collision spheres for that collision is then calculated and stored. The overlap percentage is calculated as the actor collision sphere diameter minus the min distance between the two spheres (along their respective paths) divided by the actor collision diameter. The final bit of data we store is the orthogonal vector to the agent's forward direction, away from the collider's direction of movement. This orthogonal vector is used for the path modification later on. All the necessary data we store for a detected collision is visualized in Figure 6.1b.

If no collision is detected, we calculate the collision sphere motion for the next TPM interval and repeat the check until we reach the end of the agent's collision detection range. If we have detected a collision then we immediately terminate the detection stage and move onto the trivial resolution stage. It is important to note that our system is only concerned with the first detected collision and so only tries to resolve that collision. The assumption is made that any further collisions along the agent's path will be detected and resolved on subsequent frames.

The trivial resolution stage attempts to resolve the detected collision through simple speed modification. We attempt to do this by performing the path checking algorithm at a different agent speed. If this new agent speed results in a collision-free path, then we simply instruct the agent to change speed. This adjustment is immediate, and any subsequent calls into the avoidance system will make use of the updated agent speed. This means that any other agents running an avoidance check will make use of the updated agent speed.

The speed modification check is run for all available speeds, and if all the speeds still result in a collision, then we check whether our stopping distance is collision-free; if it is then we instruct the agent to stop and wait until he can continue on a collision-free path.

This simple system resolved the bulk of our existing in-game collisions, but we needed an additional system to handle collisions that couldn't be avoided through simple speed modification (e.g., stationary agents or head-on collisions). This secondary system is used for what we termed nontrivial collision resolution, but before we carry on we need to discuss some details regarding the collision detection stage.

First, we've made an assumption that all of our characters are moving but that is not always the case. In many situations characters are stationary, either performing some level-specific or idle act (e.g., using an ATM or leaning against a wall). These stationary characters have to be handled differently since they have no paths allocated. The collision checks are performed in the same way, except now the agent is stationary so we simply don't need to calculate an update position for the collider.

Second, even though agents are moving, they might be in a transition animation for starting or stopping. In our case, our agents travel with a linear velocity, which greatly simplifies the math in the path collision check. When starting or stopping, we had a nonlinear velocity during the transition, so our prediction of agent velocity and position during those transitions was rather complex. We didn't want to unnecessarily increase complexity by modeling the nonlinear transition velocity in our avoidance code, so we simply resorted to estimating the velocity within those transitions.

Agent velocities during transitions were estimated by dividing the remaining distance of the transition by the time of the transition. We also tried to ensure that our start-and-stop animations were as short as possible, further reducing the error of this estimation. Something to keep in mind is that your transitions may have long periods wherein the agent is not actually moving. For example, we had a *turn-on-spot* starting transition where the agent would be turning for more than half of the transition, but didn't actually change position; this broke our estimation code and required us to have to pre-process all animations to determine the portion within the animations that actually move the character. Luckily, these nonmoving intervals are usually only at the start or end of an animation, which makes it easy to deal with by simply decreasing the transition time and treating the collider as stationary for that time.

Since our default avoidance query is for already moving agents, we also need to take into consideration agents that are stationary and wish to begin moving. We created a custom *'CheckForCollisionFreeStart'* avoidance query that takes into account our nonlinear start transition and determines when it is safe to start moving. This additional check allows us to wait for other agents to get out of the way before we start moving. We added two additional game-specific queries to the avoidance system dealing with combat sidesteps and *shoot-from-cover* acts. Since we don't want an agent to step out into another agent's path, we provided an interface for the combat programs to query whether a proposed new position was collision-free before issuing any move/act orders.

6.4 Nontrivial Collision Resolution through Path Modification

Our nontrivial collision resolution is a path modification system: we modify an agent's path around an obstacle without any need for replanning on a pathfinder level. Making use of the collision data stored during the detection stage, we calculate an *avoidance point* (AP) that will resolve the collision and a *reconnection point* (RP) on the original path.

The entire path starting from the agent's current position to the RP is replaced with a new path that is made up of two cubic Bézier curves and which goes through the AP. The AP is calculated as a point that lies at some distance along the orthogonal vector to the agent's forward vector at the point of collision. We apply a relatively large distance of around 5× the agent collision radius along the orthogonal vector to calculate the avoidance point. It is important to note that the actual position of the avoidance point is not all that important; in simply altering the length of the path, we also affect the time at which we would reach the previous collision point, which in itself is often enough to resolve the collision.

After calculating the avoidance point, we perform a navmesh query to ensure that the avoidance point is both on the navmesh and straight-line-reachable from the agent's collision position. If the point is off the navmesh, we simply truncate the point to the furthest on-navmesh point along the orthogonal vector that is further than some minimum avoidance threshold. We then set the tangent of the AP to be the same as the tangent on the original path at the point of collision. This means that the avoidance point simply acts as an offset to the path. If we have truncated the AP onto an exterior edge of the navmesh, we have to modify the tangent at the AP to be the same as the tangent to the exterior edge of the navmesh; doing this will help ensure that the cubic Bézier curves stay within the navmesh at the AP (refer to Figure 6.2b).

The next step is to find the furthest straight-line-reachable navmesh point along the path from the point of collision; this is the RP. It is important to ensure that the tangent at the AP and the vector to the reconnection point are dissimilar by some threshold (in our case 8 degrees) to ensure that reconnection curve doesn't cross over the original path. Finally, we then cut the path segment from the agent's current position to the RP

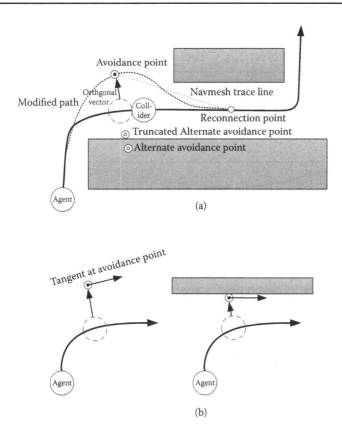

Figure 6.2

(a) Path modification. (b) Avoidance point tangents.

and replace it with the two cubic Bézier curves which pass through the avoidance point respecting the set avoidance point tangent.

Before we can accept this modified path, it is necessary to run some validation checks on it. The first check discretizes the path into short straight line segments, and we run navmesh straight-line-reachable queries for each segment to ensure that the path does not leave the navmesh. If the path leaves the navmesh, it is immediately discarded. The second check performed is a path collision detection check, exactly the same as in the detection stage, at the current agent speed on the newly modified path though. Unlike the detection stage, this check is considered successful if the result is either collision-free or is a speed modification instruction. If we receive a speed modification instruction, then we can safely accept the path, knowing that on the next frame the speed modification instruction will be received and executed.

Sometimes the modified path will result in an unavoidable collision; so what do we do in that case? We decided to try to find an alternate modified path by calculating a new AP using the negated orthogonal collision vector. We validate this alternate path and if it once again results in an unavoidable collision, then we simply pick between the two modified paths by selecting the path which results in the lowest collision overlap percentage.

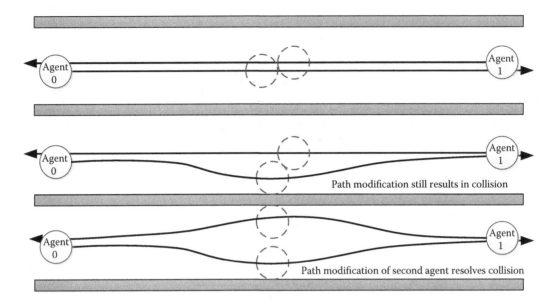

Figure 6.3

Collision resolution through multiple agent path modification.

In many cases, neither of the paths will resolve the collision, so we try to minimize the collision as much as possible. In many cases, upon running the avoidance query upon the collider and again trying to minimize the collision, you will potentially resolve it. This is exactly what we see happening when several agents try to navigate through a narrow corridor. The added benefit is that it results in flow channels forming. An example of collision resolution through collision minimization is illustrated in Figure 6.3.

6.5 Performance and Visual Quality

Visual quality was extremely important to us, so we added a few things to the avoidance system to help with the overall visual fidelity of our locomotion. We noticed that when sending groups of agents to investigate events, the agents would tend to bunch up and move together. Even though the agents were collision-free, the result looked poor. We decided to add a further check at the end of our collision detection stage (if we don't detect any collisions) to ensure that we maintain a minimum distance from any agents walking in the same direction as ourselves. We simply checked that if an agent was walking in the same direction as a collider and the agent was less than the minimum distance from the collider, we simply slowed down until we satisfied the minimum distance requirement. This simple check had a huge impact on the visual quality of our agents. We also had a problem where bugs in our AI would sometimes send more than one agent to the same position, so we leveraged the path modification to allow us to modify the end point of our path, ensuring that agents did not end up right on top of one another.

6. Collision Avoidance for Preplanned Locomotion

In general, the visual fidelity of our avoidance system is extremely high, having agents modify their speeds or simply stop and wait looks quite good (and in our opinion quite natural) especially within confined spaces. Furthermore, our system doesn't exhibit any of the oscillation side effects that are quite prevalent in the RVO family. Since our collision detection is performed along the agent's path, we have the added benefit over RVO that our detection works around corners allowing us to resolve collision well in advance of the agent reaching the corner.

It has been suggested that most of the problems with RVO can be ameliorated through tweaking of the parameters or the algorithm, but this only further increases the cost and complexity of such an approach, which is in stark contrast to the simplicity of our approach. Performance-wise, we found our system to be extremely cheap in that we are able to perform avoidance queries, in our production levels, for around 30 agents at a max total cost of around 1~1.5% (0.3~0.5 ms) of the frame time on Playstation 3.

6.6 Conclusion

We have presented a very simple alternative to RVO-based avoidance for use with preplanned locomotion. The system makes use of simple geometric intersection tests to perform collision detection and had two stages of collision resolution. The trivial stage made use of speed modification and stopping to resolve collisions, while the nontrivial stage calculated a new path in an attempt to avoid the detected collision. We discussed the high level concepts of such a system in *Hitman: Absolution* and the results thereof. This system is able to handle multiple agents in a complex environment and results in emergent flow fields developing in confined spaces. Furthermore, the premise behind the system is extremely simple and easy to extend, allowing developers a large degree of freedom in applying these concepts to their future games.

References

[Anguelov et al. 12] B. Anguelov, S. Harris, and G. Le Blanc. "Animation driven locomotion for smoother navigation." *Game Developers Conference (GDC)*, 2012.

[Champandard 09] A. J. Champandard. "Dynamic Locomotion by Example with Alex Champandard." http://aigamedev.com/premium/tutorial/dynamic-locomotion/, 2009.

[Ericson 05a] C. Ericson. *Real Time Collision Detection*. San Francisco, CA: Elsevier, 2005, pp. 88–89.

[Ericson 05b] C. Ericson. *Real Time Collision Detection*. San Francisco, CA: Elsevier, 2005, pp. 223–226.

[Guy et al. 10] S. J. Guy, M. C. Lin, and D. Manocha. "Modeling collision avoidance behavior for virtual humans." *Proc. of the 9th Int. Conf. on Autonomous Agents and Multi-agent Systems (AAMAS)*. 2010.

[Reynolds 99] C. W. Reynolds. "Steering behaviors for autonomous characters." *Game Developers Conference, 1999*. Available Online (http://www.red3d.com/cwr/steer/gdc99/).

[v.d. Berg et al. 08] J. v.d. Berg, M. Lin, and D. Manocha. "Reciprocal velocity obstacles for real-time multi-agent navigation." *IEEE International Conference on Robotics and Automation (ICRA 08)*. 2008.

7

Crowd Pathfinding and Steering Using Flow Field Tiles

Elijah Emerson

7.1 Introduction

Crowd pathfinding and steering using flow field tiles is a technique that solves the computational problem of moving hundreds to thousands of individual agents across massive maps. Through the use of *dynamic flow field tiles*, a more modern steering pipeline can be achieved with features such as obstacle avoidance, flocking, dynamic formations, crowd behavior, and support for arbitrary physics forces, all without the heavy CPU burden of repeatedly rebuilding individual paths for each agent. Furthermore, agents move instantly despite path complexity, giving AI and players immediate feedback.

7.2 Motivation

While working on *Supreme Commander 2*, we were given the task of improving movement and pathfinding behavior. As in many games with pathfinding, each unit in *Supreme*

Commander would move along a fixed, one-way A* path. Eventually, units would collide with other units, especially when they were moving in formation or moving into battle. When paths cross and units collide, the existing code would stop the units and wait for the conflict to resolve, rather than rebuilding a new path around the obstacle. This is because rebuilding a path every time there is a collision turns into a compounding problem, especially in large battles, where the new path will likely lead to a second and third collision, causing the game to grind to a halt. This behavior repeats across a thousand units, whose controlling players are all frantically clicking at each other's units, essentially begging for them to clash and collide with each other.

To overcome this path rebuilding problem, all movement was engineered to prefer to stay on the same path, resulting in limited physics, formations, AI, hit reaction, and so on. In this way, the pathfinding was limiting the entire user experience.

Because of *Supreme Commander's* one-track pathfinding solution, players would babysit their units as they moved across the map. They would spend their time watching and clicking, watching and clicking, all to help their units cope with the game's ever changing obstacles and environment.

7.3 World Layout

In the *Supreme Commander 2* engine, the world is broken up into individual sectors containing grid squares, where each grid square is 1×1 meter and each sector holds 10×10 grid squares. There are also portal windows, where each portal window crosses a sector boundary. Figure 7.1 shows an example.

In Figure 7.1, sectors are connected through pathable portal windows. Portal windows begin and end at walls on either side of sector boundaries. There is one portal for each window side, and each portal center is a node in an N-way graph with edges that connect to pathable, same sector portals.

7.4 The Three Field Types

For each 10×10 m grid sector there are three different 10×10 m 2D arrays, or fields of data, used by this algorithm. These three field types are *cost fields*, *integration fields*, and *flow fields*. Cost fields store predetermined "path cost" values for each grid square and are used as input when building an integration field. Integration fields store integrated "cost to goal" values per grid location and are used as input when building a flow field. Finally, flow fields contain path goal directions. The following sections go over each field in more detail.

7.4.1 Cost Field

A cost field is an 8-bit field containing cost values in the range 0–255, where 255 is a special case that is used to represent walls, and 1-254 represent the path cost of traversing that grid location. Varying costs can be used to represent slopes or difficult to move through areas, such as swamps. Cost fields have at least a cost of one for each grid location; if there is extra cost associated with that location, then it's added to one.

If a 10×10 m sector is clear of all cost, then a global static "clear" cost field filled with ones is referenced instead. In this way, you only spend memory on cost fields that contain

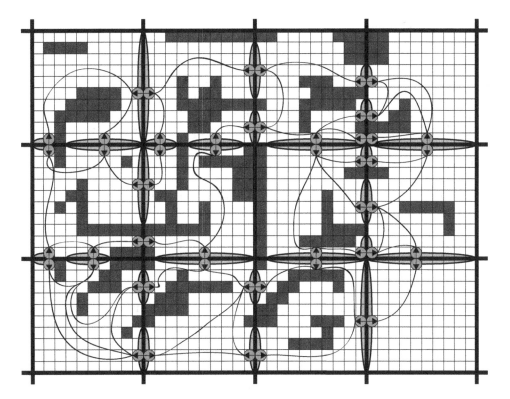

Figure 7.1

An example of the terrain representation used in *Supreme Commander 2*. Each sector is 10 x 10 grid squares with portals connecting sectors.

unique data. In an RTS game, there are a surprising number of clear sectors. In *Supreme Commander 2*, we had roughly 50–70% of the pathable space marked as clear due to widespread areas of open and flat land, lakes, and oceans.

Cost field data was prebuilt by our editor, which converted walls and geometry slope into cost values. Our design team could also visualize this path cost information, as well as make changes to it.

7.4.2 Integration Field

The integration field is a 24-bit field where the first 16 bits is the total integrated cost amount and the second 8 bits are used for integration flags such as "active wave front" and "line of sight." You can optionally spend more memory for better flow results by using a 32-bit float for your integrated cost making it a 40-bit field.

7.4.3 Flow Field

Flow fields are 8-bit fields with the first four bits used as an index into a direction lookup table and the second four bits as flags, such as "pathable" and "has line of sight." The flow field holds all the primary directions and flags used by the agent's steering pipeline for steering around hills and walls to flow toward the path goal.

7.5 Path Requests

Once you have a valid goal position and one or more source positions, you can create a *path request*. The path request will first run A* through the portal node graph. The A* walker starts at the source position, travels through portal nodes, and ends at the goal, thus producing a linked list of "next" portal nodes. This process continues with the next path request source, but this time the portal walker runs "merging" A*, in which the walker prefers to stop and point to a previously traveled portal node to "merge" with previous A* results. With "merging" A* you are more likely to share flow field results and sources are more likely to path closer together, which is the desired behavior when selecting multiple sources to move toward a single goal.

If your A* path to goal is successful, the next step is to walk through your list of next portal nodes and submit a flow field request for each one. At this point you're done with the path request and, because you've only traversed the portal node graph using merging A*, you've used very little CPU.

7.6 The Integrator

We define the *integrator* as the class responsible for taking a single flow field request and, over one or more ticks, building out a single flow field tile. This is achieved by taking the request's cost field data as well as the request's "initial wave front" as input. The initial wave front is a list of goal locations, each having a predetermined integrated cost value.

The integrator takes the initial wave front and integrates it outward using an Eikonal equation [Ki Jeong 08]. Visualize the effect of touching still water, creating a rippling wave moving across the water surface. The Integrator's active wave front behaves similarly in how it moves across the pathable surface while setting larger and larger integrated cost values into the integration field. It repeats this process until the active wave front stops moving by hitting a wall or the sector's boarders. To better understand the integration process, let's go over the Integrator's integration steps.

7.6.1 Integration Step 1: Reset the Integration Field

The integrator's first step is to reset its integration field values and apply the initial goal wave front. If the requested flow field has the final 1×1 goal, then its initial goal wave front is a single 1×1 location with a zero integrated cost value. However, if the flow field request is from a 10×1 or 1×10 portal, then there will be ten goal locations with ten different integrated cost goals.

For higher quality flow results you can integrate at least one flow field ahead in the portal path. Then you can carry over the previously integrated costs as your initial portal window costs instead of using zeros, effectively making the flow across borders seamless. This quality improvement comes at a cost of making flow tiles order dependent, and thus harder to reuse by other path requests.

7.6.2 Integration Step 2: Line Of Sight Pass

If we are integrating from the actual path goal, then we first run a line of sight (LOS) pass. We do this to have the highest quality flow directions near the path goal. When an agent is within the LOS it can ignore the Flow field results altogether and just steer toward the exact goal position. Without the LOS pass, you can have diamond-shaped flow directions around your goal due to the integrator only looking at the four up, down, left, and right neighbors.

It's possible to improve flows around your goal by looking at all eight neighbors during the cost integration pass, but we wouldn't recommend it; marking LOS is cheap and when within the LOS, you get the highest quality path direction possible by ignoring the flow field altogether.

To integrate LOS you have the initial goal wave front integrate out as you normally would, but, instead of comparing the cost field neighbor costs to determine the integrated cost, just increment the wave front cost by one as you move the wave front while flagging the location as "Has Line of Sight." Do this until the wave front hits something with any cost greater than one.

Once we hit something with a cost greater than one, we need to determine if the location is an LOS corner. We do this by looking at the location's neighbors. If one side has a cost greater than one while the other side does not, we have an LOS corner.

For all LOS corners we build out a 2D line starting at the grid square's outer edge position, in a direction away from the goal. Follow this line across the grid using Bresenham's line algorithm, flagging each grid location as "Wave Front Blocked" and putting the location in a second active wave front list to be used later, by the cost integration pass. By marking each location as "Wave Front Blocked" the LOS integration wave front will stop along the line that marks the edge of what is visible by the goal.

You can bring LOS corner lines across sector borders by carrying over the "Has Line of Sight" and "Wave Front Blocked" flags at portal window locations. Then, when you build out the neighbor's integration field, for each portal window location that has the "Wave Front Blocked" flag, consider it an LOS corner to the goal and build out the rest of the line accordingly. This will make the LOS seamless across sector borders.

Continue moving the LOS pass wave front outward until it stops moving by hitting a wall or a location that has the "Wave Front Blocked" flag. Other than the time spent using Bresenham's line algorithm, the LOS first pass is very cheap because it does not look at neighboring cost values. The wave front just sets flags and occasionally detects corners and iterates over a line.

Figure 7.2 shows the results of a LOS pass. Each clear white grid square has been flagged as "Has Line Of Sight." Each LOS corner has a line where each grid square that overlaps that line is flagged as "Wave Front Blocked."

7.6.3 Integration Step 3: Cost Integration Pass

We are now ready for cost field integration. As with the LOS pass, we start with the active wave front list. This active wave front comes from the list of "Wave Front Blocked" locations from the previous LOS pass. In this way we only integrate locations that are not visible from the goal.

We integrate this wave front out until it stops moving by hitting a wall or a sector border. At each grid location we compute the integrated cost by adding the cheapest cost field and integrated cost field's up, down, left, or right neighbors together. Then repeat this Eikonal equation process again and again, moving the wave front outward toward each location's un-integrated, non-walled neighbors.

During integration, look out for overlapping previously integrated results because of small cost differences. To fix this costly behavior, make sure your wave front stops when it hits

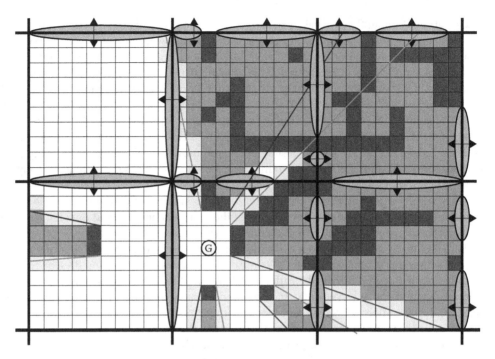

Figure 7.2

The results of an LOS pass.

previously integrated results, unless you really have a significant difference in integrated costs. If you don't do this, you risk having wave fronts bounce back and forth, eating up results when it's not necessary. In other words, if a different path is slightly cheaper to take, then don't bother backtracking across the field just to save that small pathfinding cost difference.

The following is an example of when it's appropriate to overlap previously integrated cost results. Imagine a single path that splits into two paths, where each split path leads to the same goal location. However, one split has a long and costly sand trap, while the other does not. The integration wave front will move away from the goal, split into two, and converge on each other at the beginning of the path. When they meet, the cheaper wave front will overlap the more expensive wave front's results and continue to integrate, backtracking down the expensive path until the cheaper integrated costs do not have a significant difference with the previously integrated costs. This backtracking behavior will have the effect of redirecting the flow field directions away from the sand trap and back toward the cheaper path. This is no different than backtracking in A*; it's just good to point this behavior out as it's more costly when integrating fields.

7.6.4 Integration Step 4: Flow Field Pass

We are now ready to build a flow field from our newly created integration field. This is done by iterating over each integrated cost location and either writing out the LOS flag or comparing all eight NW, N, NE, E, SE, S, SW, W neighbors to determine the "cheapest" direction we should take for that location.

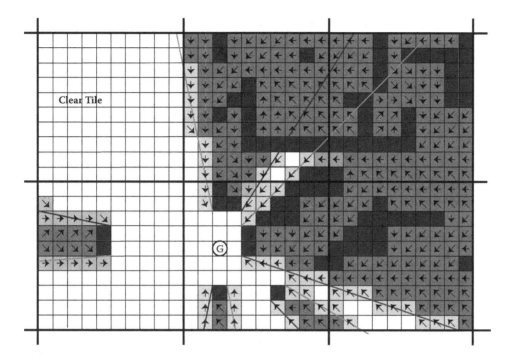

Figure 7.3

The final flow field directions.

Figure 7.3 shows what the final flow field directions look like. Notice that no work was done for locations that have goal LOS or locations within the clear tile. Once the flow field is built out we submit it to the *flow field cache*.

7.7 The Flow Field Cache

The flow field cache contains all of our built flow fields, each with their own unique ID based on the portal window they take you through. In this way, work can be shared across path requests despite having different goals.

If there is a two-way hallway in your map, the odds are pretty good that multiple paths will want the same hallway flow field results. A flow field can also be reference tracked so when there are no more references to it, it can be discarded or put on a timer to be discarded later. You can also prebuild all flow field permutations and store them on disk so that you only need to build the flow fields that have custom LOS goal information.

7.8 Supporting Dynamic Environments and Queries

The whole point of inventing this technique was to better handle the dynamic nature of our game environments in real-time. To that end, we built everything with dynamic change in mind.

We can easily support moving sources by running another "merging" A* across portal nodes if the agent's position moves outside the sectors in the planned path.

We support moving goals by rebuilding the goal's flow field. If the goal crossed a sector boundary, the path's portal nodes are rebuilt behind the scenes. Most of the flow fields requested by the new path will already have been built and will be in the cache, so very few flow fields need to be rebuilt. Once the new path is ready, the agent will seamlessly switch over to it from the old path.

We support changing walls and hills by marking the cost field of the sector that contains them and their associated portals as dirty. Then the portal graph is rebuilt for nodes that are on the borders of the dirty sectors as well as their neighbors. Finally, the paths that were affected by those changes are rebuilt.

All of this is done by marking things dirty and rebuilding them based on a priority queue, where each item in the queue is given a time slice of a fixed number of milliseconds. This allows us to control what, when, and how rebuilding happens over time.

7.9 Cost Stamp Support

Cost stamps represent a custom set of costs values you can "stamp" into the world. In *Supreme Commander 2*, we needed to place buildings down that had custom walls as well as custom pathable areas. The player can essentially paint whole new pathable landscapes by using varying sized structures, including 1×1 grid walls.

Cost stamps record the original cost field values before replacing them with a new set of costs. After placing a cost stamp down, the overlapping sectors would be flagged as dirty and the dynamic graph and path rebuilding process would take care of everything else.

7.10 Source Cost Data

The map editor would build the cost field data from looking at geometry, placing down walls and hills where appropriate. We would run a blur pass to add a cost gradient near walls to improve flow results when going down hallways and around jagged edges.

All cost data was also shown in the editor so that designers could manually add and remove path cost as they saw fit. This was a huge benefit to the design team as they could finally control where and how units moved in their maps.

7.11 Different Movement Types

Each agent in the *Supreme Commander 2* engine has its own movement type. Each movement type has its own cost field data and hence produces its own portal graph. In this way, a land-only tank would have a different path than a hovercraft that can travel over lakes and swamps.

The editor would build out the different cost data for each movement type. To support large units, a special wall cushioning process was run over the map that moved the walls outward. This had the effect of closing off skinny gaps that are too small for large units as well as pushing out wall and mountain sides so large units can't visually overlap them when near.

If the user selected units with different movement types, such as a squadron of jets, a few land-only tanks, some hovercraft, and a super large experimental robot, the game would use the "most restrictive movement type" path for all compatible units before building more paths for the incompatible units.

7.12 Steering with Flow Fields

When agents steer with flow fields, there are some if-else conditions to look out for. For starters, if the agent doesn't have a valid flow field, it should steer to the next portal position. Once the agent has a flow field, it should look for an LOS flag to steer to its goal; otherwise, it should use the specified flow field direction.

When an agent is receiving new flow field directions, we recommend storing off a path direction vector and blending in new flow directions as you cross grid squares. This has the effect of smoothing out the flow field directions as the agent traverses the field.

7.13 Walls and Physics

With flow fields, your pathfinding agents can move in any direction without the high expense of rebuilding their path. Once your agents move in any direction, they are bound to hit a wall or another agent. In the *Supreme Commander 2* engine, agents could push each other around as well as slide along walls using physics.

Having physics in our game allowed for new game play scenarios such as explosions that push back units or super large robots that could push back a hundred tanks. We had a structure that could arbitrarily push or pull units across the map, as well as a large unit that could suck units into a whirlwind, spinning them around and around until they smashed together. These new game play scenarios would not have been possible without the cheaper movement cost associated with using flow field tiles.

7.14 Island Fields

An optional *island field* type can be implemented containing island IDs, where each island ID represents a single pathable island. Imagine the different islands of Hawaii: if you are on one island, you can only drive to locations within the same island.

For each sector you store its island ID. If there is more than one island ID in the sector, then the sector has an island field breaking the IDs down to individual grid locations. With this information you can quickly determine if a path request is valid.

In the *Supreme Commander 2* engine, you can move your mouse over any location on the map and see the mouse icon change from an arrow to a stop sign, indicating that you cannot reach that location. This feature was implemented by retrieving Island IDs at the source and destination locations to see if they match.

7.15 Minimizing CPU Footprint

You can enforce low CPU usage by capping the number of tiles or grid squares you commit to per tick. You can also easily spread out integration work across threads because the Integration Field memory is separate from everything else.

7.16 Future Work

The following is a list of ideas to further improve this technique.

- Support 3D spaces by connecting portal graph nodes across overlapping sectors.
- Pre-process and compress *all* flow field permutations and stream them from disk.
- Add support for arbitrarily sized maps by using a hierarchy of sectors and N-way graphs.
- Build out the flow field using the GPU instead of the CPU [Ki Jeong 07].
- Support multiple goals. Multiple goal flow fields are perfect for zombies chasing heroes.

7.17 Conclusion

Our work on *Supreme Commander 2* shows that it's advantageous to move beyond single path-based solutions and start looking at field-based solutions to support dynamic crowd pathing and steering in RTS games with hundreds to thousands of agents. In this article, we demonstrated how to represent and analyze the pathable terrain to generate flow fields that can drive hundreds of units to a goal. Additionally, we showed that this method is computationally cheap, compared with individual unit pathfinding requests, even in the face of dynamic terrain and queries. Hopefully you can benefit from our experience with the *Supreme Commander 2* engine and continue to expand and refine field-based pathfinding in your next game.

References

[Ki Jeong 07] W. Ki Jeong and R. Whitaker. "A fast Eikonal equation solver for parallel systems." *SIAM Conference on Computational Science and Engineering*, 2007.
[Ki Jeong 08] W. Ki Jeong and R. Whitaker. "A fast iterative method for Eikonal equations." *SIAM Journal on Scientific Computing* 30(5), 2008.

8

Efficient Crowd Simulation for Mobile Games

Graham Pentheny

8.1 Introduction

Crowd simulation is a topic of ongoing exploration and experimentation in the game AI industry [Pelechano et al. 07, Sung et al. 04]. Modern games are filled with more and more AI-controlled agents. It is therefore imperative to create a movement system that is realistic, robust, and designer-friendly.

Traditional pathfinding approaches compute separate paths for individual agents, even though many paths may have similar sections. These redundant path calculations inhibit simulations of large numbers of units on mobile hardware.

The mobile tower defense game *Fieldrunners 2* used a combination of vector flow fields and steering behaviors to efficiently simulate thousands of agents, referred to as units. This article will describe the systems of flow-field generation, flow sampling, and unit movement employed by *Fieldrunners 2*. The process of constructing and balancing a dynamic crowd simulation system will be described in detail from the ground up.

8.2 Grid

The grid provides a discretization of the game world and defines the areas within which units may travel. For *Fieldrunners 2,* a grid cell was sized slightly wider than the widest unit, so that every computed path was traversable by every unit. Each grid cell can either be *open*, indicating that a unit may pass through it, or *blocked* indicating that the cell is impassible.

8.3 Flow Field

Units move through the grid following a static vector *flow field*. The flow field represents the optimal path direction at every cell in the grid, and is an approximation of a continuous *flow function*. Given a set of destination points, the flow function defines a vector field of normalized vectors, indicating the direction of the optimal path to the nearest destination. The flow function is similar to common methods for describing flows in fluid dynamics [Cabral and Leedom 93], with the difference that all flow vectors are normalized. Given this definition, we can define a flow field to be a discretization of a *flow function*.

Flow fields guide units to the nearest destination in the same manner as a standard pathfinding system; however, the units' pathing information is encoded in a flow field, removing the need for units to compute paths individually.

The vector flow field is specific to each set of potential destinations and thus can be used by all units sharing a set of destination points. Because the flow field expresses pathing information for the entire game world, it does not need to be updated unless the pathable areas of the grid or the set of destination points changes.

For example, if a bridge across a river is destroyed, the flow field only needs to be recomputed once to account for the change to pathable areas. Units following that flow field will implicitly change their respective paths in response to the change in the game world.

The flow field is comprised of a single normalized vector for each grid cell, as shown in Figure 8.1. A flow field and a unique set of destination points together are called a *path*. For example, a path corresponding to an *m* by *n* grid is a set of *m*n* normalized vectors and a set of one or more destination points. Due to the number of vectors required to represent the flow function, this approach can potentially yield prohibitively high memory usage. Memory consumption is linearly dependent on the product of the number of grid cells and the number of independent paths. Maps in *Fieldrunners 2* were restricted to three unique paths at most, and map grid sizes were small enough that flow-field memory usage did not prove to be a significant issue.

The grid size, and thus the resolution of the flow field, does not need to be high to yield believable movement characteristics. Using bilinear interpolation, a continuous flow function can be approximated from the four closest vectors in the low-resolution flow field [Alexander 06]. As the grid resolution increases, the flow field computes a higher and higher sampling of the same flow function. Bilinear interpolation of vectors in a flow field improves the continuity and organicity of unit paths.

8.4 Generating the Flow Field

The flow field is generated via a modified traditional point-to-point pathfinding function. The algorithm used in *Fieldrunners 2* was based on Dijkstra's algorithm

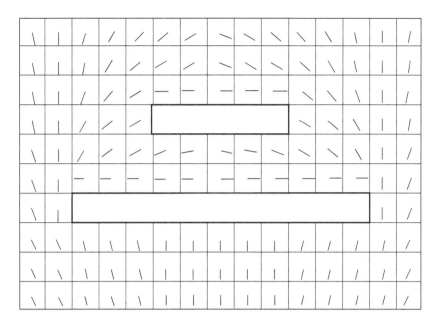

Figure 8.1

A flow field for a sample environment. The flow for a given cell is shown as a line starting at the center of the cell and pointing in the flow direction. Blocked cells are outlined with a thick black line. This particular flow field moves characters around the two rectangle obstacles and towards a destination along the bottom edge of the environment.

Dijkstra [59]; however, alternate pathfinding algorithms are aptly capable of generating a flow field.

The algorithm used in *Fieldrunners 2* begins by adding the grid cells for each of the paths' destinations to the open list. As the normal iterations of Dijkstra's algorithm progress, nodes are removed from the open list and linked to a nearby cell with the lowest computed path cost. As cells from the open list are expanded, the flow vector for the newly expanded cell is set to point in the direction of the cell it was linked to. Instead of terminating when a path is found, the algorithm expands all traversable cells added to the open list, assigning a flow vector to each, and terminating when the open list is empty. The demo code included with this article on the book's website (http://www.gameaipro.com) contains a full implementation of flow-field generation within the `GenerateFlowField()` function.

This preceding algorithm is used to generate a flow field for each path every time a change is made to either the path's destination set or the traversable area of the grid.

8.5 Units

Fieldrunners 2 required a crowd dynamics system capable of supporting dozens of different units, each with unique movement characteristics. Units in *Fieldrunners 2* are simple autonomous agents based on Craig Reynolds' *Boid* model [Reynolds 99]. Each unit has a set of both physical attributes and steering behaviors that together control its movement.

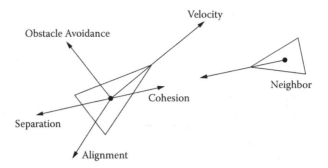

Figure 8.2

This figure shows all the steering forces acting on the left unit, with the exception of flow-field following.

The set of steering behaviors and their implementations are consistent across all unit types. A unit's physical attributes (e.g., total mass, size, agility) define its unique movement characteristics.

Units in *Fieldrunners 2* are represented as point-masses with respective velocities. A unit's steering behaviors control its point-mass by applying a set of forces to it. The prioritized combination of these steering forces imparts an acceleration on the unit, resulting in realistic, perceptively intelligent movement. Steering behaviors are widely used in games to control unit movement, and are described in numerous publications [Reynolds 99, Millington and Funge 09]. In *Fieldrunners 2*, specific modifications were made to the standard implementations of some steering behaviors to support more dynamic unit interactions.

Units in *Fieldrunners 2* use a limited, greedy, prioritized summation of five steering behaviors (four of which are shown in Figure 8.2). The five behaviors listed in descending order of priority include flow-field following, obstacle avoidance, separation, alignment, and cohesion. In each simulation step, a unit is only influenced by a specified total magnitude of steering forces. The forces resulting from steering behaviors are added to the running total in priority order until the maximum magnitude has been reached. Any steering forces that have not been added to the total are ignored.

The separation, alignment, and cohesion steering forces together describe flocking behavior [Reynolds 99]. In *Fieldrunners 2*, flocking is used to encourage units to move cohesively as a group when near other units.

Obstacle avoidance helps faster units maneuver intelligently around slower units. The implementations of the obstacle avoidance and separation behaviors differ slightly from Reynolds' original implementation [Reynolds 99]. The obstacle avoidance steering behavior generates a "side stepping" force perpendicular to the unit's velocity, and proportional to the position and relative velocity of the neighbor. The force generated by the separation steering behavior is scaled by the ratio of the kinetic energy of the neighbor to the kinetic energy of the unit the force is applied to. Units with smaller masses and velocities (presumably being more nimble) will more readily yield to larger, less maneuverable units.

Finally, flow-field following moves the unit in the direction specified by the flow field. The flow-field direction at the position of the unit is computed by linearly interpolating the four closest flow vectors.

The mass, maximum force, maximum velocity, and neighbor radius attributes describe a unit's unique behavior. The mass is used to calculate the unit's kinetic energy in addition to the accelerations resulting from steering behaviors. The maximum force value dictates the maximum combined magnitude of steering forces that can influence the unit in a single simulation step. A unit's agility value is defined as the ratio of a unit's maximum force to its mass—the unit's maximum acceleration. Finally, the maximum velocity attribute limits the magnitude of the unit's velocity, and the neighbor radius attribute restricts the set of neighbors used in calculating flocking forces to those within a certain radius.

8.6 Adjusting Unit Movement Values

It is necessary to find the correct set of attribute values for a unit to yield a desired behavior. In simulations based on steering behaviors, this is notoriously difficult and arduous. A systematic approach was developed and used by designers to balance unit attributes in *Fieldrunners 2*. For reasons of simplicity, all units used an identical set of weighted, prioritized steering behaviors, relying on their physical attributes for unique behavior.

First, the maximum velocity attribute is set to a reasonable value, and the remaining attributes are given an arbitrary base value. Because the maximum velocity of a unit is most easily visualized, it provides a good starting point. The remaining values will each be adjusted individually.

Next, the maximum force value is adjusted to yield believable movement characteristics for a single unit of that type. Because the maximum force affects the agility of the unit, it will alter visual aspects such as turning speed and braking.

Given a group of homogeneous units, the result of changes to the unit's neighbor radius attribute can easily be observed in isolation. Smaller neighbor radiuses will allow units to cluster more closely, while increasing the neighbor radius will spread units out.

Finally, all units' masses are adjusted relative to each other. When adjusting the mass of a unit, its agility must remain constant, or the previously adjusted movement characteristics of the unit will change.

8.7 Mobile Limitations and Performance Considerations

The largest runtime performance issue in this approach is the generation and processing of neighboring unit lists used in computing the flocking steering forces. In *Fieldrunners 2*, performance issues were mitigated through use of a *loose quad tree* [Ulrich 00] to reduce the neighboring unit search space. Units with large neighbor radiuses will yield a large set of neighbors to consider, decreasing performance. Combining the calculations of flocking forces can provide measurable performance improvements, as intermediary values can be reused in subsequent computations.

Floating-point operations on mobile processors can be slow, and minimizing the number of operations required in pathing and movement calculations can also yield improvements. Storing scalars that represent vector magnitudes as their respective squared values was a common optimization in *Fieldrunners 2*. This allowed vector length comparisons to use the squared vector magnitude, removing the need to compute many floating-point square root values.

Flow-field-based systems provide the greatest benefits when large numbers of units need to navigate to a set of common goals. A separate flow field is required for each unique set of goal positions among units. As the number of unique sets of goals increases, the calculations and memory required to maintain the necessary flow fields can become prohibitively complex and large. The memory required to represent a flow field grows linearly with the number of grid cells, while the pathfinding computational complexity is equivalent to the worst-case complexity of the pathfinding algorithm used. In the case of *Fieldrunners 2*, Dijkstra's algorithm was used, which yielded quasi-linear time complexity dependent on the number of grid cells. One approach to minimizing flow-field memory consumption is to save flow vectors as a specific rotation of the "north" vector (usually <0,1>). When accessing the flow direction for a given cell, the known basis vector is recreated and rotated the amount specific to that cell. Alternatively, if flow vectors are restricted to specific directions (e.g., cardinal directions), they can be stored as a one byte integer where its value corresponds to the specific potential direction.

As mobile hardware moves towards multicore processors, correct utilization of multi-threaded algorithms becomes important. The problem of generating multiple flow fields can easily be modeled as a parallel process. The mutual independence of flow fields allows each to be computed in parallel with the rest, potentially in different threads or processes. The composition and independence of steering behaviors allows them to be computed in parallel as well, so long as they're accumulated and applied to the unit collectively. Together, the intrinsic parallelizability of flow-field generation and steering behavior computation make multithreading optimizations trivial.

8.8 Benefits

This approach to unit movement was chosen for *Fieldrunners 2* due to a specific set of unique benefits that it provided. Pathing information is precomputed and stored in the flow field; thus it is only ever calculated once for a given world configuration. This property of flow fields offered notable performance benefits in *Fieldrunners 2*, as the pathability of the world is modified infrequently.

Pathing information for all locations in the world is computed in a single pass, yielding a grid size-based complexity comparable to Dijkstra's algorithm. Compared to traditional pathfinding methods where the time complexity is linear with respect to the number of units, this approach is constant with respect to the number of units simulated. For *Fieldrunners 2*, this enabled complex scenarios with thousands of independent and diverse units to run on mobile devices at interactive frame rates.

Steering behavior-based approaches like this one provide great flexibility in defining unique unit behavior. Steering behaviors rely on composition to define complex behavior, making specializations and additions modular and encapsulated. The composition of a new steering behavior or the modification of an existing steering behavior can both easily be applied to a unit to define a unique movement style.

8.9 Conclusion and Future Work

The system used in *Fieldrunners 2* used static vector flow fields and steering behaviors to simulate thousands of units on mobile devices. Unlike traditional pathfinding techniques, the proposed navigation system minimizes redundant path calculations by encoding pathing information from all areas in a vector flow field.

Flow-field-based pathfinding techniques provide a unique way to reduce redundant pathfinding computations by computing the optimal path from every point. The flow-field generation technique used in *Fieldrunners 2* was based on Dijkstra's algorithm for simplicity and design reasons. More advanced pathfinding algorithms, such as Theta* [Nash et al. 07], can generate smoother, more organic flow fields. Flow fields can be extended to incorporate alternate motivations and concerns for units by blending static and dynamic flow fields [Alexander 06]. Despite this potential improvement, static flow fields and steering behaviors provided a robust, realistic crowd simulation for *Fieldrunners 2*.

References

[Alexander 06] B. Alexander. "Flow fields for movement and obstacle avoidance." In *AI Game Programming Wisdom 3*, edited by Steve Rabin, pp. 159–172. Boston, MA: Charles River Media, 2006.

[Cabral and Leedom 93] B. Cabral and L. Leedom. "Imaging vector fields using line integral convolution." *SIGGRAPH '93 Proceedings of the 20th Annual Conference on Computer Graphics and Interactive Techniques*, pp. 263–270, 1993. Available online (http://www.cg.inf.ethz.ch/teaching/scivis_common/Literature/CabralLeedom93.pdf).

[Dijkstra 59] E. Dijkstra. "A note on two problems in connexion with graphs." *Numerische Mathematik* 1, pp. 261–271, 1959. Available online (http://www-m3.ma.tum.de/foswiki/pub/MN0506/WebHome/dijkstra.pdf).

[Millington and Funge 09] I. Millington and J. Funge. *Artificial Intelligence for Games*, pp. 55–95. Burlington, MA: Morgan Kaufmann, 2009.

[Nash et al. 07] A. Nash, K. Daniel, S. Koenig, and A. Felner. "Theta*: Any-angle path planning on grids." *Proceedings of the AAAI Conference on Artificial Intelligence (2007)*, pp. 1177–1183, 2007. Available online (http://idm-lab.org/bib/abstracts/papers/aaai07a.pdf).

[Pelechano et al. 07] N. Pelechano, J. M. Allbeck, and N. I. Badler. "Controlling individual agents in high-density crowd simulation." *SCA '07 Proceedings of the 2007 ACM SIGGRAPH/Eurographics Symposium on Computer Animation*, pp. 99–108, 2007. Available online (http://www.computingscience.nl/docs/vakken/mpp/papers/12.pdf).

[Reynolds 99] C. W. Reynolds. "Steering behaviors for autonomous characters." *Proceedings of the Game Developers Conference (1999)*, pp. 763–782, 1999. Available online (http://www.red3d.com/cwr/papers/1999/gdc99steer.pdf).

[Sung et al. 04] M. Sung, M. Gleichar, and S. Chenney. "Scalable behaviors for crowd simulation." *Computer Graphics Forum*, Volume 23, Issue 3, pp. 519–528. September 2004. Available online (http://www.computingscience.nl/docs/vakken/mpp/papers/21.pdf).

[Ulrich 00] T. Ulrich. "Loose octrees." In *Game Programming Gems*, edited by Mark DeLoura, pp. 444–453. Hingham, MA: Charles River Media, 2000.

9

Animation-Driven Locomotion with Locomotion Planning

Jarosław Ciupiński

9.1 Introduction

In the race to increase immersion in video games, every aspect of a game has to be improved. Animation-driven locomotion is one way to increase the realism of character movement. This doesn't just mean having lots of animations, as playing them in a random order will look unrealistic. The solution to this problem is to plan actions so that every animation is perfectly coordinated with *future* movement. To sum it up in few words: in animation-driven locomotion, a character's movement comes directly from the animations.

However, due to the dynamic nature of games, just playing the animations is not enough. Some adjustments are required to move a character in the desired direction and to the desired spot. For that reason, the execution of a plan is important for making animation-driven locomotion work and using it to fulfill its aesthetic requirements.

This article approaches the task as follows: A high-level path is used to guide the incremental generation of an animation-driven path. An animation-driven path is comprised of *actions*, which are broken into three categories. *Transfer actions* are used to cover longer distances in roughly a straight line. *Pretransfer* and *posttransfer* actions are optionally used to move into and out of transfer actions. The entire system described here is a revised version of what shipped in the game *Bulletstorm*.

9.2 Animation and Movement Architectures

In many cases, locomotion does not exist as a separate subsystem. Responsibility for a character's movement is often divided between the AI, gameplay, physics, and animation systems. To have more control over "what is happening and why" in locomotion, it is better to move as many responsibilities related to movement (creation of the navigation path, taking care of actual movement, queuing, checking if the target is reached, etc.) together, providing a clean and easy-to-use interface. The best place to put locomotion code, if not in a separate layer between AI/gameplay/scripting and animation, is in an animation subsystem itself.

Animation-driven locomotion uses data from animation to move a character. What this means is that movement conforms to animation data and velocity data contained in the animations. Locomotion subsystems may make further changes to adjust velocities to fulfill movement requests. To make animations easier to work with, they should follow some basic rules. For example, the root bone (if root motion in your animation code translates directly to the character's velocity) should move as closely as possible to a straight line or curve.

While this is not a hard requirement and in some cases may not even be desired (e.g., for drunk characters), it will make locomotion planning more predictable (characters will be less likely to leave the planned path), and move execution will be easier.

If only simple looped animations are used, then there is no need for any planning and the locomotion can be fully reactive. This means that played animations are chosen to match movement which is already planned. The character's AI then selects its own velocity and animations to try and make everything look appropriate. Such approaches are simple to implement, but in many cases do not look natural, especially when movement is starting or stopping.

To make movement look more natural, transition animations are used. These are animations for starting, stopping, changing directions, and other nonlooped actions. Note that these animations take time and require space to be played properly. Therefore, a system that just responds to current requests will work, but only in some simple and straightforward situations. For example, such a system will have no problem with a character running forward 10 meters and starting to stop 2 meters before the destination point. But, if the path is more complicated, a character may easily miss the point where it was requested to stop. There are often several variants for stopping animations, but checking against all possibilities for every frame is too expensive. As the AI knows what path to take to get to its final destination, preplanning animations is the natural solution.

9.3 Preparation

When starting work on animation-driven locomotion, it is strongly advised that you talk to animators and AI programmers as much as possible to decide what you want to achieve. For example, animators may desire really long, nice-looking animations to cover various situations in order to achieve nice aesthetics. However, these may be problematic to handle, as long animations will result in a less responsive system and will require more physical space to perform. This may mean that the system will need to plan ahead more than just a few steps.

You should also decide the kinds of movement that you want to have. Running and walking, for example, might only be done in the forward direction, while other directions will be covered with short steps or in sequence (making turns and moving forward). Also, it is important to decide whether obstacles can be traversed before starting work on animations and the planning system. If so, consider what kind of obstacles there will be, how they should be approached by the character, how they should be stored in the navmesh, and how they are processed. Animators, AI programmers, and/or designers may want to have other features and rules present. An example might be a rule to have specific animations for shooting when taking steps in any direction, instead of allowing shooting to be overlaid onto walking or running animations.

9.4 Locomotion Planning

It is best to divide planning for locomotion into separate modules, each having a distinct and clearly defined purpose:

1. A navigation path-processor
2. A planner that creates an action-stack
3. An animation system that executes the action-stack

It is strongly advised to add an additional module that works as an interface to other game subsystems. This module would accept new requests, prepare orders for animation modules (what they should do now), and work as a central hub for exchanging data. Such a module really helps with finding problems with locomotion; it makes it easier to find invalid requests and decide whether it was the animation/locomotion subsystem problem or another module that failed.

9.4.1 Navigation Path-Processor

The handling of movement requests starts with the creation of a navigation path. It is worthwhile to store the navigation path as both polygons and points. Due to unexpected events that may take place during movement (e.g., other objects moving in the way), the navigation path might require adjustment or complete recreation of the whole path. Storing polygon data will reduce the need to access the navmesh. It also gives more freedom when adjusting point-based paths, which are the base representation of the planner (Figure 9.1).

The creation of point-based paths should start with a simple approach such as string-pulling or the funnel algorithm that will give the shortest path connecting the start and end points. Please refer to the following resources for more information on pathfinding, string-pulling, and the funnel algorithm [Demyen et al. 06, Cui et al. 11].

The first job for the path processor is to take care of points that are close to each other, as they don't provide any extra information and may just complicate the subsequent steps in locomotion planning. It is easier to assume that every segment of the path is of minimum length, chosen arbitrarily, or based on the shortest stopping animation. This means that the three subsequent segments (starting at the current location of the character) will cover, for example, at least 2 or 3 meters.

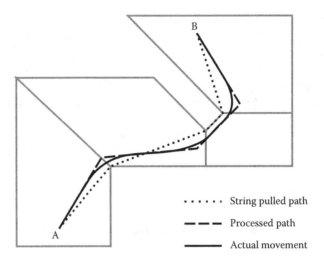

String pulled path

Processed path

Actual movement

Figure 9.1

A path from point A to point B is provided to the locomotion system as polygons and is further processed. Actual movement doesn't exactly correlate to the processed path, as for locomotion planning it is more important where the animation should start and where it will end.

In some cases, when dealing with longer movement animations (that require more space), it is better to do further adjustments to the location of points. For example, after string-pulling a path, there might be two subsequent points that change the direction of movement by 90° in opposite directions and are very close to each other. If they are too close, it will be impossible to play two "sharp-turn-while-running animations" one after another and to (roughly) stay on path. If there is enough space around these points, they might be moved further away from each other to give enough space to play both animations. If it isn't possible to move the points further away, there should still be a fail-safe solution provided: stopping at the first turn point, taking a step towards the next point, and starting to run from there. In order to avoid affecting the fluidity of movement, such fail-safe solutions should be used rarely.

In some cases it might be useful to add extra points along the path that would make approaching some locations easier. For example, instead of running to an obstacle that should be jumped over, stopping next to it, and then jumping, an extra point could be used to run at the obstacle from a better angle. Due to memory limitations, there might be just two animations for "jumping from standing" and for "jumping while running straightforward" and both might look terrible when running toward an obstacle from a wide angle; therefore, approaching from a better angle is critical to making it look good.

9.4.2 Action-Stack

The *action-stack* is a list of actions required to follow the current segment of the path. It is more feasible to choose actions starting from the end (from the desired goal state). This means that the first actions to be chosen are last to be executed (Figure 9.2).

When the path has been processed, it should be in the form of points with some extra data describing how to behave at each given time (crouch, do not run, jump over). Only

9. Animation-Driven Locomotion with Locomotion Planning

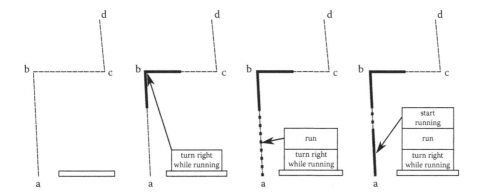

Figure 9.2

In this example we are creating an action-stack for segment "ab" of the path, starting at point "a". It is essential to know how much space animations need (for animation-based actions this is marked as a thick line) so only animations that can fit in given segment are chosen. The space required to execute an animation-based action is also used to determine when to first trigger the action (a dotted line represents a "run" action that at some point should be interrupted with the "turn right while running" action).

two or three segments of the path should be considered when creating an action-stack for the following reasons:

1. The creation of the action-stack is computationally intensive, and if done for whole path, would result in significant performance spikes.
2. We have no idea what will happen in the future, so there really is no need to plan everything ahead. A character may run into another character or may be ordered to do something else.

Ideally, just one segment of the path needs to be covered by the action-stack. When all actions from the stack are performed, the character should be at the best point to go on to the next segment, and a new action-stack can be created at that time. However, the two or three subsequent segments should still be considered when creating the first action-stack, in order to best enter subsequent segments. There is also another reason for considering subsequent segments: In some of the cases it might be possible to use one animation to cover several segments. One example might be entering cover behind a corner.

Even if planning actions are only performed for one segment, knowledge of what the character will be doing afterwards is valuable. Will the character run or slide? Does it need to stop there or should it proceed at full speed? This tells it what state (location, direction, gait, or pose) the character should be in at the end of the current segment. There is also, of course, the current state of the character. Other information might describe the current segment, such as distance, and what animations are allowed or disallowed (e.g., character can't run here). Given this data we have two options to cover the segment:

1. Do one action that will directly transition the character from current state straight to the desired state.

2. Do several actions:

A pretransfer action that will ready the character for a transfer action (e.g., start running in specific direction).

A transfer action that will move the character over longer distances (e.g., walk, run).

A posttransfer action that will bring the character into the desired state (e.g., stop at a point, perform sharp-turn while running).

9.4.2.1 Direct Transition

A direct transition gives the best-looking results but requires lots of animations that cover many possibilities. In an actual game these should only be used to cover special cases. For example, walking extremely short distances can be accomplished by an animation taking a single step or two steps. For such short distances there is no need, and it might look strange to start running and then immediately stop.

9.4.2.2 Transfer Action

Using a transfer action is more feasible for longer distances. It requires animations to be divided into three basic groups (as described previously: pretransfer, transfer, and posttransfer), which can be heavily reused in different combinations resulting in smooth character animation.

Each action (pretransfer, transfer, and posttransfer) is optional. Since a character may already be in a "transfer" state, there may be no need to do anything at the end of the segment. Additionally, the transfer itself may be omitted as in some cases it might be practical to just play pretransfer and posttransfer animations back-to-back.

In games, it is not possible to have pretransfer or posttransfer animations for all possible situations. This may happen because of memory limitations, budget limitations, or development time limitations. Therefore, we might remove or not create animations for rare situations. When dealing with cases for which there is no appropriate animation, the planner will have to solve the problem in a different way.

An example of such a case is starting to run when the character is crouching. Let's assume that there is no animation for this case and follow what the planner does. The planner first tries to find one animation that will take the character from a crouched stance (current state) to running 20 meters away (desired state). There, of course, is no such animation. The planner then tries to find posttransfer, transfer, and pretransfer actions, but it can't find an action to take the character from crouching to running. Suppose there are just animations for "character starting to run from standing" in eight directions, and there are animations that bring a character from a crouch to a standing stance. The planner should then try to use the crouch to standing animation, execute one action-stack, and try to approach the problem again. After playing the animation of the character crouching to standing, it is possible to use one of eight "stand to run" animations.

In some cases it might be possible to use actions or animations that take a character from the current state to the desired state, but only with an extra action. For example, there could be an animation that is walking to the right while shooting, but in the beginning the character faces away from the target, so before the walking-shooting animation plays, the character should turn toward the enemy.

Similar extra actions may be required when a transfer action brings a character to a desired location, but it is not yet in the desired state (e.g., the character isn't turned in the right direction or is not in the desired stance).

9.4.2.3 Implementation Suggestions

For implementation, we strongly suggest dividing data into three groups:

1. **Transfer information (walk, run, walk crouched, jump over, slide under) that has:**
   A list of transfer animations.
   A list of posttransfer animations with info about the final character state (e.g., rotation, stance, how much space does it take, or any other information needed). Note that some of the posttransfer animation entries may store that this is not the final animation to reach a desired state and the planner needs to do something more.

2. **Stance information (standing, crouching, stealthy) that has**
   A list of stance idle animations.
   A list of pretransfer animations with information about the state they take a character into (transfer state, in which direction the character will move, how much space is required, etc.).
   A list of animations that change directly from one stance to another.

3. **Direct transitions:**
   A list of animations that take a character from any state to any other state, although in most of the cases it might be enough to have such a list just for stances.

Pretransfer, posttransfer, and direct transition animations may also be described in a separate place with details irrelevant to the decision taken by the planner, but having general information about the transfer which is useful during execution.

Some of this information can be collected algorithmically. For example, how does every animation connect to the transfer animation (to start a transfer animation, to match a pose, or to adjust movement in such a manner that the posttransfer animation will be triggered at the right moment).

Other information (mostly those required by the planner) may be collected automatically, although it is often useful to enter the data or at least tweak it by hand. An example is the space required for an animation. Some "starting to run" animations may need 2 meters of space. Some animations that are taking characters from one spot to another may only cover from 1 to 3 meters. While this can be computed automatically, entering data by hand gives much more cohesion and control over what each system will do in a given situation.

Note that it is important to have fail-safe solutions that would prevent the character from being stuck in one pose, even if it means turning towards the final destination and walking there step-by-step.

9.4.3 Executing Actions

During planning, actions are divided into a few different types, including pretransfer, transfer, posttransfer, whole segment animations, and extra actions. Conversely, *execution* of actions can be divided into only two groups: transfer and nontransfer actions. The following sections describe the execution of each group.

9.4.3.1 Nontransfer Actions

Nontransfer actions just play an assigned animation with small adjustments to velocity and rotation, if required.

When changing stance (standing up or crouching), it is enough to play an animation without any adjustments. For pretransfer actions, a directional adjustment is required in order to get the character moving in the correct direction when the pretransfer animation reaches its end. Most of the posttransfer actions require characters to be at a precise spot facing the right direction, so there is a requirement to adjust these as well. Adjustments to both location and direction are needed for actions that take a character from one place to another.

Parameter adjustments should be determined by the planner, meaning that the execution of all such actions does not differ.

9.4.3.2 Transfer Actions

Transfer actions are looped animations (although there can be random or in-order animations following one another) that take a character from one point in space to another. Besides matching the correct direction and ending at the required location, a character might be required to end in a specific pose in order to make a seamless blend to a post-transfer action. For example, a stopping animation that starts with a character on the right foot requires a character to be on that same foot when the stopping animation begins.

This may require altering character velocity, such as slightly speeding up or slowing down movement. This works nicely for longer distances, but adjusting a pose over short distances can result in a velocity adjustment that is too big or results in the character switching to a posttransfer animation too far away from the target location. In such cases the pose either has to be ignored, or there should be posttransfer animations that differ in the starting pose (on the left foot or right foot). Although variants can be decided during planning, they can also be picked up during execution. This may come in handy if a character had to adjust its path slightly for other reasons.

An alternative to speeding up or slowing down the character's velocity is modifying the playback rate of the animation. It is important to remember to maintain the playback rate when switching animations and to adjust the playback rate gradually. If the playback rate is not kept, animations may seem to speed up and slow down immediately, resulting in strange-looking character behavior.

Code for handling transfer actions should try to deal with any obstacles, keep characters in formation, or perform any required path adjustments. With navigation corridors and information about the end-point of transfer actions, it is possible to do some adjustments to the movement of a character and still end at the point requested by subsequent actions. For example, if a character runs and notices a new obstacle in front of it, it may alter the direction of movement early enough to avoid hitting the obstacle, without risking that the character won't be able to end at a point where the next action should start.

There are also situations in which a character will end up outside of a known navigation corridor or at some point of execution it might become obvious that it will miss the next action's starting point or won't get there at all. In such cases, either the action-stack should be rebuilt or the whole navigation path should be reconsidered.

Hitting an obstacle should be handled in a similar way. It may be impossible to avoid hitting an obstacle or it may be decided that a character may not even try to avoid running into one. The latter solution works well enough in practice. When a character hits an obstacle, it can play an evasive animation and, after it is finished, request a new navigation path (although in some cases rebuilding of action-stack may be enough).

9.4.4 Inverse Kinematic (IK) Controllers

As the system makes lots of adjustments to movement, IK controllers for feet should be used to cover corrections by removing, hiding, or at least reducing the foot-sliding effect. A simple two-bone IK solver is enough for human limbs [Juckett 08]. A proper animation will have no foot-slide, which means that when a foot is put down on the ground, it doesn't move until it is picked up.

During execution of the action-stack, the velocity of a movement animation is increased or decreased without speeding up or slowing down the animation playback rate (as the reason to speed up or slow down is to match a pose at a given point), which unfortunately results in foot sliding. For example, if the velocity is increased, the foot will slide forward; if there are additional rotations or other adjustments, the foot may also slide sideways. In these cases, an IK controller tries to keep the foot where it was originally placed.

Other IK controllers may be used to adjust the torso location in reference to the feet to help with situations in which the feet are kept behind or in front of the character. This may happen if the character stopped and antisliding controllers kept the feet in places other than originally expected.

9.5 Other Information about Locomotion Planning

The following is additional information about locomotion planning.

9.5.1 Performance

Locomotion does not require significant CPU resources during the execution stage. Everything is already planned, and it is just about keeping the character's movement faithful to the plan. In contrast, reactive locomotion requires checking and possibly updating all possible actions during every frame.

However, while the execution stage causes no problems with performance, it is important to note that locomotion planning may cause significant CPU spikes. If there is a need, most of the spikes can be neutralized by delaying any of the following processes, trying to delay actions with lowest priority first:

1. Lowest priority: handling a new navigation path
2. Middle priority: action-stack creation for standing characters
3. Highest priority: action-stack creation for moving characters

In the worst-case scenario, some characters might get stopped. Please keep in mind that when a character is stopped (playing a stopping animation), the CPU situation may get much better. In-game, the resulting behavior may look like a bug, as the character has stopped and started running again, but remember that there is always the potential to play a new animation. In particular, an animation for looking around, scratching your head, or stumbling will all offset the user perception of poor AI behavior.

9.5.2 AI Requests for Movement

An AI that relies on animation-driven locomotion should be patient; that is, it should not send too many requests in too short of a time period. If the AI changes its mind too often, a character may get stuck in repeating "start" and "stop" animations over and over. This can be partially prevented through locomotion systems that provide extensive feedback, so the AI does not have to "worry" that a character is not moving yet or is doing something else. Not every AI request can be handled immediately, as pre- and posttransfer actions are usually not interruptible and should be left until they're finished.

The locomotion system should be careful not to treat every AI request as something completely new and unconnected, as this results in creating completely new paths. New paths often mean that the character will stop and start to move again in the same direction. In many situations, the AI just needs to change the very end of a requested path, so the currently executed action-stack (with part of the navigation path already processed) is still sufficient for local movement.

9.6 Commercial Implementation

Planning, as described in this article, is a revised version of the planning implemented for *Bulletstorm* (developed by People Can Fly, part of Epic, published by Electronic Arts in 2011). The actual implementation relied on finite-state machines—generalized versions of transfer and stance descriptions mentioned in previous sections. This means that the whole system was data driven, although some cases required a separate approach, which was handled by special code. Mantling over and sliding under objects, for example, were added late in production.

The code for this implementation was part of the animation tree (distributed over a few animation nodes) with a separate structure (called AnimationProxy) used for communication with other game systems. Source code is available for UE3 licensees.

9.7 Conclusion

Animation-driven locomotion with planning brings a believable look and feel to a game. Characters move in a more natural and fluid manner. The basic implementation of planning is quite easy and, as it is data driven, adding more animations is simple. The same code can be used for characters that have different behaviors, although the fine-tuning of the system may require experience and time.

References

[Cui et al. 11] X. Cui and H. Shi. "Direction oriented pathfinding in video games." *International Journal of Artificial Intelligence & Applications (IJAIA)*, Vol. 2, No. 4, October 2011. Available online (http://airccse.org/journal/ijaia/papers/1011ijaia01.pdf).
[Demyen et al. 06] D. Demyen and M. Buro. "Efficient Triangulation-Based Pathfinding." Department of Computing Science, University of Alberta Edmonton, 2006. Available online (http://www.aaai.org/Papers/AAAI/2006/AAAI06-148.pdf).
[Juckett 08] R. Juckett. "Analytic Two-Bone IK in 2D." http://www.ryanjuckett.com/programming/animation/16-analytic-two-bone-ik-in-2d, 2008.

JPS+

An Extreme A* Speed Optimization for Static Uniform Cost Grids

Steve Rabin and Fernando Silva

10.1 Introduction

Jump point search (JPS) is a recently devised optimal pathfinding algorithm that can speed up searches on uniform cost grid maps by up to an order of magnitude over traditional A* [Harabor 12]. However, by statically analyzing a map and burning in directions to walls and jump points, it is possible to dramatically speed up searches even further, up to *two orders of magnitude* over traditional A*. To illustrate the difference in speed on a particular 40 × 40 map, A* found an optimal solution in 180.05 ns, JPS in 15.04 ns, and JPS+ in 1.55 ns. In this example, JPS+ was 116x faster than traditional A*, while remaining perfectly optimal.

Both JPS and JPS+ use a state-space pruning strategy that only works for grid search spaces where the cost of traversal is uniform with regard to distance. This chapter will explain in detail how JPS+ works and the exact specifics on how to implement it. JPS+ was first unveiled on June 2014 at the International Conference on Automated Planning and Scheduling (ICAPS); however, one of the authors of this chapter (Steve Rabin) independently invented the improved algorithm for storing directions to walls and jump points a month before Harabor's initial publication. For consistency, the terms in this chapter will be from the original ICAPS paper [Harabor 14].

The code from this chapter, along with a full source demo, can be found on the book's website (http://www.gameaipro.com).

10.2 Pruning Strategy

JPS gets its tremendous speed from pruning the search space at runtime. This exploit exists because open areas in grids can be visited multiple times through equivalent paths. Consider a uniform cost grid space of 2×5 that contains no walls, as in Figure 10.1. Now consider how many optimal paths exist from the bottom left to the top right of this search space. Figure 10.1 shows that there are four identical cost paths. In many problems, traditional A* will redundantly check the same nodes along these paths to verify that a shorter path cannot be found. This is wasted work; with the ideas behind JPS+, we can avoid it.

JPS has a clever method for systematically choosing a single route through these equivalent paths. Figure 10.2 shows how JPS searches from the start node, visiting each node only once. That is, JPS will only consider the successors of a state in the direction of the arrows; all other successors are ignored. Of the total JPS speedup over A*, this pruning strategy accounts for roughly 50% of the speed improvement.

To understand this strategy in more detail, consider the node east of the center node in Figure 10.2. This is a node visited straight (nondiagonally) from the parent. Nodes visited straight from their parent only have successors that continue on in that same direction. In this case, the node east of the center node only considers the node to the east as a possible neighbor (pruning from considering the other seven directions).

Now consider the node northeast of the center node in Figure 10.2. This is a node visited diagonally from the parent. Nodes visited diagonally only consider three neighbors in the diagonal direction. The node northeast of the center node only considers nodes to the north, northeast, and east as possible neighbors (pruning from consideration the northwest, west, southwest, south, and southeast nodes).

JPS has another trick where it only puts relevant nodes, called *jump points*, on the open list. Since the open list is a bottleneck in traditional A*, a dramatic reduction in nodes on

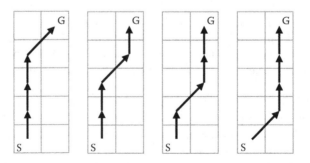

Figure 10.1

Four equivalent and optimal paths exist from the start node to the goal node.

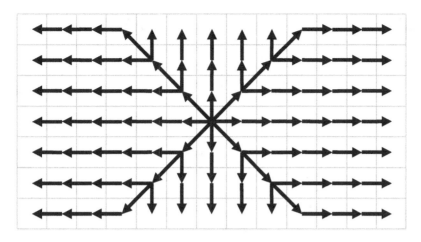

Figure 10.2

Systematic pruning rules keep nodes from being visited multiple times.

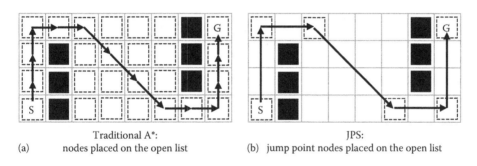

Traditional A*:	JPS:
(a) nodes placed on the open list	(b) jump point nodes placed on the open list

Figure 10.3

Nodes put on the open list in (a) traditional A* versus (b) JPS.

the open list results in a tremendous runtime savings. This second trick accounts for the other 50% speedup over traditional A*. Figure 10.3 illustrates the difference in the number of nodes that get placed on the open list.

Assuming that these two general ideas are understood, the rest of this chapter will provide a detailed explanation of how to correctly and efficiently implement them.

10.3 Forced Neighbors

There are certain cases where the pruning strategy from Figure 10.2 fails to visit a node due to walls in the search space. To address this, JPS introduced the concept of *forced neighbors*. Figure 10.4 shows the eight forced neighbor cases. Forced neighbors only occur when traveling in a straight or *cardinal* direction (north, south, west, or east). Forced neighbors are a signal that the normal pruning strategy will fail and that the current node must consider additional nodes.

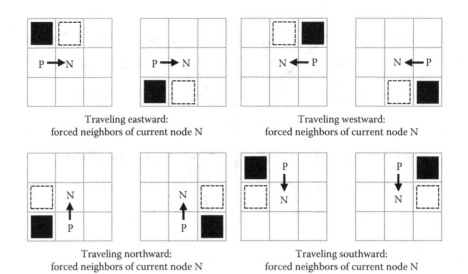

Traveling eastward:
forced neighbors of current node N

Traveling westward:
forced neighbors of current node N

Traveling northward:
forced neighbors of current node N

Traveling southward:
forced neighbors of current node N

Figure 10.4

The eight forced neighbor cases. Forced neighbor nodes are outlined with a dashed line. Node P is the parent node and node N is the current node being explored. Note that forced neighbors are dependent on the direction of travel from the parent node.

10.4 Jump Points

Jump points are another concept introduced by JPS. Jump points are the intermediate points on the map that are necessary to travel through for at least one optimal path. JPS+ introduces four flavors of jump points: *primary*, *straight*, *diagonal*, and *target*.

10.4.1 Primary Jump Points

Primary jump points are easy to identify because they have a forced neighbor. In Figure 10.4, the primary jump points are the current node, N, for each situation shown. In Figure 10.5, we introduce a new map that shows the primary jump points, given the travel direction from the parent node.

Note that a node is only a primary jump point when traveling to the node in the direction indicated. So the same node can both be a jump point and not a jump point depending on the direction of travel during the search. Given that jump points only occur when traveling in a cardinal direction, there are four possible jump point flags for each node.

10.4.2 Straight Jump Points

Once all primary jump points have been identified, the straight jump points can be found. The straight jump points are nodes where traveling in a cardinal direction will eventually run into a primary jump point for that direction of travel (before running into a wall), as shown in Figure 10.6.

Note that a node can be both a primary and straight jump point for each direction of travel. Think of straight jump points as directions on how to get to the next primary jump point for that direction of travel.

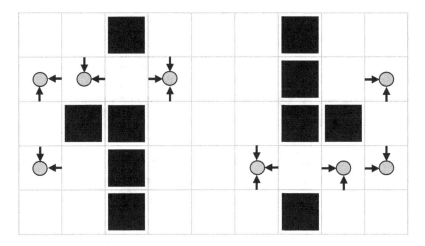

Figure 10.5

Primary jump points due to forced neighbors. Nodes marked with a circle are the jump points. The arrow direction indicates the direction of travel from the parent node for that node to be a jump point in that direction of travel.

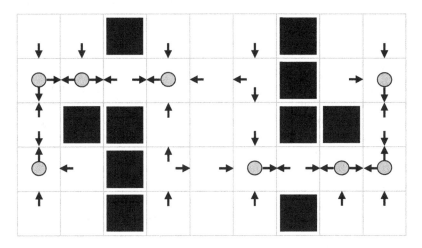

Figure 10.6

Straight jump points point to primary jump points. Primary jump points are marked with a circle. Straight jump points are any node with an arrow in it.

Figure 10.7 is a more detailed version of Figure 10.6 where the arrows have been replaced with distances. The distances indicate how many nodes away is the next primary jump point for that direction of travel. However, there is a very tricky thing going on in Figure 10.7 that wasn't apparent in Figure 10.6. The distance values aren't the distance to just any primary jump point, but only to primary jump points *in that direction of travel*. For example, the node on the very bottom left has a distance value of 3 in the up direction.

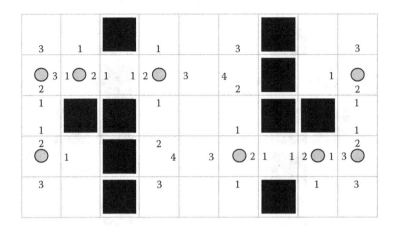

Figure 10.7

Straight jump points are marked with a distance indicating how many nodes away the next primary jump point is for that direction of travel.

It looks as if it should be a 1, but the primary jump point in the node above it is not a primary jump point *for that direction of travel* (double check Figure 10.5 to confirm). The actual primary jump point for traveling up is 3 nodes above.

10.4.3 Diagonal Jump Points

After straight jump points and their respective distances to primary jump points have been identified, we need to identify diagonal jump points. Diagonal jump points are any node in which a diagonal direction of travel will reach either a primary jump point or a straight jump point *that is traveling in a direction related to the diagonal direction* (before hitting a wall). For example, a node with a diagonal direction moving northeast is only a diagonal jump point if it runs into a primary or straight jump point traveling either north or east. This is consistent with the pruning strategy introduced in Figure 10.2.

As we did with straight jump points, we need to fill diagonal jump points with distances to the other jump points. Figure 10.8 shows our map with the diagonal jump points filled in.

10.5 Wall Distances

The information built up in Figure 10.8 is very close to the finished preprocessed map, but it needs wall distance information to be complete. In an effort to minimize the memory required for each node, we will represent wall distances as zero or negative numbers. Any node direction that is not marked with a straight or diagonal distance will be given a distance to the wall in that direction. Figure 10.9 shows the completed map where every node has distances for all eight directions. Additionally, we have deleted the primary jump point markers since they were only used to build up the distance map and are not needed at runtime.

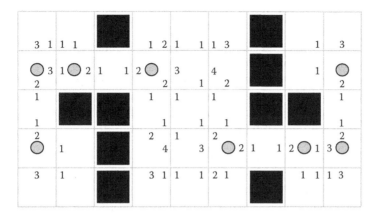

Figure 10.8

Diagonal jump points filled in with distances to primary and straight jump points.

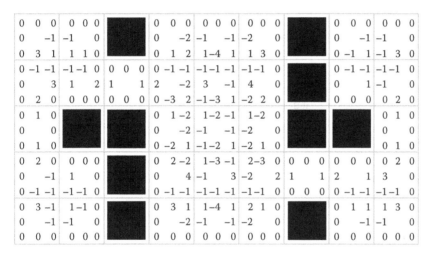

Figure 10.9

Wall distances added to all unmarked directions. Walls are either zero or negative and represent the distance to a wall (discard the negative sign).

10.6 Map Preprocess Implementation

As a practical matter, the complete precomputed map in Figure 10.9 can be created with the following strategy:

1. Identify all primary jump points by setting a directional flag in each node.
2. Mark with distance all westward straight jump points and westward walls by sweeping the map left to right.
3. Mark with distance all eastward straight jump points and eastward walls by sweeping the map right to left.

4. Mark with distance all northward straight jump points and northward walls by sweeping the map up to down.
5. Mark with distance all southward straight jump points and southward walls by sweeping the map down to up.
6. Mark with distance all southwest/southeast diagonal jump points and southwest/southeast walls by sweeping the map down to up.
7. Mark with distance all northwest/northeast diagonal jump points and northwest/northeast walls by sweeping the map up to down.

Listing 10.1 provides an example of the sweep to compute westward numbers in step 2. Similar code must be written for the other three sweep directions in steps 3–5. Listing 10.2 provides an example of the sweep to compute southwest numbers as part of step 6. Similar code must be written to compute southeast, northeast, and northwest numbers.

Listing 10.1. Left to right sweep to mark all westward straight jump points and all westward walls.

```
for (int r = 0; r < mapHeight; ++r)
{
    int count = -1;
    bool jumpPointLastSeen = false;

    for (int c = 0; c < mapWidth; ++c)
    {
        if (m_terrain[r][c] == TILE_WALL)
        {
            count = -1;
            jumpPointLastSeen = false;
            distance[r][c][West] = 0;
            continue;
        }

        count++;

        if (jumpPointLastSeen)
        {
            distance[r][c][West] = count;
        }
        else //Wall last seen
        {
            distance[r][c][West] = -count;
        }

        if (jumpPoints[r][c][West])
        {
            count = 0;
            jumpPointLastSeen = true;
        }
    }
}
```

Listing 10.2. Down to up sweep to mark all southwest diagonal jump points and all southwest diagonal walls.

```
for (int r = 0; r < mapHeight; ++r)
{
    for (int c = 0; c < mapWidth; ++c)
    {
        if (!IsWall(r, c))
        {
            if (r == 0 || c == 0 || IsWall(r-1, c) ||
                IsWall(r, c-1) || IsWall(r-1, c-1))
            {
                //Wall one away
                distance[r][c][Southwest] = 0;
            }
            else if (!IsWall(r-1, c) && !IsWall(r, c-1) &&
                (distance[r-1][c-1][South] > 0 ||
                 distance[r-1][c-1][West] > 0))
            {
                //Straight jump point one away
                distance[r][c][Southwest] = 1;
            }
            else
            {
                //Increment from last
                int jumpDistance =
                    distance[r-1][c-1][Southwest];

                if (jumpDistance > 0)
                {
                    distance[r][c][Southwest] =
                        1 + jumpDistance;
                }
                else
                {
                    distance[r][c][Southwest] =
                        -1 + jumpDistance;
                }
            }
        }
    }
}
```

10.7 Runtime Implementation

The genius of the preprocessed map is that it contains many of the decisions required for the search, thus making the runtime code much simpler and faster than traditional JPS. For example, the recursive step from JPS is completely eliminated and only jump points are ever examined.

The pseudocode in Listing 10.3 is the complete JPS+ runtime algorithm. However, there are several aspects that need clarification. The first is the ValidDirLookUpTable. This table is used to only consider directions in the spirit of Figure 10.1. For example, if traveling in a diagonal direction such as northeast, the directions east, northeast, and north

Listing 10.3. Complete runtime pseudocode for JPS+.

```
ValidDirLookUpTable
    Traveling South: West, Southwest, South, Southeast, East
    Traveling Southeast: South, Southeast, East
    Traveling East: South, Southeast, East, Northeast, North
    Traveling Northeast: East, Northeast, North
    Traveling North: East, Northeast, North, Northwest, West
    Traveling Northwest: North, Northwest, West
    Traveling West: North, Northwest, West, Southwest, South
    Traveling Southwest: West, Southwest, South

while (!OpenList.IsEmpty())
{
    Node* curNode = OpenList.Pop();
    Node* parentNode = curNode->parent;

    if (curNode == goalNode)
        return PathFound;

    foreach (direction in ValidDirLookUpTable
            given parentNode)
    {
        Node* newSuccessor = NULL;
        float givenCost;

        if (direction is cardinal &&
            goal is in exact direction &&
            DiffNodes(curNode, goalNode) <=
            abs(curNode->distances[direction]))
        {
            //Goal is closer than wall distance or
            //closer than or equal to jump point distance
            newSuccessor = goalNode;
            givenCost = curNode->givenCost +
                        DiffNodes(curNode, goalNode);
        }
        else if (direction is diagonal &&
                goal is in general direction &&
                (DiffNodesRow(curNode, goalNode) <=
                abs(curNode->distances[direction]) ||
                (DiffNodesCol(curNode, goalNode) <=
                abs(curNode->distances[direction]))))
        {
            //Goal is closer or equal in either row or
            //column than wall or jump point distance

            //Create a target jump point
            int minDiff = min(RowDiff(curNode, goalNode),
                            ColDiff(curNode, goalNode));
            newSuccessor =
                GetNode(curNode, minDiff, direction);
            givenCost = curNode->givenCost +
                (SQRT2 * minDiff);
        }
```

```
        else if (curNode->distances[direction] > 0)
        {
            //Jump point in this direction
            newSuccessor = GetNode(curNode, direction);
            givenCost = DiffNodes(curNode, newSuccessor);
            if (diagonal direction) {givenCost *= SQRT2;}
            givenCost += curNode->givenCost;
        }

        //Traditional A* from this point
        if (newSuccessor != NULL)
        {
            if (newSuccessor not on OpenList or ClosedList)
            {
                newSuccessor->parent = curNode;
                newSuccessor->givenCost = givenCost;
                newSuccessor->finalCost = givenCost +
                    CalculateHeuristic(newSuccessor, goalNode);
                OpenList.Push(newSuccessor);
            }
            else if(givenCost < newSuccessor->givenCost)
            {
                newSuccessor->parent = curNode;
                newSuccessor->givenCost = givenCost;
                newSuccessor->finalCost = givenCost +
                    CalculateHeuristic(newSuccessor, goalNode);
                OpenList.Update(newSuccessor);
            }
        }
    }
}

return NoPathExists;
```

must be considered. If traveling in a cardinal direction, continued movement in the cardinal direction plus any possible forced neighbor directions plus the diagonal between the forced neighbor and the original cardinal direction must be considered. For example, if traveling east, the directions east plus the possible forced neighbors of north and south plus the diagonals northeast and southeast must be considered. The actual distances in each node will further clarify if these are worth exploring, but this is a first-pass pruning. Figure 10.10 shows an example computed path where you can see the directions considered at each node based on the ValidDirLookUpTable.

Consider another important clarification regarding the middle conditional in the for loop to create a target jump point (Listing 10.3). The need for this is subtle and nonobvious. When approaching the goal node, we might need a *target* jump point (our fourth type of jump point) between the current node and the goal node in order to find a path that is grid aligned to the goal. This arises only when traveling diagonally, the direction of travel is toward the goal node, and the distance to the goal node in row distance or column distance is less than or equal to the current node's diagonal distance to a wall or jump point. The newly synthesized target jump point will be constructed by taking the minimum of the row distance and the column distance to the goal node and continuing travel diagonally by that amount. If the goal node is directly diagonal in the direction of travel, this new target

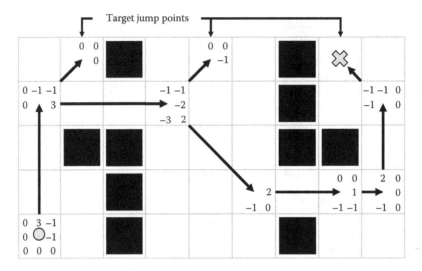

Figure 10.10

Runtime search from bottom left node to top right goal node. Only node distances used in the search are included in the figure. Note that three target jump points are created along the top row based on potential intermediate routes to the goal.

jump point will be equal to the goal node. Otherwise, this target jump point is a possible intermediate jump point between the current node and the goal node. Figure 10.10 shows an example computed path where three target jump points are created at runtime.

To appreciate the speed of JPS+, consider the search in Figure 10.10. Only 10 nodes are even considered during the entire search with 7 of them being absolutely necessary for an optimal path. Contrast this with traditional JPS that would look at every node on the map during its recursive step. Additionally, since all wall information is stored in the grid cells themselves as distances, this data structure is extremely cache friendly since neighboring rows or columns aren't constantly checked for the existence of walls. The cumulative result is that JPS+ does very little runtime processing and considers an extremely limited number of nodes. This accounts for the tremendous improvement over traditional JPS.

In order to achieve good results with JPS+, it is advised to use a heapsort algorithm for the open list, preallocate all node memory along with a dirty bit for cheap initialization, and use an octile heuristic [Rabin 13]. If you have between 1 and 10 MB of extra memory available, you can achieve a ~10x speed increase by using a bucket-sorted priority queue for the open list. Create a bucket for every 0.1 cost and then use an unsorted preallocated array for each bucket. If you use a LIFO strategy in each bucket, the final path won't be more than 0.1 worse than optimal and it will be blazing fast. For A*, this data structure would require 10 to 100 MB, but JPS+ puts far fewer nodes on the open list, which makes this optimization much more practical.

10.8 Conclusion

JPS+ takes a great deal of the runtime computation from JPS and stores it directly in the map. As a result, the algorithm is up to an order of magnitude faster than traditional JPS and two orders of magnitude faster than a highly optimized A*. The trade-off for this speed is that the map is static (walls can't be added or removed), the map must be preprocessed with eight numbers stored per grid cell, and the map is a uniform cost grid.

The degree of speed gains is directly proportional to the openness of the map. If the map contains large open areas, JPS+ is extremely fast and will achieve up to two orders of magnitude speed improvement over A*. If the map is intensely mazelike consisting primarily of jagged diagonal walls, then JPS+ is more conservatively around 20% faster than traditional JPS and about 2.5x faster than a highly optimized A* solution.

References

[Harabor 12] Harabor, D. and Grastien, A. 2012. The JPS pathfinding system. In *Proceedings of the Fifth Symposium on Combinatorial Search* (*SoCS*), Niagara Falls, Ontario, Canada. Available online at: http://users.cecs.anu.edu.au/~dharabor/data/papers/harabor-grastien-socs12.pdf (accessed September 10, 2014).

[Harabor 14] Harabor, D. and Grastien, A. 2014. Improving jump point search. In *International Conference on Automated Planning and Scheduling (ICAPS)*, Portsmouth, NH. Video available at: https://www.youtube.com/watch?v=NmM4pv8uQwI (accessed September 10, 2014).

[Rabin 13] Rabin, S. and Sturtevant, N. 2013. Pathfinding architecture optimizations. In *Game AI Pro: Collected Wisdom of Game AI Professionals*. A K Peters/CRC Press, Boca Raton, FL.

Subgoal Graphs for Fast Optimal Pathfinding

Tansel Uras and Sven Koenig

11.1 Introduction

Paths for game agents are often found by representing the map that the agents move on as a graph and using a search algorithm, such as A*, to search this graph. Pathfinding in games needs to be fast, especially if many agents are moving on the map. To speed up path planning, maps can often be preprocessed before games are released or when they are loaded into memory. The data produced by preprocessing should use a small amount of memory, and preprocessing should be fast if it is performed at runtime.

In this chapter, we present *subgoal graphs*, which are constructed by preprocessing maps that are represented as grids. Subgoal graphs use a small amount of memory and can be used to find shortest paths fast by ignoring most of the grid cells during search. We describe several variants of subgoal graphs, each being a more sophisticated version of the previous one and each requiring more preprocessing time in return for faster searches. Even though subgoal graphs are specific to grids, the ideas behind them can be generalized to any graph representation of a map.

Table 11.1 summarizes the results from the original paper on subgoal graphs [Uras 14] on maps from the video games *Dragon Age: Origins*, *StarCraft*, *Warcraft III*, and *Baldur's*

Table 11.1 Comparison of Subgoal Graph Variants on Game Maps

Subgoal Graph Variant	Preprocessing Time (s)	Memory Used (MBytes)	Runtime of A* on Subgoal Graphs Rather Than Grids	Optimal?
Simple subgoal graphs	0.022	1.172	24 times faster	Yes
Two-level subgoal graphs	2.031	1.223	71 times faster	Yes
N-level subgoal graphs	2.195	1.223	112 times faster	Yes

Note: The average runtime of A* is 12.69 ms on these maps.

Gate II [Sturtevant 12]. The two-level subgoal graph (TSG) entry was one of the nondominated entries in the Grid-Based Path Planning Competitions 2012 and 2013. That is, if another entry was faster, it either was suboptimal or required more memory.

11.2 Preliminaries

We assume that the map is represented as a uniform-cost eight-neighbor grid with obstacles consisting of contiguous segments of blocked cells. The agent moves from grid center to grid center and can move to an unblocked cell in any cardinal or diagonal direction, with one exception: we assume that the agent is not a point and, therefore, can move diagonally only if both associated cardinal directions are also unblocked. For example, in Figure 11.1, the agent cannot move diagonally from B2 to A1 because A2 is blocked. The lengths of cardinal and diagonal moves are 1 and $\sqrt{2}$, respectively.

A* is a commonly used algorithm for pathfinding. It is an informed search algorithm that uses a heuristic to guide the search to find paths faster. The heuristic estimates the distance between any two locations on the map and, in order for A* to find shortest paths, needs to be admissible, that is, never overestimate the distance between two locations [Hart 68].

One common heuristic used when solving pathfinding problems is the Euclidean distance, which is the straight-line distance between two locations. For instance, the Euclidean distance between s and r in Figure 11.1 is $\sqrt{5^2+2^2}=5.39$. The Euclidean

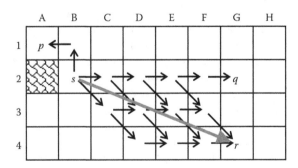

Figure 11.1

Shortest paths from s to some other cells on an eight-neighbor grid and the straight line between s and r.

distance is guaranteed to be admissible on maps with uniform traversal costs since the shortest path between two locations cannot be shorter than the straight line between them.

On eight-neighbor grids with uniform traversal costs, however, there is a more informed heuristic. The octile distance between two cells on the grid is the length of a shortest path between (that is, between their centers) assuming there are no obstacles on the grid. On a grid with no obstacles, the shortest path between two cells contains moves in only two directions. For instance, in Figure 11.1, all shortest paths between s and r contain exactly two diagonal moves toward the southeast and three cardinal moves toward the east. Therefore, the octile distance between two cells can be computed by simply comparing their x and y coordinates to figure out exactly how many diagonal and cardinal moves would be on a shortest path between them if the grid had no obstacles. For instance, the octile distance between s and r is $3 + 2 \times \sqrt{2} = 5.83$.

The octile distance is guaranteed to be admissible on eight-neighbor grids with uniform traversal costs since the shortest path between two cells cannot be shorter than on a grid with no obstacles. It is more informed than the Euclidean distance because the octile distance between two cells cannot be smaller than the Euclidean distance but is sometimes larger. Searching with a more informed heuristic means that the search typically performs fewer expansions before it finds a path and is then faster.

11.3 Simple Subgoal Graphs

Simple subgoal graphs (SSGs) are an adaptation of visibility graphs to grids. Visibility graphs abstract continuous environments with polygonal obstacles. The vertices of a visibility graph are the convex corners of obstacles, and the edges connect vertices that are visible from each other. The length of an edge is equal to the Euclidean distance between the vertices it connects. To find a shortest path between given start and goal locations in a continuous environment, one simply adds the vertices for them to the visibility graph, connects them to all vertices visible from them, and searches the resulting graph for a shortest path from the start vertex (which corresponds to the start location) to the goal vertex (which corresponds to the goal location). Figure 11.2 shows an example of a visibility graph and a path found by searching this graph. If an optimal search algorithm is used to search this graph (such as a suitable version of A* with the

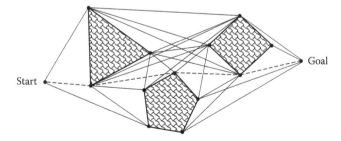

Figure 11.2

A visibility graph and the shortest path between the start and goal vertices.

Euclidean distance as heuristic), the resulting path is also a shortest path from the start location to the goal location in the continuous environment.

SSGs, on the other hand, abstract grids. The vertices of an SSG are called subgoals and are placed at the convex corners of obstacles on the grid. The edges connect subgoals that satisfy a certain connection strategy that we describe later. The length of an edge is equal to the octile distance between the vertices it connects. To find a shortest path between given start and goal cells on a grid, one can use the following steps: First, vertices are added to the SSG for the start and goal cells. Then, edges are added to connect them to the other vertices using the given connection strategy. Finally, the resulting graph is searched with A* with the octile distance as heuristic. The resulting high-level path is a series of subgoals connecting the start and goal vertices. One can then connect the subgoals on this high-level path on the grid to obtain a shortest low-level path on the grid.

Visibility graphs have strengths that SSGs aim to preserve. For instance, they can be used to find shortest paths and can be precomputed and stored. Visibility graphs also have some weaknesses that SSGs aim to fix. For instance, they can result in search trees with high branching factors, which is bad for both memory consumption and search time. The construction of visibility graphs can also be time consuming since one needs to perform visibility checks between all pairs of vertices. Even if preprocessing time is not an issue, visibility checks need to be performed when connecting the start and goal vertices to the visibility graph at runtime, namely, from the start and goal vertices to all other vertices of the visibility graph.

11.3.1 Constructing Simple Subgoal Graphs

Similar to visibility graphs, SSGs place subgoals at the corners of obstacles. Formally, we say that a cell s is a subgoal if and only if s is unblocked, s has a blocked diagonal neighbor t, and the two cells that are neighbors of both s and t are unblocked. For instance, in Figure 11.1, B1 is a subgoal because A2 is blocked and both A1 and B2 are unblocked. The idea is the same as for visibility graphs, namely, that one can use the convex corners of obstacles to navigate around them optimally.

We now introduce the concept of *h-reachability*. We say that two vertices of a graph are h-reachable if and only if there is a shortest path between them whose length is equal to the heuristic between them. H-reachability is a generalization of the concept of visibility in visibility graphs. Since visibility graphs abstract continuous environments, the heuristic used is the Euclidean distance. Thus, two vertices in a continuous environment are h-reachable if and only if they are visible from each other. Therefore, edges in visibility graphs connect exactly the h-reachable vertices.

Now, we discuss how h-reachable subgoals are connected. Since SSGs abstract grids, we use the octile distance as heuristic, and the length of an edge is equal to the octile distance between the subgoals it connects. Figure 11.3 shows an SSG constructed by connecting all h-reachable subgoals.

We now explain three properties that a connection strategy should possess and check whether the strategy of connecting h-reachable subgoals satisfies them:

1. *Edges are easy to follow on the grid*: If two cells on the grid are h-reachable, we can navigate from one cell to the other by moving in only two directions, as discussed in the preliminaries. This certainly makes it easier to follow h-reachable edges (edges that

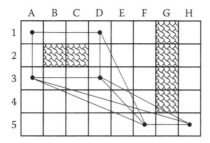

Figure 11.3

An SSG constructed by connecting all h-reachable subgoals.

connect two h-reachable cells) compared to doing an A* search on the grid between the two subgoals they connect since we know how many cardinal and diagonal moves to make in which directions. All we have to figure out is the order of the moves.

2. *Searches find shortest paths*: Adding edges between all h-reachable subgoals (plus the start and goal cells) also allows us to find shortest paths on the grid. The proof follows from the observation that, if two cells are not h-reachable, then there must be an obstacle that makes the path between the two cells longer than the octile distance between them. This obstacle introduces a subgoal that can be used to optimally circumnavigate it [Uras 13].

3. *Search trees have low branching factors*: Unfortunately, with this connection strategy, SSGs can have many more edges than the corresponding visibility graphs. For instance, in Figure 11.3, D3 and H5 are not visible from each other, but they are h-reachable.

The branching factors are a deal breaker for us, so we need to modify our connection strategy. H-reachability is still a valuable concept that will be used later when we generate two-level subgoal graphs from SSGs.

Fortunately, it is easy to address this issue. Consider the edge between D3 and H5 in Figure 11.3. This edge corresponds to the grid path D3-E4-F5-G5-H5. But there is already a subgoal at F5, and there are edges in the SSG between D3 and F5 and between F5 and H7. The sum of the lengths of these two edges is equal to the length of the edge between D3 and H5. Therefore, the edge between D3 and H5 is redundant and can be removed from the SSG without affecting the optimality of the resulting paths. When we remove all such redundant edges from the SSG in Figure 11.3, we end up with the SSG in Figure 11.4. We call the remaining edges *direct-h-reachable* edges and the subgoals they connect direct-h-reachable subgoals.

Formally, we say that two cells are direct-h-reachable if and only if they are h-reachable and none of the shortest paths between them pass through a subgoal. Direct-h-reachable edges are easier to follow than h-reachable edges. As mentioned before, h-reachable edges are easy to follow because we know exactly how many cardinal and diagonal moves we have to make in each direction. The problem is that we have to figure out the order of the moves. This is not the case for direct-h-reachable edges. Observe that, in Figure 11.1, all shortest paths between *s* and *r* cover a parallelogram-shaped area. As an equivalent definition of direct-h-reachability, we say that two cells are direct-h-reachable if and only if the parallelogram-shaped area between them does not contain any subgoals and that the

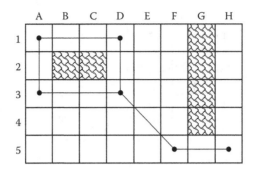

Figure 11.4

An SSG constructed by connecting all direct-h-reachable subgoals.

movement inside the parallelogram-shaped area is not blocked. Therefore, when following direct-h-reachable edges, we can make the cardinal and diagonal moves in any order. The equivalence of the two definitions follows from the observation that obstacles that block movement in the parallelogram-shaped area between two cells either introduce subgoals in the parallelogram-shaped area (meaning that the two cells are not direct-h-reachable) or block all shortest paths between the two cells (meaning that the two cells are not even h-reachable) [Uras 13].

The definition of parallelogram-shaped areas is also useful for showing that the branching factors of the search trees generated when using SSGs are lower than when using visibility graphs. If the movement inside the parallelogram-shaped area between two cells is not blocked, then the straight line between the two cells cannot be blocked either, which means that they must be visible from each other. Therefore, every direct-h-reachable edge in an SSG corresponds to a straight-line edge in the visibility graph. The converse is not true. For instance, in Figure 11.4, A3 and F5 are visible from each other but not direct-h-reachable.

To summarize, SSGs are constructed by placing subgoals at the corners of obstacles and adding edges between subgoals that are direct-h-reachable. Section 11.3.3 describes an algorithm to identify all direct-h-reachable subgoals from a given cell.

11.3.2 Searching Using Simple Subgoal Graphs

Once an SSG has been constructed, it can be used to find shortest paths between any two cells on the grid. Given a start cell and a goal cell, we connect them to their direct-h-reachable subgoals using the algorithm described in the next section. We then search the resulting graph with an optimal search algorithm, such as a suitable version of A* with the octile distance heuristic, to find a shortest high-level path. We then follow the edges of this path by simply moving in the direction of the next cell on the high-level path, to find a shortest low-level path on the grid. This process is illustrated in Figure 11.5.

There are some subtle points to the algorithm. If either the start or goal cell is a subgoal, we do not need to identify the subgoals that are direct-h-reachable from them since they are already in the SSG. Also, since the algorithm described in the next section finds only the subgoals that are direct-h-reachable from a given cell, it might not connect the start cell to the goal cell if they are direct-h-reachable but neither of them is a subgoal. In this case, we might not be able to find a shortest path between them. Before connecting the

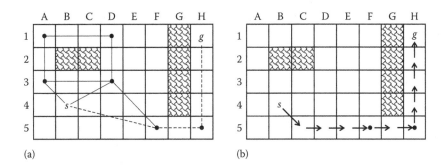

(a)   (b)

Figure 11.5

Connecting the start and goal cells to the SSG and finding a shortest high-level path on the resulting graph (a). Then, following the edges on this high-level path to find a shortest low-level path on the grid (b).

start and goal cells to the SSG, we therefore first generate a possible shortest path between them (for instance, by first moving diagonally and then moving cardinally). If the path is not blocked, we return it as the shortest path. Otherwise, the start and goal cells cannot be direct-h-reachable, and we therefore search using the SSG as described earlier.

11.3.3 Identifying All Direct-H-Reachable Subgoals from a Given Cell

Being able to identify all direct-h-reachable subgoals from a given cell quickly is important both during the construction of SSGs and when connecting the start and goal cells to SSGs. The algorithm we propose is a dynamic programming algorithm that identifies all direct-h-reachable cells from a given cell s and returns all subgoals among them. Figure 11.6 shows an example.

Our algorithm uses clearance values. The clearance value of a cell s in a direction d, called $Clearance(s, d)$, is the maximum number of moves the agent can make from s

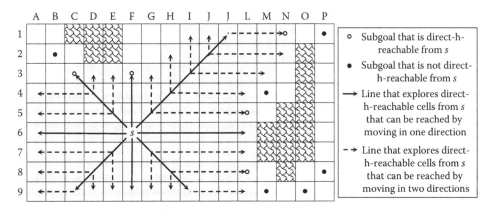

Figure 11.6

Identifying the direct-h-reachable area around s (shown in gray), which contains all direct-h-reachable subgoals from s.

toward d without reaching a subgoal or being blocked. For instance, the east clearance of s in Figure 11.6 is 6 because M6 is blocked. The north clearance of s is 2 because F3 is a subgoal. Clearance values can be either computed at runtime or be precomputed, although the algorithm does not benefit much from storing clearance values in diagonal directions. The algorithm works in two phases:

The first phase identifies all direct-h-reachable cells from s that can be reached by moving in only one direction. This is achieved by looking at the clearance values of s in all eight directions to figure out if there are direct-h-reachable subgoals in these directions. For instance, since the north clearance of s in Figure 11.6 is 2, the algorithm checks the cell 2 + 1 moves north of s, F3, to see if it is a subgoal. In Figure 11.6, the first phase determines that C3 and F3 are direct-h-reachable subgoals from s.

The second phase identifies all direct-h-reachable cells from s that can be reached by a combination of moves in a cardinal and a diagonal direction. There are eight combinations of cardinal and diagonal directions that can appear on a shortest path between two direct-h-reachable cells, and each of them identifies an area. Figure 11.6 shows these combinations, divided by the solid lines emanating from s in eight directions. The algorithm explores each area line by line (using the dashed lines in Figure 11.6). Assume that it is exploring the area that is associated with cardinal direction c and diagonal direction d. For each cell that is direct-h-reachable from s by moving toward d, it casts a line that starts at that cell and travels toward c. It starts with the line closest to s and continues until all lines are cast.

We now present three rules to determine how far each line extends. The first rule is simple: *a line stops when it reaches a subgoal or directly before it reaches an obstacle*. This is so because the additional cells the line would reach cannot be direct-h-reachable from s according to the definition of direct-h-reachability. Otherwise, the parallelogram-shaped area between s and the next cell the line would reach contained a subgoal or obstacle. The second rule follows from the following observation: if cell t is direct-h-reachable from cell s, then any cell u that lies in the parallelogram-shaped area between s and t is also direct-h-reachable from s. This is so because the parallelogram-shaped area between s and u is a subarea of the parallelogram-shaped area between s and t and, therefore, does not contain any subgoals and the movement inside the area is not blocked (since s and t are direct-h-reachable). Therefore, the area of cells that are direct-h-reachable from s is a union of parallelogram-shaped areas, each area between s and some other cell. This results in the second rule: *a line cannot be longer than the previous line*. Otherwise, the area cannot be a union of parallelogram-shaped areas. The third rule is a refinement of the second rule: *a line cannot be longer than the previous line minus one cell if the previous line ends in a subgoal*.

The algorithm uses these rules to determine quickly how far each line extends. For instance, in Figure 11.6, when the algorithm explores the east–northeast area around s, the first line it casts travels along row 5 toward east and reaches subgoal L5 after 5 moves. Since the first line ends in a subgoal, the second line can only travel 5 − 1 = 4 moves and stops before reaching subgoal M4, which is not direct-h-reachable from s. Instead of explicitly casting lines, the algorithm can use the clearance values of the cells in which the lines originate. Listing 11.1 shows pseudocode that uses the clearance values.

Listing 11.1. Identify all direct-h-reachable subgoals in an area.

```
GetDirectHReachable(cell s, cardinal dir. c, diagonal dir. d)
    SubgoalVector list = {};
    int maxLineLength = Clearance(s,c);
    int nDiagMoves = Clearance(s,d);
    for int i = 1 … nDiagMoves
        s = neighbor of s toward d;
        l = Clearance(s,c);
        if (l < maxLineLength)
            maxLineLength = l;
            s' = the cell l+1 moves away from s toward c;
            if (s' is a subgoal)
                list.add(s');
    return list;
```

11.4 Two-Level Subgoal Graphs

Searches using SSGs are faster than searches of grids because SSGs are smaller than grids and searching them expands fewer cells on average. In a way, SSGs partition the cells into subgoals and nonsubgoals, and the search ignores all nonsubgoals other than the start and goal cells.

Two-level subgoal graphs (TSGs) apply this idea to SSGs instead of grids. TSGs are constructed from SSGs by partitioning the subgoals into local and global subgoals. The search ignores all local subgoals that are not direct-h-reachable from the start or goal cells, allowing us to search even smaller graphs. TSGs satisfy the following property, called the *two-level property (TLP)*:

> The length of a shortest path between any two (local or global) subgoals s and t on the SSG is equal to the length of a shortest path between *s* and *t* on the graph consisting of all global subgoals of the TSG plus s and t (and all edges between these subgoals in the TSG).

In other words, if we remove all local subgoals except for *s* and *t* (and their associated edges) from the TSG, then the length of a shortest path between *s* and *t* does not change.

This property guarantees that TSGs can be used to find shortest paths on grids [Uras 13]. Figure 11.7 shows an SSG and a TSG constructed from the SSG. Observe that the subgraph of the TSG consisting of A1, D1, D3, and H5 contains the shortest path between A1 and H5. Also, observe that the edge between D3 and H5 is not direct-h-reachable. During the construction of TSGs, h-reachable edges can be added to the graph if this allows classifying more subgoals as local subgoals.

11.4.1 Constructing Two-Level Subgoal Graphs

Constructing TSGs from SSGs is different from constructing SSGs from grids. When constructing SSGs from grids, we identify some cells as subgoals and connect them with a connection strategy that allows them to be used to find shortest paths on the grids. This is possible because grids have structure, and visibility graphs provide some intuition for exploiting it.

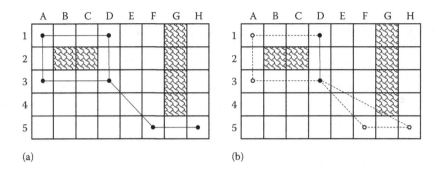

Figure 11.7

An SSG (a) and a TSG constructed from the SSG (b). Hollow circles indicate local subgoals, and solid circles indicate global subgoals.

On the other hand, there is little structure to exploit when constructing TSGs from SSGs. Therefore, we start by assuming that all subgoals are global subgoals. At this point, the TLP is satisfied since the TSG is identical to the SSG. We then iterate over all global subgoals and classify them as local subgoals if doing so does not violate the TLP. We are allowed to add edges between h-reachable subgoals if doing so helps to preserve the TLP and allows us to classify a global subgoal as a local subgoal.

The question remains how to determine quickly whether a subgoal s can be classified as a local subgoal. The straightforward method is to check if removing s from the TSG increases the length of a shortest path between two other subgoals that are not h-reachable (if they are h-reachable, we can simply add an edge between them). It is faster to check if removing s from the TSG increases the length of a shortest path between two of its neighbors that are not h-reachable, because any path that passes through s must also pass through its neighbors. The process of removing s in this way is called a contraction [Geisberger 08]. Listing 11.2 shows pseudocode for constructing a TSG from an SSG.

For each global subgoal s, we accumulate a list of edges that would need to be added to the TSG if s were classified as a local subgoal. We iterate over all pairs of neighbors of s. If there exists a pair of neighbors such that all shortest paths between the two neighbors pass through s and the neighbors are not h-reachable, then s cannot be classified as a local subgoal because doing so would violate the TLP. Otherwise, we classify s as a local subgoal and add all necessary edges to the TSG.

SSGs do not necessarily have unique TSGs since the resulting TSG can depend on the order in which the subgoals are processed. For instance, in Figure 11.7, if D1 were a local subgoal and A3 were a global subgoal, the resulting TSG would still satisfy the TLP. No research has been done so far on how the order in which the subgoals are processed affects the resulting TSG.

11.4.2 Searching Using Two-Level Subgoal Graphs

Search using TSGs is similar to search using SSGs. We start with a core graph that consists of all global subgoals and the edges between them. We then connect the start and goal cells to their respective direct-h-reachable (local or global) subgoals. Next, local subgoals

Listing 11.2. Constructing a TSG from an SSG.

```
ConstructTSG(SSG S)
    SubgoalList G = subgoals of S; //Global subgoals
    SubgoalList L = {}; //Local subgoals
    EdgeList E = edges of S;
    for all s in G
        EdgeList E+ = {}; //Extra edges
        bool local = true; //Assume s can be a local subgoal
        for all p, q in Neighbors(s) //Neighbors wrt E
            d = length of a shortest path between p and q
                (wrt E) that does not pass through s or any
                subgoal in L;
            if (d > c(p,s) + c(s,q))
                if (p and q are h-reachable)
                    E+.add((p,q));
                else //s is necessary to connect p and q
                    local = false; //Can't make s local
                    break;
        if (local)
            G.remove(s); //Classify s as a local subgoal
            L.add(s);
            E.append(E+); //Add the extra edges to the TSG
    return (G, L, E);
```

that are direct-h-reachable from the start or goal cells using edges not in the core graph are added to the graph. Once a high-level shortest path from the start cell to the goal cell is found on this graph, we follow its edges to find a low-level path on the grid. We might have to follow edges between cells that are h-reachable but not direct-h-reachable. This means that we have to identify the order of cardinal and diagonal moves, which can be achieved with a depth-first search. Figure 11.8 shows an example of this search graph. The number of subgoals excluded from the search can be much larger for larger TSGs.

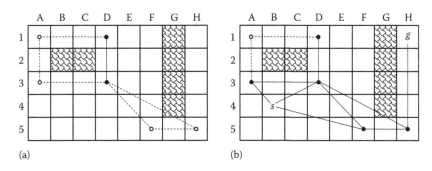

Figure 11.8

A TSG (a) and a search using this TSG (b). The graph that is searched consists of the solid circles.

11.4 Two-Level Subgoal Graphs

11.5 N-Level Graphs

We now generalize the ideas behind the construction of TSGs to be able to generate graphs with more than two levels from any given undirected graph [Uras 14].

Observe that only the terms "subgoal" and "h-reachable" are specific to subgoal graphs in the partitioning algorithm shown in Listing 11.2 and can be replaced by the terms "vertex" and "a property P that all extra edges need to satisfy," making the partitioning algorithm applicable to any undirected graph. The lengths of the edges added to the graph should always be equal to the lengths of shortest paths on the original graph between the two vertices they connect. We need to specify a property P that all extra edges need to satisfy. Otherwise, all vertices of a graph can be classified as local by adding edges between all vertices, which would create a pairwise distance matrix for the graph. P should be chosen such that the extra edges can easily be followed on the original graph and the branching factors of the search trees do not increase too much. H-reachability satisfies these criteria for subgoal graphs, although other properties could exist that would result in even faster searches. If it is hard to come up with such a property, one can always choose P such that no extra edges are added to the graph, resulting in fewer vertices being excluded from the search. *Two-level graphs* can be constructed by applying the general version of the partitioning algorithm described in Listing 11.2 to any undirected graph. Figure 11.9 shows an example with an undirected graph with unit edge costs and a two-level graph constructed from the undirected graph without adding extra edges.

The general version of the algorithm described in Listing 11.2 partitions the vertices of an undirected graph into local and global vertices. Call local vertices *level 1 vertices* and global vertices *level 2 vertices*. Level 2 vertices and the edges between them form a graph, and one can apply the general version of the algorithm described in Listing 11.2 to this graph to partition the level 2 vertices into level 2 and level 3 vertices. Figure 11.10 shows an example of a *three-level graph*, constructed from the two-level graph shown in Figure 11.9 by partitioning its level 2 vertices into level 2 and level 3 vertices.

One can keep adding levels to the graphs by recursively partitioning the highest-level vertices until they can no longer be partitioned. Adding more levels to the graph means

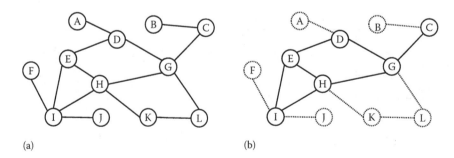

(a)   (b)

Figure 11.9

An undirected graph with unit edge costs (a) and a two-level graph constructed from the undirected graph without adding extra edges (b). Solid circles indicate global vertices, and dashed circles indicate local vertices.

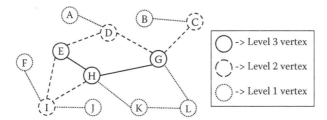

Figure 11.10

A three-level graph constructed from the undirected graph in Figure 11.9.

that the graphs that are searched are getting smaller but also that one needs to spend more time constructing the graph for each search.

Once an n-level graph has been constructed, it can be used to find shortest paths between any two vertices of the original graph. Call the graph consisting of all highest-level vertices (and the edges between them) the *core graph* since it appears in every search. When using a two-level graph to find a shortest path between given start and goal vertices, one adds them to the core graph and searches the resulting graph with an optimal search algorithm to find a high-level path. When using a three-level graph to find a shortest path between given start and goal vertices, one also adds any level 2 vertices that are neighbors of the start or goal vertices. This process is illustrated in Figure 11.11. Listing 11.3 shows pseudocode to determine which vertices need to be added to the core graph when using n-level graphs, for any value of N. This algorithm needs to be called for both the start and goal vertices. When this algorithm is called for an SSG, it creates an n-level subgoal graph.

SSGs are essentially *two-level grid graphs*. If one were to allow the addition of extra edges between direct-h-reachable vertices of the grid graph, the general version of the algorithm described in Listing 11.2 could classify all subgoals as level 2 vertices and all nonsubgoals as level 1 vertices [Uras 14], although it could take a long time to run and the extra edges between direct-h-reachable cells could require a lot of memory to store. The construction of SSGs, as described previously, avoids these issues by exploiting the structure of grids and by only storing direct-h-reachable edges between subgoals. Direct-h-reachable edges that are not stored are reconstructed

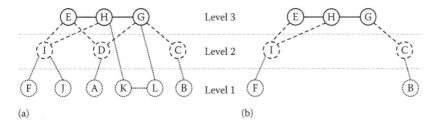

Figure 11.11

The three-level graph from Figure 11.10 with vertices rearranged in layers (a) and the graph searched for a shortest path between vertices F and B of the three-level graph (b).

```
IdentifyConnectingVertices(vertex s, Graph G, int graphLevel)
    VertexList open = {s};
    VertexList closed = {};
    while (open != {})
        vertex p = open.getVertexWithSmallestLevel();
        open.remove(p);
        if (p.level == graphLevel)
            break;
        if (!closed.contains(p))
            closed.add(p);
            for all neighbors q of p in G
                if (q.level > p.level && !closed.contains(q))
                    open.add(q);
    return closed;
```

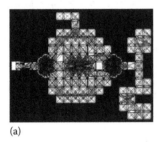 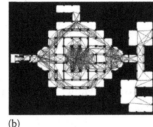 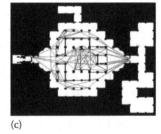

(a)　　　　　　　　　　　(b)　　　　　　　　　　　(c)

Figure 11.12

An SSG (a), TSG (b), and a five-level subgoal graph (c). Only the highest-level subgoals and the edges between them are shown.

before a search when connecting the start and goal cells to the SSG or when checking if the start and goal cells are direct-h-reachable. Figure 11.12 shows an SSG, a TSG, and a five-level subgoal graph (six-level grid graph).

The ideas behind n-level graphs are also closely related to contraction hierarchies [Geisberger 08], where the vertices of a graph are first ordered by "importance" and then iteratively contracted, starting from the least important vertex. Contracting a vertex v means replacing unique shortest paths between the neighbors of v that go through v by shortcut edges. The resulting graphs are searched with a bidirectional search algorithm, where the forward search uses only edges leading to more important vertices and the backward search uses only edges coming from more important vertices. Vertex contraction is used during the construction of n-level graphs whenever the level of a vertex is decreased. In essence, n-level graphs are contraction hierarchies where there are constraints on adding new edges to the graph but each level is not limited to contain only one vertex.

11.6 Conclusion

Subgoal graphs are generated by preprocessing grids and can be used to significantly speed up searches on grids, with little memory overhead. The ideas behind them apply to any undirected graph, although it might need some ingenuity to figure out a suitable property that all extra edges need to satisfy. We have, so far, only tested n-level graphs on grids.

Acknowledgments

The research at USC was supported by NSF under grant numbers 1409987 and 1319966. The views and conclusions contained in this document are those of the authors and should not be interpreted as representing the official policies, either expressed or implied, of the sponsoring organizations, agencies or the U.S. government.

References

[Geisberger 08] Geisberger, R., Sanders, P., Schultes, D., and Delling, D. 2008. Contraction hierarchies: Faster and simpler hierarchical routing in road networks. *Proceedings of the International Workshop on Experimental Algorithms,* Provincetown, MA, 319–333.

[Hart 68] Hart, P., Nilsson, N., and Raphael, B. 1968. A formal basis for the heuristic determination of minimum cost paths. *IEEE Transactions on Systems Science and Cybernetics* 4(2):100–107.

[Sturtevant 12] Sturtevant, N. 2012. Benchmarks for grid-based pathfinding. *Transactions on Computational Intelligence and AI in Games* 4(2):144–148.

[Uras 13] Uras, T., Koenig, S., and Hernandez, C. 2013. Subgoal graphs for optimal pathfinding in eight-neighbor grids. *Proceedings of the International Conference on Automated Planning and Scheduling*, Rome, Italy, 224–232.

[Uras 14] Uras, T. and Koenig, S. 2014. Identifying hierarchies for fast optimal search. *Proceedings of the AAAI Conference on Artificial Intelligence*, Quebec City, Quebec, Canada, pp. 878–884.

12

Theta* for Any-Angle Pathfinding

Alex Nash and Sven Koenig

12.1 Introduction

One of the central problems in game AI is finding short and realistic-looking paths. Pathfinding is typically divided into two steps: discretize and search. First, the **discretize** step simplifies a continuous environment into a graph. Second, the **search** step propagates information along this graph to find a path from a given start vertex to a given goal vertex. Video game developers (and roboticists) have developed several methods for discretizing continuous environments into graphs, such as 2D regular grids composed of squares (square grids), hexagons or triangles, 3D regular grids composed of cubes, visibility graphs, circle-based waypoint graphs, space-filling volumes, navigation meshes, framed quad trees, probabilistic road maps, and rapidly exploring random trees [Björnsson 03, Choset 04, Tozour 04].

Due to its simplicity and optimality guarantees, A* is almost always the search method of choice. A* is guaranteed to find shortest paths on graphs, but shortest paths on graphs are not equivalent to shortest paths in the continuous environments. A* propagates information along graph edges and constrains paths to graph edges, which artificially constrains path headings. Consider Figures 12.1 and 12.2, in which two different continuous environments have been discretized into a square grid and a navigation mesh, respectively. The shortest paths on the square grid and the navigation mesh (Figure 12.1) are longer than the shortest paths in the continuous environment (Figure 12.2) and are unrealistic looking due to either a heading change in free space or a heading change that does not *hug* a blocked cell.

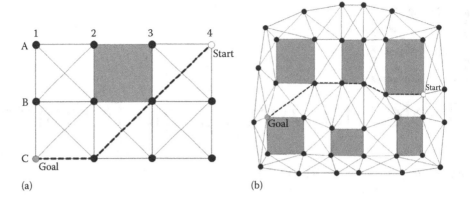

Figure 12.1

Grid paths: square grid (a) and navigation mesh (b). (Adapted from Patel, A., Amit's game programming information, 2000, Retrieved from http://www-cs-students.stanford. edu/~amitp/gameprog.html, accessed September 10, 2014.)

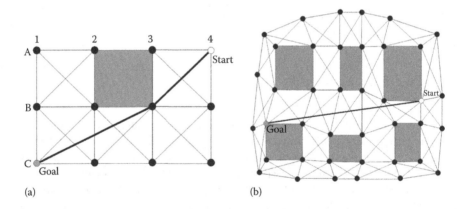

Figure 12.2

Any-angle paths: square grid (a) and navigation mesh (b). (Adapted from Patel, A., Amit's game programming information, 2000, Retrieved from http://www-cs-students.stanford. edu/~amitp/gameprog.html, accessed September 10, 2014.)

The fact that A* paths can be long and unrealistic looking is well known in the video game community [Rabin 00]. The paths found by A* on eight-neighbor square grids can be approximately 8% longer than the shortest paths in the continuous environment [Nash 12]. The typical solution to this problem is to use a postprocessing technique to shorten the A* paths. One such technique is to remove vertices from the path, such that they look like *rubber bands* around obstacles (A* PS). This technique shortens paths such that all of the heading changes on the path *hug* a blocked cell.

However, choosing a postprocessing technique that consistently shortens paths is difficult because there are often several shortest paths on a given graph, and a

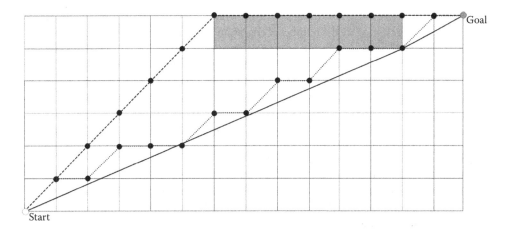

Figure 12.3

A* paths with different postprocessing techniques.

postprocessing technique typically shortens some of them more effectively than others. For example, A* with the octile distance heuristic finds paths very efficiently on eight-neighbor square grids. (The octile distance is the shortest distance between two vertices on an eight-neighbor square grid with no blocked cells.) However, these paths are often difficult to shorten because the search tends to find paths in which moves in the diagonal directions appear before moves in the cardinal directions (for the tie-breaking scheme explained in the next section). The dashed path in Figure 12.3 depicts this behavior.

On the other hand, A* with the straight-line distance heuristic finds paths that are of the same lengths as those found by A* with the octile distance heuristic, albeit more slowly due to additional vertex expansions. However, paths found using the straight-line distance heuristic are often shortened more effectively because they tend to follow the shortest paths in the continuous environment. The dotted path in Figure 12.3 depicts this behavior. In general, postprocessing techniques do improve paths, but they provide trade-offs between path length and runtime that are difficult to chose between, and they do not address the fundamental issue, namely, that the search only considers paths that are constrained to graph edges [Nash 07, Ferguson 06].

We address this issue by describing a different approach to the search problem, called any-angle pathfinding. Specifically, we describe Theta*, a popular any-angle pathfinding algorithm. The development of Theta* was motivated by combining the desirable properties of A* on two different discretizations of the continuous environment:

- *Visibility graphs*: Visibility graphs contain the start vertex, the goal vertex, and the convex corners of all blocked cells [Lorzano-Perez 79]. A vertex is connected via a straight line to another vertex if and only if it has line of sight to the other vertex, that is, the straight line from it to the other vertex does not pass through a blocked cell or between blocked cells that share a side. Shortest paths on visibility graphs are also shortest paths in the continuous environment. However, pathfinding is slow on large visibility graphs since the number of edges can be quadratic in the number of vertices.

- *Grids*: Pathfinding is faster on grids than visibility graphs since the number of edges is linear in the number of cells. However, shortest paths on grids can be longer than shortest paths in the continuous environment and unrealistic looking since the path headings are artificially constrained to grid edges [Nash 07].

Theta* combines the desirable properties of these pathfinding techniques by propagating information along graph edges (to achieve short runtimes) without constraining paths to graph edges (to find short *any-angle* paths).

Theta* is easy to understand, quick to implement and provides a good trade-off between path length and runtime. It quickly finds short and realistic-looking paths and can be used to search any Euclidean graph. The pseudocode for Theta* is very similar to the pseudocode for A*, and both pathfinding algorithms have similar runtimes. Despite this, Theta* finds paths that have nearly the same length as the shortest paths in the continuous environments without the need for postprocessing techniques.

12.2 Problem Formalization

For simplicity, this article focuses on eight-neighbor square grids in which a 2D continuous environment is discretized into square cells that are either blocked (gray) or unblocked (white). Vertices are placed at cell corners rather than cell centers, and paths are allowed to pass between diagonally touching blocked cells. Neither of these two assumptions are required for Theta* to function correctly. Our goal is to find a short and realistic-looking path from a given start vertex to a given goal vertex (both at the corners of cells) that does not pass through blocked cells or between blocked cells that share a side.

In the following pseudocode, s_{start} is the start vertex of the search, and s_{goal} is the goal vertex of the search. $c(s, s')$ is the straight-line distance between vertices s and s', and $lineofsight(s, s')$ is true if and only if they have line of sight or, synonymously, they are visible from each other. $open.Insert(s, x)$ inserts vertex s with key x into the priority queue $open$. $open.Remove(s)$ removes vertex s from $open$. $open.Pop()$ removes a vertex with the smallest key from $open$ and returns it. For A*, we break ties among vertices with the smallest key in the open list in favor of vertices with the largest g-value. This tiebreaking scheme can reduce the runtimes of A*, especially when used with the octile distance heuristic. Finally, $neighbor_{vis}(s)$ is the set of neighbors of vertex s that have line of sight to s.

12.3 A* Algorithm

Theta* builds upon A* [Nilsson 68], and thus we introduce it here. The pseudocode for A* can be found in Figure 12.4. A* uses heuristic values (h-values) $h(s)$ for each vertex s that approximate the goal distances and focus the search. A* maintains two values for every vertex s: the g-value and the parent. The g-value $g(s)$ is the length of the shortest path from the start vertex to s found so far. The parent $parent(s)$ is used to extract the path after the search terminates. Path extraction is performed by repeatedly following parents from the goal vertex to the start vertex. A* also maintains two global data structures: the open list and the closed list. The open list $open$ is a priority queue that contains the vertices to be considered

```
 1  Main()
 2      open:=closed:=∅;
 3      g(S_start):=0;
 4      parent(S_start):=S_start;
 5      open.Insert(S_start,S_start)+h(S_start));
 6      While open≠∅ do
 7          s:=open.Pop();
 8          if s=s_goal then
 9              return "path found";
10          closed:=closed ∪{s};
11          foreach s'∈neighbor_vis(s)do
12              if s'∉closed then
13                  if s'∉open then
14                      g(s'):=∞;
15                      parent(s'):=NULL;
16                  UpdateVertex(s,s');
17      return "no path found";
18  end
19  Update Vertex(s,s')
20      g_old:=g(s');
21      ComputeCost(s,s');
22      if g(s')<g_old then
23          if s'∈open then
24              open.Remove(s');
25          open.Insert(s',g(s')+h(s'));
26  end
27  ComputeCost(s,s')
28      /* Path 1 */
29      if g(s)+c(s,s')<g(s') then
30          parent(s'):=s;
31          g(s'):=g(s)+c(s,s');
32  end
```

Figure 12.4

Pseudocode for A*.

for expansion. For A*, we break ties among vertices with the smallest key in the open list in favor of vertices with the larger g-value. This tiebreaking scheme can reduce the runtimes of A*, especially when used with the octile distance heuristic. The closed list $closed$ is a set that contains the vertices that have already been expanded. A* updates the g-value and parent of an unexpanded visible neighbor s' of vertex s (procedure **ComputeCost**) by considering the path from the start vertex to s [$= g(s)$] and from s to s' in a straight line [$= c(s, s')$], resulting in a length of $g(s) + c(s, s')$ (Line 29). It updates the g-value and parent of s' if this path is shorter than the shortest path from the start vertex to s' found so far [$= g(s')$].

As noted by Rabin [Rabin 00], A* paths often appear as though they were constructed by someone who was drunk. This is both because the paths are longer than the shortest paths in the continuous environment and because the path headings are artificially constrained by the grid. As we mentioned earlier, postprocessing techniques can shorten A* paths but are often ineffective. This is because A* only considers paths that are constrained to grid edges during the search and thus cannot make informed decisions about other paths. Theta*, on the other hand, also considers paths that are not constrained to grid edges during the search and thus can make more informed decisions during the search.

12.4 Theta* Algorithm

The key difference between Theta* and A* is that Theta* allows the parent of a vertex to be any visible vertex, whereas A* requires the parent to be a visible neighbor. So, the pseudocode for Theta* is nearly identical to the pseudocode for A*. Only the procedure ComputeCost is changed; the new code can be found in Figure 12.5. We use the straight-line distance heuristic $h(s) = c(s, s_{goal})$ to focus the search. Theta* is identical to A* except that Theta* updates the g-value and parent of an unexpanded visible neighbor s' of vertex s by considering the following two paths in procedure ComputeCost, as shown in Figure 12.5.

- *Path 1*: As done by A*, Theta* considers the path from the start vertex to s [$= g(s)$] and from s to s' in a straight line [$= c(s, s')$], resulting in a length of $g(s) + c(s, s')$ (Line 41).
- *Path 2*: To allow for any-angle paths, Theta* also considers the path from the start vertex to parent(s) [$= g(parent(s))$] and from *parent(s)* to s' in a straight line [$= c(parent(s),s')$], resulting in a length of $g(parent(s)) + c(parent(s),s')$, if s' has line of sight to *parent(s)* (Line 36). The idea behind considering Path 2 is that Path 2 is guaranteed to be no longer than Path 1 due to the triangle inequality if s' has line of sight to *parent(s)*.

Theta* updates the g-value and parent of s' if either path is shorter than the shortest path from the start vertex to s' found so far [$= g(s')$]. For example, consider Figure 12.6, where B3

```
33 ComputeCost(s,s')
34   if lineofsight(parent(s),s') then
35       /* Path 2 */
36       if g(parent(s)) + c(parent(s),s')< g(s') then
37           parent(s') := parent(s);
38           g(s') := g(parent(s)) + c(parent(s),s');
39   else
40       / * Path 1 */
41       if g(s) + c(s,s')< g(s') then
42           parent(s'):= s;
43           g(s'):= g(s) + c(s,s');
44 end
```

Figure 12.5

Pseudocode for Theta*.

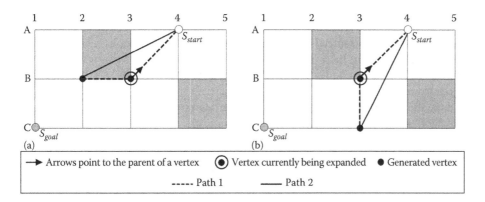

Figure 12.6

Theta* updates a vertex according to Path 1 (a) and Path 2 (b).

(with parent A4) gets expanded. The Path 1 rule is used when generating B2 because it *does not* have line of sight to A4. This is depicted in Figure 12.6a. The Path 2 rule is used when generating C3 because it *does* have line of sight to A4. This is depicted in Figure 12.6b.

Figure 12.7 shows a complete trace of Theta*. Arrows point from vertices to their parents. The concentric circles indicate the vertex that is currently being expanded and solid circles indicate vertices that have already been generated. The start vertex A4 is expanded first, followed by B3, B2, and C1.

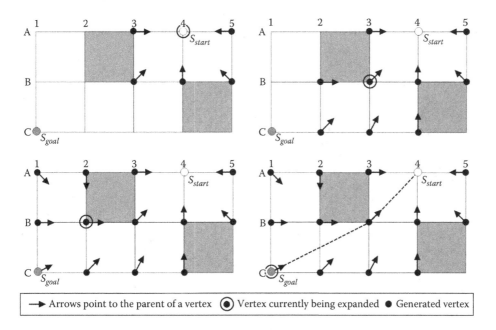

Figure 12.7

Example trace of Theta*.

12.5 Theta* Paths

While Theta* is not guaranteed to find shortest paths in the continuous environment (for the reasons explained in the work of Nash et al. [Nash 07]), it finds shortest paths in the continuous environment quite frequently, as demonstrated in Figure 12.8. We performed a search from the center of the grid to all of the vertices in the grid. In Figure 12.8a, A* PS found the shortest path in the continuous environment from the center of the grid to each shaded dot. Similarly, in Figure 12.8b, Theta* found the shortest path in the continuous environment from the center of the grid to each shaded dot. There are far more shaded dots in Figure 12.8b than Figure 12.8a.

Figure 12.9 compares a Theta* path (bottom) and an A* path (top) on a game map from BioWare's popular RPG *Baldur's Gate II*, which has been discretized into a 100 × 100 eight-neighbor square grid. The Theta* path is significantly shorter and appears more realistic than the A* path. Furthermore, most postprocessing techniques are unable to shorten the A* path into the Theta* path since the A* path circumnavigates blocked cells in a different way.

12.6 Analysis

Researchers have performed experiments comparing the path lengths and runtimes of A*, A* PS, and Theta* using eight-neighbor square grids that either correspond to game maps or contain a given percentage of randomly blocked cells [Nash 12, Yap 11, Sislak 09]. The relationships between the lengths of the paths found by A*, A* PS, and Theta* are relatively consistent. The Theta* paths are approximately 4% shorter than the A* paths. The A* PS paths are approximately 1%–3% shorter than the A* paths depending on the type of environment and the heuristic (e.g., straight-line distance or octile

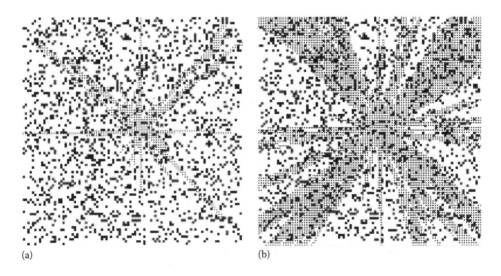

(a)   (b)

Figure 12.8

Shortest paths found by A* PS (a) and Theta* (b).

12. Theta* for Any-Angle Pathfinding

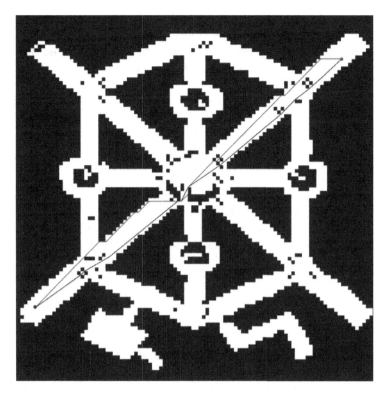

Figure 12.9

Theta* path (bottom path) versus A* path (top path).

distance heuristic). The shortest paths in the continuous environment are approximately 0.1% shorter than the Theta* paths.

The relationships between the runtimes of A*, A* PS, and Theta* are less consistent. This is because the results vary significantly with different experimental setups (such as grid size, placement of blocked cells, locations of start and goal vertices, h-values, and tiebreaking scheme for selecting a vertex among those with the smallest key in the open list). Currently, there is no agreement on standard experimental setups in the literature. We therefore broadly average over all reported results to give the reader an approximate idea of the efficiency of Theta*. Theta* is approximately two to three times slower than A* with the octile distance heuristic and approximately two times *faster* than A* PS with the straight-line distance heuristic. The significant difference in runtime between A* with the octile distance heuristic and A* PS with the straight-line distance heuristic is due to a large difference in the number of vertex expansions. However, highly informed heuristics, such as the octile distance heuristic on grids, do not exist for many discretizations of continuous environments, such as navigation meshes. If A*, A* PS, and Theta* all use the straight-line distance heuristic, then Theta* might find shorter paths faster than A*, and A* PS.

In general, Theta* provides a good trade-off between path length and runtime. On the one hand, Theta* is orders of magnitude faster than standard implementations of

A* on visibility graphs and finds paths that have nearly the same length. On the other hand, Theta* is approximately two to three times slower than versions of A* on eight-neighbor square grids that are optimized for performance but finds much shorter and more realistic-looking paths. The efficiency of Theta* is dependent on efficient line-of-sight checks. For applications in which line-of-sight checks are slow and thus a bottleneck, we suggest taking a look at Lazy Theta* [Nash 10] and Optimized Lazy Theta* [Nash 12]. These are optimized versions of Theta* that are easy to understand, quick to implement, and often provide an even better trade-off between path length and runtime.

12.7 Conclusion

We hope that this chapter serves to highlight the usefulness of any-angle pathfinding for efficiently finding short and realistic-looking paths. For more information on Theta*, we suggest visiting our any-angle pathfinding web page [Koenig 14] and reading the publications that this article is derived from [Daniel 10, Nash 07, Nash 12, Nash 13]. If you are interested in Theta*, you may also like other any-angle pathfinding algorithms such as Field D* [Ferguson 06], Accelerated A* [Sislak 09], Block A* [Yap 11], and Anya [Harabour 13].

Acknowledgment

The research at USC was supported by NSF under grant numbers 1409987 and 1319966. The views and conclusions contained in this document are those of the authors and should not be interpreted as representing the official policies, either expressed or implied, of the sponsoring organizations, agencies or the U.S. government.

References

[Björnsson 03] Björnsson, Y., Enzenberger, M., Holte, R., Schaeffer, J., and Yap, P. 2003. Comparison of different grid abstractions for pathfinding on maps. *Proceedings of the International Joint Conference on Artificial Intelligence*, 1511–1512.

[Choset 04] Choset, H., Hutchinson, S., Kantor, G., Burgard, W., Lydia, K., and Thrun, S. 2004. *Principles of Robot Motion*. MIT Press, Cambridge, MA.

[Daniel 10] Daniel, K., Nash, A., and Koenig, S. 2010. Theta*: Any-angle path planning on grids. *Journal of Artificial Intelligence Research*, 39, 533–579.

[Ferguson 06] Ferguson, D. and Stentz, A. 2006. Using interpolation to improve path planning: The Field D* algorithm. *Journal of Field Robotics*, 23(2), 79–101.

[Harabor 13] Harabor, D. and Grastien, A. 2013. An optimal any-angle pathfinding algorithm. *Proceedings of the International Conference on Automated Planning and Scheduling*, Rome, Italy, 308–344.

[Koenig 14] Koenig, S. 2014. Project "Any-angle path planning". Retrieved from http://idm-lab.org/project-o.html (accessed September 10, 2014).

[Lorzano-Perez 79] Lozano-Perez, T. and Wesley, M. 1979. An algorithm for planning collision-free paths among polyhedral obstacles. *Communication of the ACM*, 22, 560–570.

[Nash 07] Nash, A., Daniel, K., Koenig, S., and Felner, A. 2007. Theta*: Any-angle path planning on grids. *Proceedings of the AAAI Conference on Artificial Intelligence,* 1177–1183.

[Nash 10] Nash, A., Koenig, S., and Tovey, C. 2010. Lazy Theta*: Any-angle path planning and path length analysis in 3D. In *Proceedings of the AAAI Conference on Artificial Intelligence,* 147–154.

[Nash 12] Nash, A. 2012. Any-angle path planning. PhD dissertation, University of Southern California, Los Angeles, CA.

[Nash 13] Nash, A. and Koenig, S. 2013. Any-angle path planning. *Artificial Intelligence Magazine,* 34(3), 85–107.

[Nilsson 68] Nilsson, N., Hart, P., and Raphael, B. 1968. Formal basis for the heuristic determination of minimum cost paths. *IEEE Transactions on Systems Science and Cybernetics,* 4(2), 100–107.

[Patel 00] Patel, A. 2000. Amit's game programming information. Retrieved from http://www-cs-students.stanford.edu/~amitp/gameprog.html (accessed September 10, 2014).

[Rabin 00] Rabin, S. 2000. A* aesthetic optimizations. In *Game Programming Gems,* ed. DeLoura, M., 264–271. Charles River Media, Hingham, MA.

[Sislak 09] Sislak, D., Volf, P., Pechoucek, M., Suri, N., Nicholson, D., and Woodhouse, D. 2009. Accelerated A* path planning. *Proceedings of the International Conference on Autonomous Agents and Multiagent Systems,* 375–378.

[Tozour 04] Tozour, P. 2004. Search space representations. In *AI Game Programming Wisdom 2,* ed. Rabin, S., 85–102. Charles River Media, Hingham, MA.

[Yap 11] Yap, P., Burch, N., Holte, R., and Schaeffer, J. 2011. Block A*: Database-driven search with applications in any-angle path-planning. *Proceedings of the AAAI Conference on Artificial Intelligence,* 120–125.

13

Advanced Techniques for Robust, Efficient Crowds

Graham Pentheny

13.1 Introduction

To date, crowds in games are usually driven by static pathfinding combined with localized steering and collision avoidance. This technique is well understood and works well for small or moderate crowd sizes that are sparsely distributed in their environment. As crowd density increases and the agents' goals converge, this approach falls apart. In situations like this, agents fight the rest of the crowd to follow their ideal path as closely as possible, seemingly ignoring all other possible routes.

Congestion maps provide a simple means of modeling aggregate behavior in large crowds of tens or hundreds of thousands of agents. Combined with *vector flow fields*, congestion maps can be used to elegantly handle large variations in path travel times due to congestion and crowding from other agents in the scene. Agents controlled by this technique appear to be more aware of their surroundings, reconsidering their current path choice if a less-congested alternative exists.

13.2 Pathfinding's Utopian Worldview

Current solutions for pathfinding compute paths in an idealized environment. They compute the shortest distance path from the current agent position to its goal through a given environment as if no other agents existed. Some variations of common pathfinding approaches such as Partial Refinement A* [Sturtevant 05] repeatedly perform partial path calculations to account for changes in the environment. This is ideal for rapidly changing environments as much of a full path calculation is likely to never be used before it is necessary to repath. Despite adeptly handling changes to the open areas in the environment, Partial Refinement variants of A* operate on the principle that the only obstacles in the environment are static and binary. Either the agent can move through a given location or it can't. These approaches cannot handle situations where certain path directions are obstructed by large groups of other agents, because they do not consider other agents in their calculations. This can be thought of as optimizing for total path length, rather than for the actual travel time. In an empty environment, the travel time is simply the distance inversely scaled by the agent's velocity. However, in a crowded world, other agents increase the travel time through certain points in the environment.

Collision avoidance algorithms attempt to avoid other agents in the local vicinity by either restricting or augmenting the agent's velocity. These techniques are well suited for avoiding localized collisions and are often used to complement idealized pathfinding. Collision avoidance algorithms, however, fail to account for situations where movement is significantly impacted by other agents. Collision avoidance helps avoid other agents that may obstruct travel along the ideal, shortest path, but does not deviate the path direction. In games using this dual-layered pathing and collision avoidance approach, repathing occurs only when the collision avoidance solver pushes the agent far enough away from their current, ideal path so that it no longer remains the ideal movement direction. The implications of this are most easily seen in the following example, illustrated in Figure 13.1.

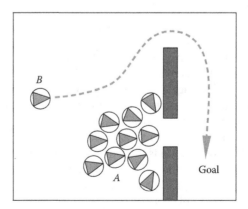

Figure 13.1

Two groups of agents attempting to reach a shared goal. The dashed line indicates the time-optimal path for agent *B*.

13. Advanced Techniques for Robust, Efficient Crowds

In this scenario, the agents are attempting to reach a common goal. There are a large number of agents in group A, and therefore they will take a considerable amount of time to move through the lower opening. Because all agents follow their ideal shortest path, both groups attempt to move through the lower opening. The agent marked as "B" in this example could path through the upper unobstructed opening, resulting in a shorter travel time to its goal. This alternative path is indicated as a gray dashed line in Figure 13.1. With just path planning and collision avoidance, agent B will consider the alternative path only when its collision avoidance moves the agent close to the upper opening. Only then, when the agent's shortest path is through the upper opening, will it consider this alternative route.

Both approaches that compute individual paths, and those like flow fields that aggregate pathfinding information across a group, suffer from this lack of contextual awareness. These algorithms are designed to minimize the total path distance, as this is a measurable and easily optimized metric. Alternatively, full movement-planning approaches involve predicting and planning movement for all agents through the scene and solving for collisions and congestion over their entire respective paths. These approaches can be too resource intensive to compute for large numbers of agents in real time. Additionally, motion planning does not account for future environmental or goal changes that may affect the computed movement information. As such, motion planning is only seen in situations requiring high-quality movement for small numbers of agents.

13.3 Congestion Map Approach

The solution we propose is a hybrid of static, idealized pathfinding, with a simplification of motion planning. The approach computes aggregate crowd density and movement across the environment and then compares that to the idealized path direction and movement. This information, called a *congestion map*, is then used to augment pathfinding computations by discouraging movement through crowded areas. Congestion maps offer significant advantages over *direction maps* (DMs) [Jansen 08], an approach we will compare later in this chapter.

This approach is based on the observation that moving against or across a crowd is much more difficult than movement aligned with the flow of the crowd. Additionally, the more densely crowded an area is, the more time it will cost to move through.

Because information on crowd dynamics is computed for groups of agents as a whole, the computational complexity is far less than that of full motion planning. Combined with aggregate pathfinding techniques such as flow fields, this approach scales well to large numbers of agents, making it ideal for large crowd simulations.

13.4 Augmenting Path Planning with Congestion Maps

The first step in the process is to compute the aggregate crowd density across the environment. For each agent in the scene, we record its current velocity and position. We then use the agent positions to construct an agent influence map [Champandard 11] across the environment space. This is used as an estimation of agent density, where larger influence values correspond to a denser crowd at that position. Conversely, lower values indicate more sparsely distributed agents.

Velocity information is plotted and distributed over the environmental space in the same manner. In addition, we compute a rolling average of the agent velocity vectors, providing a map of the average velocity of the crowd at each point. For clarity, both the average velocity and the crowd density information are referred to collectively as a "congestion map." The congestion map indicates areas that are likely to experience increased travel costs due to crowd congestion.

The congestion map information is then used as a means of computing path traversal cost in a heuristic pathfinding algorithm, such as A*. Crowd density alone could be interpreted as a traversal cost; however, this would cause agents moving together at a uniform velocity to unnecessarily avoid each other. Instead, we use the aggregate crowd velocity information to ensure that we only add traversal costs when necessary. Using an unmodified pathfinding algorithm, we begin to compute the ideal path from the agent to the goal. In the pathfinding process, we use the congestion map to augment the computed traversal cost from one step in the path to the next. This is done by computing the difference in the aggregate crowd velocity and the agent's ideal path velocity. The scalar magnitude of this vector difference is then scaled by the crowd density value, resulting in the "congestion penalty" for that movement. Pseudocode for computing the traversal cost is shown in Listing 13.1. The congestion penalty can then be easily integrated into existing calculations as an additional path traversal cost. Furthermore, because the crowd congestion penalty is never negative, it maintains heuristic admissibility in the path planner.

As agents move through the scene, they use the congestion map to augment their pathfinding queries. This ensures that they will favor paths that offer the shortest travel time, even if they are not the shortest in distance. Each agent performs a traditional pathfinding query, or an aggregate pathfinding pass is performed in the case of using flow fields. The normal behavior of the heuristic path planner uses the "congestion map" information to choose paths with lower costs and thus minimal travel times. Alternatively, if a congested path still remains better than any alternative, the path planner will correctly choose the congested path.

Listing 13.1. Traversal cost computation using the congestion map information.

```
float congestionPenalty(Vec2 ideal,
                        Vec2 aggregate,
                        float density)
{
    //Projection of aggregate onto ideal, represented
    //as a scalar multiple of ideal.
    float cost = Vec2.dot(ideal, aggregate);
    cost /= ideal.mag() * ideal.mag();

    //If cost is > 1, the crowd is moving faster along the
    //ideal direction than the agent's ideal velocity.
    if (cost >= 1) return 0.0f;

    //Cost is transformed to be positive,
    //and scaled by crowd density
    return (1 - cost) * density;
}
```

13. Advanced Techniques for Robust, Efficient Crowds

The final step in the process involves adding in local collision avoidance. While the congestion map will help deal with macrolevel collision avoidance, we still rely, albeit far less, on collision avoidance algorithms to resolve local agent collisions.

13.5 Path Smoothing

Because the congestion coefficients are used by the pathfinder as traversal cost values, unmodified path-smoothing algorithms will not maintain this information. Path smoothing relies on line-of-sight collision checks to determine whether a waypoint in a path is considered redundant and can be removed. This process creates a final, smoothed path containing the minimal number of waypoints necessary to accurately guide the agent through the static obstacles in the environment to its goal. Because the heuristic for skipping path nodes only considers line of sight, it will not produce smoothed paths that respect congestion map information.

Smoothing of paths computed with congestion map information involves comparing the movement cost of smoothed routes. Classic path-smoothing approaches assume the movement cost in the world is invariant and thus optimize for the shortest total path distance. To incorporate the congestion map information, the path-smoothing algorithm must compare the ultimate time cost of moving along both paths. To accurately compare two potential smoothed versions of a path, the smoothing algorithm must produce a heuristic that accounts for both the traversal cost and total distance of each. The heuristic estimates the total travel cost for a path by computing the line integral along path direction over the congestion penalty function. This can be easily computed over a discretized world (such as a grid) by computing the sum of each step's movement distance scaled by its corresponding traversal cost. The result of this summation (more generally of the line integral) constitutes the overall traversal cost for a path. The path-smoothing algorithm can use this value as a heuristic, allowing it to accurately compare two potential smoothed paths.

13.6 Flow Fields with Congestion Maps and Theta

In dense crowd simulations, many agents will be considering movement in a shared space. Additionally, many agents may share a set of goal destinations. As such, pathfinding approaches that exploit this uniformity across the agent population are ideal. Flow fields provide these benefits, as they unify pathfinding information for all agents with a shared goal. Flow fields compute ideal path directions for every discretized point in a given world. This provides constant computation and look-up cost for paths for any number of agents with a shared set of goals. The increased pathfinding complexity of congestion map aware algorithms amplifies the benefits of flow fields for large crowds. When using flow fields with congestion maps, the special path-smoothing considerations can be combined into the flow vector calculation process.

Flow fields are generated by back-propagating ideal path directions from the goal position using an unbounded Dijkstra's algorithm. While this is efficient and easily implemented for simple applications, it does not offer smoothed paths. Additionally, adding smoothing as a postprocess step (as in single-source pathfinding) does not scale well to large crowds due to the number of line-of-sight calculations required. These restrictions make the Theta* [Nash 07, Nash 15] algorithm ideal for generating flow fields.

Theta* operates identically to Dijkstra's algorithm when generating flow fields; however, it performs path-smoothing calculations as paths are being constructed. As Theta* creates a path link between two nodes *A* and *B*, it performs a line-of-sight check between the new node *A* and the parent of the previously expanded node *B*. This line-of-sight check then exists through the remainder of all path calculations and can be reused in subsequent path-smoothing calculations. The line-of-sight check can also incorporate congestion map information by computing and memoizing the path traversal cost via the process defined in the previous section. Theta* combined with these path cost calculations allows it to efficiently generate congestion map aware flow fields. Please see the chapter on Theta* in this book for more details on Theta* [Nash 15].

13.7 Current Alternatives

Current crowd dynamics solutions generally involve two layers: pathfinding and local collision avoidance. These approaches offer a few noteworthy benefits. They produce high-quality movement and avoidance on small scales and are well understood and researched by the community. There are many open-source and off-the-shelf implementations of these techniques, and they integrate well into existing technology. A popular choice for many games is the combination of A* with velocity obstacle [van den Berg 08] approaches such as ORCA [van den Berg 09] or ClearPath [Guy 09]. These offer an enticing combination of fast, inexpensive pathfinding with robust, high-quality collision avoidance.

In high-density crowd situations, solely relying on local collision avoidance and idealized pathfinding will cause agents to pile up at popular, shared path waypoints. Collision avoidance algorithms only help avoid local collisions in the pursuit of following the ideal path. Often games rely on these algorithms to divert agents to less-congested, less-direct routes in high-density situations. In certain situations, collision avoidance can lead to this desired behavior, though it is always a side effect of the system and not a deliberate consideration.

Work has been done in incorporating aggregate crowd movement and crowd density into pathfinding computations [van Toll 12, Karamouzas 09, Jansen 08]. Approaches that augment pathing via crowd density [van Toll 12, Karamouzas 09] do not take into account the aggregate movement or direction of movement of the crowd. This leads to overcorrection of the phenomenon illustrated in Figure 13.1.

Congestion maps are similar in many ways to existing cooperative pathfinding algorithms, such as "DMs" [Jansen 08], but differ in a few key respects. DMs use average crowd motion over time to encourage agents to move with the flow of the crowd. Because of this, many of the oscillations present in the congestion map approach are smoothly resolved. Conversely, this temporal smoothing prevents DMs from quickly and accurately reacting to changes in the environment and crowd behavior. Both congestion maps and DMs apply the aggregate crowd movement information to the path planning process in much the same way; however, congestion maps handle agents of varying size and shape, while DMs traditionally assume homogeneity. The final major difference between DMs and congestion maps is that congestion maps weight movement penalties proportional to the density of the crowd. Without taking density into account, DMs display overly pessimistic pathing behavior, where agents are encouraged to path around sparse groups of agents blocking the ideal path.

13. Advanced Techniques for Robust, Efficient Crowds

13.8 Benefits

Congestion maps offer an effective way of enhancing crowd behavior at scale. Compared to motion planning approaches that predict movement and interactions of all agents in a given time interval, congestion maps are an inexpensive addition to established character movement systems. Additionally, the simplicity of congestion maps makes them easy to implement and optimize.

Congestion maps augment agent pathfinding to work as it should. Instead of optimizing for minimal path distance, path planners using congestion maps correctly optimize for path travel time. This ensures agents will consider less-crowded alternative routes that may be slightly longer but ultimately faster than the ideal path.

Though congestion maps can be added to any existing path planning system, flow fields are ideal for exploiting the benefits of this approach. Using Theta* to generate flow fields results in drastically fewer line-of-sight checks, as their results can be shared across path calculations. Theta* minimizes the impact of the increase in path-smoothing computations with congestion maps, without reducing the technique's effectiveness.

13.9 Drawbacks

Despite the many benefits congestion maps offer, they are not a replacement for full motion planning. Congestion maps are a reactive, macrolevel collision avoidance technique. Changes to crowd density over time are not taken into account when augmenting unit paths. As such, an agent may avoid a congested area along its ideal path that, by the time the agent would reach that area, would no longer be congested. This can lead to agents appearing to "change their mind" as congestion eases in specific locations. Conversely, an agent can begin moving toward a location that is not currently congested, but that will become so once the agent reaches the area. This will cause the agent to change directions toward a longer, less-congested path. Depending on the application of the congestion map approach, these behavioral flaws may be acceptable, as they mimic the fallibility of human path planning. In other applications, their impact may be negligible.

Due to the dynamic nature of crowd density, congestion maps are best suited for highly dynamic environments and techniques. As crowd density changes, existing paths become less ideal in both distance and traversal time. This necessitates replanning existing paths to account for changes in the environment. Hierarchical discretization helps alleviate some of the costs of consistent repathing by shrinking the search space, speeding up individual pathfinding computations.

Finally, by their nature, congestion maps weaken the heuristic used for search, increasing the cost of path planning. Again, hierarchical methods or weighted A* can be used to reduce this overhead [Jansen 08].

13.10 Performance Considerations

Congestion maps compute crowd density and aggregate information across the entire environment. This requires discretizing the continuous space at some granularity. As the resolution of the congestion map data increases, the memory required to store the congestion data also increases. Additionally, the cost of computing blended moving averages of aggregate crowd movement vectors increases with the resolution of the congestion map.

Despite holding information for every position in the environment, the congestion map doesn't need to correspond directly to the existing world discretization. In fact, the congestion map resolution can be much smaller than the world discretization resolution and still maintain much of its effectiveness. However, the coarser the congestion map resolution, the more likely agents will exhibit strange behavior, such as avoiding areas that don't need to be avoided. The overall macrolevel behavior will be correct and consistent; however, individuals may show odd patterns of behavior.

13.11 Future Work

Hysteresis can be added to the system to prevent agents from oscillating between potential paths quickly due to rapid changes in congestion information. With hysteresis, an agent will remain on its current path until the congestion values have surpassed a certain value for a certain amount of time. Likewise, the agent will not consider a shorter path until that path has been uncongested for a certain amount of time. These time intervals and congestion thresholds are user defined, offering high-level control over the behavior of the agents in the scene. Additional realism is obtained by authoring congestion coefficient levels and time delays as random distributions over specific value ranges.

Because the congestion map only offers a snapshot of the current crowd density and aggregate velocity, it is not perfectly accurate to the realities of the agents' theoretically ideal behavior. This inaccuracy is introduced as a means of improving runtime performance and simplifying implementation details. Computing the full crowd density over time would allow the path planner to more accurately compute traversal cost. With this method, the path planner can base the traversal cost on the crowd state at the time when the agent would be at the considered position in its path. This is similar to motion planning approaches, in that each agent must know the expected behavior of the other agents in the scene to compute an ideal path. Because they only require computing aggregate agent behavior, congestion maps evaluated over time intervals may also prove to be less computationally expensive than full motion planning.

13.12 Conclusion

A combination of static, idealized pathfinding and localized collision avoidance algorithms are often used to simulate crowds in games. While effective for small numbers of sparse agents, these approaches lack consideration of the effects of crowd dynamics on agents' path planning calculations.

Congestion maps introduce context awareness to the path planning system and allow individual agents to react to the agents around them on a large scale. Together with Theta*, congestion maps can generate ideal pathing information for an entire environment in the form of a vector flow field. By maximally reusing shared path computations, flow fields help reduce the cost of smoothing individually computed paths.

Adding congestion maps to a path planning system allows agents, in situations of high crowd density, to find alternative, longer paths that will ultimately take less time to follow.

13. Advanced Techniques for Robust, Efficient Crowds

This is a behavior not previously possible without expensive motion planning approaches, which provides opportunities for games to create more compelling, realistic, and interesting crowds.

References

[Champandard 11] Champandard, A. 2011. The mechanics of influence mapping: Representation, algorithm and parameters. http://aigamedev.com/open/tutorial/influence-map-mechanics/ (accessed June 1, 2014).

[Guy 09] Guy, S., Chhugani, J., Kim, C., Satish, N., Lin, M., Manocha, D., Dubey, P. 2009. ClearPath: Highly parallel collision avoidance for multi-agent simulation. *Proceedings of the Eurographics/ACM SIGGRAPH Symposium on Computer Animation (2009)*, pp. 177–187.

[Jansen 08] Jansen, M. and Sturtevant, N. 2008. Direction maps for cooperative pathfinding. *Proceedings of the AAAI Conference on Artificial Intelligence and Interactive Digital Entertainment.*

[Karamouzas 09] Karamouzas, I., Bakker, J., and Overmars, M. 2009. Density constraints for crowd simulation. *Proceedings of the ICE Games Innovations Conference*, pp. 160–168.

[Nash 07] Nash, A., Daniel, K., Koenig, S., and Felner, A. 2007. Theta*: Any-angle path planning on grids. *Proceedings of the AAAI Conference on Artificial Intelligence*, pp. 1177–1183.

[Nash 15] Nash, A. and Koenig, S. 2015. Theta* for Any-Angle Pathfinding. In *Game AI Pro²: Collected Wisdom of Game AI Professionals*, ed. S. Rabin. A K Peters/CRC Press, Boca Raton, FL.

[Sturtevant 05] Sturtevant, N. and Buro, M. 2005. Partial pathfinding using map abstraction and refinement. *Proceedings of the National Conference on Artificial Intelligence*, July 2005, Vol. 5, pp. 1392–1397.

[van den Berg 08] van den Berg, J., Lin, M., and Manocha, D. 2008. Reciprocal velocity obstacles for real-time multi-agent navigation. *IEEE International Conference on Robotics and Automation*, 1928–1935.

[van den Berg 09] van den Berg, J., Guy, S., Lin, M., and Manocha, D. 2009. Reciprocal n-body collision avoidance. *Proceedings of the International Symposium on Robotics Research.*

[van Toll 12] van Toll, W., Cook IV, A., and Geraerts, R. 2012. Real-time density-based crowd simulation. *Computer Animation and Virtual Worlds*, 23, 59–69.

14

Context Steering
Behavior-Driven Steering at the Macro Scale

Andrew Fray

14.1 Introduction

Steering behaviors are extremely common in the games industry [Reynolds 87, Reynolds 99]. Their popularity is with good cause, promising a fast-to-implement core with emergent behavior from simple components.

However, steering behaviors are not suited for some types of game. When the player can pick out and watch individual entities, collision avoidance and consistent movement become very important. Achieving this can cause behavior components to balloon in size and become tightly coupled. Entity movement then becomes fragile and hard to tune.

In this chapter, we'll outline how you can identify the games for which steering behaviors aren't a good fit and describe a new approach for those problems called *context steering*. Context steering behaviors are small and stateless and guarantee any desired movement constraint. When used to replace steering behaviors on the game *F1 2011*, the codebase shrunk by 4000 lines, yet the AI were better at avoiding collisions, overtaking, and performing other interesting behaviors.

14.2 When Steering Behaviors Go Bad

A steering behavior system is used to move an entity through a world. The system consists of multiple child behaviors. During each update, the child behaviors are asked for a vector representing how they would like the entity to move. The vectors are combined to produce a final velocity. That's really it; the simplicity of the system is one of its strengths.

Note that the behavior vectors can be either a desired final velocity or a corrective force to the current velocity. This chapter will show behavior output as a final velocity. It doesn't change the arguments either way, but it makes the diagrams easier to arrange and understand.

Imagine an entity with free movement on a 2D plane. The entity cares about avoiding *obstacles* and chasing *targets*. At the instant of time shown in Figure 14.1, there are two possible targets in the scene and one obstacle.

What's the ideal result here? Assuming our only concern on choosing a target is distance, the entity should move toward target A. However, there's an obstacle in the way, so moving toward target B would be best. Can that decision emerge from small simple behaviors?

We start with two simple steering behaviors: *chase*, for approaching targets, and *avoid*, for not hitting obstacles. Our avoid behavior sees the nearby obstacle and returns a velocity to avoid it. The chase behavior knows nothing about obstacles and so returns a velocity toward the nearest target, target A.

The behavior system combines these behaviors. Let's assume they're just averaged for now, although you can use more complex combination techniques. The final vector is very close to 0, and the entity hardly moves. Players are not going to think this is an intelligent entity!

Steering behavior systems have evolved some Band-Aids to deal with this situation over the years. Here's a few ways this stalemate might be solved:

We could add *weighting* to our behaviors, so avoid heavily outweighs chase when there is an obstacle nearby. Now the entity has a strong northward velocity, but at some point, it will reach equilibrium again. We've only succeeded in moving the problem, at the cost of a new weighting parameter. That parameter will invariably need tweaking any time we change any of the affected behaviors.

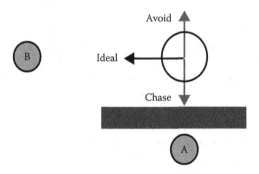

Figure 14.1

Entity layout, ideal path, and first path.

We could add *prioritization*, so avoid is the only behavior that runs when near obstacles, but then movement near obstacles is very single minded, and not very expressive.

Finally, we could add some *awareness* of obstacles to the chase behavior. It could raycast to reject targets that don't have a clear path or pathfind to all targets and select the one with the shortest path. Both of these introduce the concept of obstacles into chase, which increases coupling. In most game engines, raycasts and pathfinds are going to be either expensive or asynchronous, both of which introduce different types of complexity. This makes chase neither "small" nor "stateless."

There doesn't seem to be a good way to fix this.

This may sound like a forced example, but it's based on a real experience. In *F1 2010*, our equivalent of the avoid behavior had to be incredibly robust, which meant it often demanded to run frequently and in isolation, dominating how the opponent cars moved. To put some expressiveness back into the AI, we extended the avoid behavior over and over again to make it avoid in intelligent ways, coupling it to multiple other behaviors and making it monolithic. By the end, it had decomposed into an old-school sequence of if/else blocks with a thin steering behavior wrapper and was a maintenance nightmare.

14.2.1 Flocks versus Groups

If steering behaviors are so broken, why are they so popular? Because not all games expose the right conditions to make the problems apparent. Steering behaviors are a statistical steering method. Most of the time, they will give you mostly the right direction. How often they give you inconsistent or bad results, and how bad that is for the player, is a per-game decision.

It's no coincidence that the most famous application of steering behaviors is flocking [Reynolds 87]. In flocking, the user is typically an external observer of many entities moving as a semicohesive group. The group seems to have lifelike properties and unpredictable but believable behavior. Really, the "entity" here is the flock, not the individual. The size of the flock can hide the odd inconsistent movement or collision of individuals.

In the racing genre, the player is often inside the "flock," wheel to wheel with AI cars. Here, inconsistent movements can be glaring and immersion breaking. They can result in missed overtaking opportunities, poor overtake blocking, or at worst collisions with other cars. Steering behaviors were not a good fit for *F1*.

14.2.2 Lack of Context

We now understand what steering behavior failure looks like and what types of games that matters for. But we don't yet know *why* steering behavior systems have this flaw. Once we understand that, we can design a solution.

A single steering behavior component is asked to return a vector representing its decision, considering the current state of the world. The framework then tries to merge multiple decisions. However, there just isn't enough information to make merging these decisions possible. Adding prioritization or weighting attempts to make merging easier by adding more information to the behavior's result, but it translates to louder shouting rather than more nuanced debate. By making chase aware of obstacles, we can make it produce more sensible results, yet this is just special casing the merge step. That is not a scalable solution.

Sometimes, the reasons why a behavior didn't want to go any other way—the *context* in which the decision was made—is just as important as the decision itself. This is a particular problem for collision avoidance behaviors, because they can only communicate in the language of desired velocity, not undesired velocity.

14.3 Toward Why, Not How

Returning a decision, even with some metadata, just isn't going to work. Instead, what if we could ask a behavior for the context in which it would make the decision, but skip the actual decision step? If we could then somehow merge all those contexts, some external behavior-agnostic processor could produce a final decision, fully aware of everything.

The context of avoid could be, "I feel moderately strongly we shouldn't go south," and the chase context could be, "it's a little interesting to go west and quite interesting to go south." It's a holistic view rather than a resolute decision. The framework then waves a magic wand and combines these contexts, revealing that the ideal decision is to go west.

The end result is as if chase was aware of obstacles and disregarded its favorite target because it was blocked, yet the individual behaviors were focused only on their concerns. The system is emergent and has consistent collision avoidance and small stateless behaviors.

14.3.1 Context Maps

The context steering framework deals in the currency of *context maps*. Imagine everything the entity cares about in the world projected onto the circumference of a circle around the entity, as shown in Figure 14.2. It's like a 1D image, and in fact, many of the tricks we'll show you later in the chapter follow from this image metaphor.

Internally, the context map is an array of scalar values, with each slot of the array representing a possible heading, and the contents of the slot representing how strongly the behavior feels about this heading. How many slots the array has is the "resolution" of the context map. (If you're already wondering if you need huge resolutions to have decent movement, then relax. I'll show you later why you need many less than you think.) By using this array format, we can easily correlate and merge different context maps and go from slots to headings and vice versa. This is our data structure for arbitrating between different behaviors.

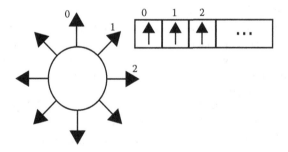

Figure 14.2

Mapping headings to context map slots.

In each frame, the framework will ask every behavior for two different context maps: the *danger* map and the *interest* map. The danger map is a view of everything the behavior would like to stay away from. As you'd suspect, the interest map is everything the behavior would like to move toward.

14.4 Context Maps by Example

What does our previous entity example look like, rewritten to use context maps? We can translate it by thinking about the information that informed the old behavior's decision and storing that information in the correct context map.

14.4.1 Chase Behavior

The chase behavior wants the entity to move toward targets, preferring near targets to far. However, choosing the best target requires making a decision, and we don't want to do that. So we're going to write all the targets into the interest map, with farther targets represented with lower intensity.

We could take a vector directly toward a target, translate that into a map slot, and write only into that slot. That captures that moving toward the target is desirable. However, we can also write over a range of slots, centered on the target with configurable falloff to zero. This captures that passing the target but just missing it is also an interesting thing to do, even if not the best. There's a lot of power and nuance in how this falloff works, giving you a lot of control over how the entity moves.

All this can be done with a quick for-each over all targets, some tuning constants, and no state. The resultant interest map is shown in Figure 14.3.

14.4.2 Avoid Behavior

The avoid behavior wants the entity to keep at least a minimum distance away from obstacles. We're going to render all obstacles into the danger map, in a very similar for-each loop to chase. The intensity of an obstacle in the danger map represents the distance to the obstacle. If the obstacle is beyond the minimum distance, it can be ignored. Again, falloff around the obstacle can be used in an interesting way. Here, it represents the heading

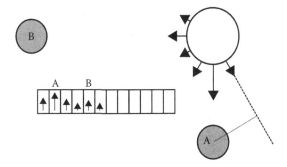

Figure 14.3

Chase behavior, writing into interest map.

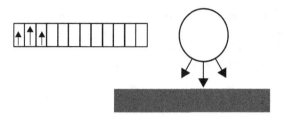

Figure 14.4

Avoid behavior, writing into danger map.

required to pass it without reentering the exclusion zone around it. This behavior is also stateless and small. The avoid behavior is shown in Figure 14.4.

14.4.3 Combining and Parsing

The output of each behavior can be combined with others by comparing each slot across multiple maps and taking a maximum. We could sum or average the slots, but we're not going to avoid a particular obstacle any more just because there's another obstacle behind it. We already must avoid the first obstacle, and that obscures any danger from the second. Through combining, we can reduce all output to a single interest and danger map pair.

The next step processes the maps, boiling down the entire shared context into a single final velocity. How this happens is game specific; the racing game example will have its own implementation.

First, we traverse the danger map to find the lowest danger and mask out all slots that have higher danger. In our example, there are some empty slots in the danger map, so our lowest danger is zero, and therefore, we mask out any slot with nonzero danger, shown in Figure 14.5(i). We take that mask and apply it to the interest map, zeroing out any masked slots (ii). Finally, we pick the interest map slot with the highest remaining interest (iii) and move in that direction (iv). The speed we move is proportional to the strength of interest in the slot; a lot of interest means we move quickly.

The final decision here is the correct decision. It is emergent—preserving collision avoidance while chasing a sensible target—yet we did it with small, stateless, and decoupled behaviors. It is the promise of steering behaviors at the macro scale.

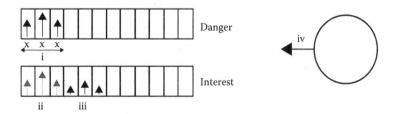

Figure 14.5

Processing the final maps.

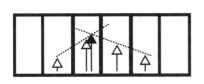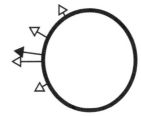

Figure 14.6

Subslot calculations.

14.4.4 Subslot Movement

You might initially think the context map is too limiting a system. The entity will always be locked to one of the slot directions, so either you need a bucketful, which sounds expensive, or you are stuck with robotic entities that can only move in very coarse directions.

It turns out we can keep the slot count low, for speed, and yet have movements in a continuous range. Once we have our target slot, we can evaluate the gradients of the interest around it and estimate where those gradients would have met. We then back-project this *virtual* slot index into world space, producing a direction to steer toward, as shown in Figure 14.6.

14.5 Racing with Context

Context steering doesn't just work for 2D entities on a plane. In fact, it is easily portable to any decision made in 1D or 2D space. Let's look at how the context steering for *F1* was implemented and how it differs from the entity example.

14.5.1 Coordinate System

We could pretend race cars moved with freedom in 2D space, but they don't. In *F1*, a low-level driver system followed a hand-placed *racing line* spline, braking for corners and accelerating down straights. The behavior system only needed to manage position on the track, rather than driving. This was done with a scalar left or right offset from the racing line. That's one of our dimensions. Although the driver will brake for corners for us, the behavior system must handle collision avoidance, so it needs to be able to slow down for emergencies. How much we want to slow down, if at all, is another scalar making our second dimension.

You can visualize the context map as a cross section of the track, with each slot representing a specific offset of the racing line, as shown in Figure 14.7. The map scales with the width of the track, with the left and right edges of the map lining up with the track edges. The racing line doesn't always map to the same slot; it will sweep from one edge of the map to the other as it moves across the track. In this and the following figures, the AI car is white.

14.5.2 Racing Line Behavior

The racing line behavior maps interest all across the track, with a peak around the racing line. It never quite reaches zero no matter how wide the track is. We only want to create a

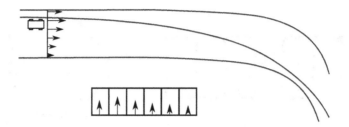

Figure 14.7

Racing line writing into interest map.

differential from slot to slot, so if the car is trapped at a far edge of the track by traffic, it always has an idea of which way is closer to the racing line and can tuck in tightly.

The behavior will write the most interest at the racing line, but never very much. Being able to reach the racing line should be good, but we want lots of room to be expressive about other interest map behaviors, while still having that important differential across the whole map.

14.5.3 Avoid Behavior

For an open-wheel racer, collision avoidance is paramount. Any type of connection (side to side or front to back) would be catastrophic. The avoid behavior evaluates all cars in the vicinity and writes danger into the map corresponding to the other car's racing line offset, with intensity proportional to the presented danger, as shown in Figure 14.8. Evaluating the danger of a car is complex. If a car is in front but at racing speed, then you should ignore them—writing danger for them will only make overtaking difficult. However, if a car is substantially below racing speed, you may need to take evasive action, so should write danger. Cars alongside are always considered dangerous. This is a good benefit of using the racing line as a coordinate system: the behavior system can be aware of a stationary car around a corner, where a raycasting approach might not see it until after the corner has been turned.

We've already seen how context steering can guarantee collision avoidance, but it can also be used more subtly. *F1* wrote high danger into the map over the width of the other car, but also a decreasing skirt of danger at the edges. This kept a minimum lateral separation between cars. The driver personality fed into this, writing wider skirts for drivers that were more cautious.

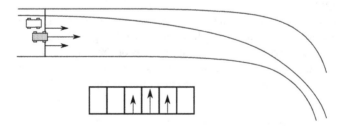

Figure 14.8

Avoid behavior written into the danger map.

14.5.4 Drafting Behavior

These two behaviors are enough for collision avoidance around a track, but it would make for quite a dull race. *F1* had four or five other behaviors that made the AI more expressive, but we'll just cover the drafting behavior.

Drafting happens when one car follows another closely and at high speeds. The trailing car doesn't need to do so much work to push air out of the way, so it can match the leading car's speed without using as much energy. At the right moment, the spare energy can be used to overtake.

F1's drafting behavior evaluated all the cars in front of the AI and scored each for "draftability." Cars going fast and near to us would score lots of points. Then the behavior would write pyramids of interest into the context maps at the corresponding racing line offset of each car, with more interest for more draftable cars, as shown in Figure 14.9.

14.5.5 Processing Context Maps

Now we have a pair of complex maps, with danger and interest in different places. How do we go from that to an actual movement? There are probably a few ways to do this that produce good consistent movement, but this is how *F1* did it.

First, we find the slot of the danger map corresponding to the car's current position on the track, shown in Figure 14.10(i). Then we walk left and right along the map, continuing as long as the danger in the next slot is less than the current. Once we cannot expand any

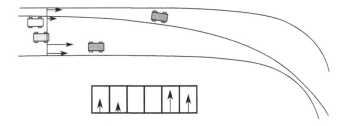

Figure 14.9

Draft behavior writing into interest map.

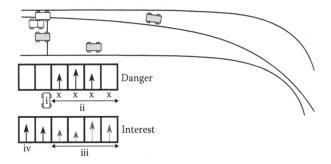

Figure 14.10

Processing the maps for a final racing line offset.

more, we mask all slots we can't reach (ii). We apply the mask to the interest map (iii) and pick the highest remaining slot (iv). The resulting movement picks the car in the far right of the figure to draft, avoiding the nearer car because it can't be reached without a collision.

This approach avoids moving into higher danger, which might represent a physical obstacle. It also stops us remaining in high danger because of high interest when there's an obvious escape route. Once we have all valid movements, it picks the most interesting of those movements.

To find out if we need to do emergency braking, we look at the highest danger across the planned journey from our current slot to the most interesting. If any slot is over some threshold of danger, we ask for braking with intensity proportional to the danger strength. We use a threshold because some danger can be informative without being a real issue, a developing situation to be aware of rather than a problem.

14.6 Advanced Techniques

There are several improvements we can make to the simple implementations outlined. These improvements are often easier to implement and maintain than their steering behavior counterparts, because they work at the level of the context map, not the individual behavior components.

14.6.1 Post-Processing

To avoid sharp spikes or troughs, we can apply a blurring function over the context maps after the behaviors have acted. As it's a global effect, it's easy to tweak and cheap to implement.

The chase behavior from our original steering behaviors example suffers from flip-flopping if the closest target oscillates back and forth between two choices. We can fix this with per-behavior hysteresis, but that adds state and complexity to behaviors. Context steering allows us to avoid flip-flopping much more easily. We can take the last update's context map and blend it with the current one, making high values emerge over time rather than instantly. This is a kind of global hysteresis that requires no support from the behaviors at all.

14.6.2 Optimizations

The overall complexity of the system is dependent on your implementation, but everything we've outlined here is linear in memory and CPU in proportion to the context map resolution. Doubling the size of the map will require twice as much memory and probably be twice as slow.

On the other hand, halving the map will double the speed. Because the system can still provide consistent collision avoidance and continuous steering even with a low-resolution map, you can construct a very granular level-of-detail controller to manage system load. Entities far from the player can be allocated small maps, producing coarser movements but requiring less system resources. Entities near the player can have more resolution, reacting to very fine details in the map. It's not very common to find an AI system that can be tweaked as subtly as this without compromising integrity.

Since the context maps are essentially 1D images, we can further optimize them using techniques from graphics programming. We can use vector intrinsics to write to and process the map in chunks, providing a massive speed up. *F1* shipped like that, and although it made the guts of the processing harder to read, the payoff was worth it. We did that late in the project, when the implementation was nailed down.

Because the behaviors are stateless, and context maps merge easily, we can multithread them or put them on a PS3 SPU. You might also consider doing the behaviors and processing in a compute shader. Be sure to profile before and after, because some behaviors may be so simple that the setup and teardown costs of this kind of solution would be dominant. Batching behaviors into jobs or structuring the whole system in a data-orientated way is also possible. Doing this with more stateful and coupled steering behaviors would be difficult.

14.7 Conclusion

Steering behaviors remains extremely useful in many situations. If your game has individual entities that will be closely watched by the player and a world with strong physical constraints, steering behaviors can break down. For games that can be represented in two dimensions, context steering offers strong movement guarantees and simple, stateless, decoupled behaviors.

References

[Reynolds 87] Reynolds, C. 1987. Flocks, herds and schools: A distributed behavioral model. *International Conference and Exhibition on Computer Graphics and Interactive Techniques,* Anaheim, CA, pp. 25–34.
[Reynolds 99] Reynolds, C. 1999. Steering behaviors for autonomous characters. *Game Developers Conference,* San Francisco, CA.

15

Guide to Anticipatory Collision Avoidance

Stephen J. Guy and Ioannis Karamouzas

15.1 Introduction

Anticipation is a key aspect of human motion. Unlike simple physical systems, like falling rocks or bouncing balls, moving humans interact with each other well before the moment of actual collision. This type of forethought in planning is a unique aspect to the motion of intelligent beings. While physical systems (e.g., interacting electrons or magnets) show evidence of oriented action at a distance, the intelligence humans show in their paths is a unique phenomenon in nature, and special techniques are needed to capture it well.

In games, the act of computing paths that reach a character's current goal is typically accomplished using some form of global planning technique (see, e.g., [Snook 00, Stout 00]). As a character moves along the path toward its goal, it still needs to intelligently react to its local environment. While, typically, there are not computational resources available to plan paths that account for every local detail, we can quickly modify a character's path to stay free of collisions with any local neighbors. In order to keep this motion looking realistic and intelligent, it is important that our characters show clear anticipation even for this local collision-avoidance routine. Consider, for example, the scenario shown in Figure 15.1, where two agents pass each other walking down the

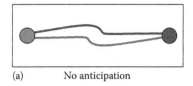
(a)   No anticipation

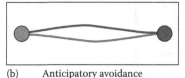
(b)   Anticipatory avoidance

Figure 15.1

(a) Simple reactive agents versus (b) anticipatory agents. Anticipatory agents exhibit smooth and efficient motion as compared to simple reactive agents.

same path. On the left, we see the result of a last second, "bouncy-ball" style reaction—the characters will get to their goals, but the resulting motion does not display much anticipation. In contrast, the right half of the figure shows our desired, humanlike behavior, where characters are able to anticipate the upcoming collision and efficiently adapt their motions early on.

In this chapter, we will present the key ideas needed to implement this type of high-quality, anticipatory collision avoidance for characters in your game. After explaining the main concepts, we will provide a step-by-step explanation of a modern anticipatory collision-avoidance algorithm and discuss how to optimize its implementation. We will also walk through the approaches taken by modern systems used in commercial games and explain how they relate to the algorithm presented here.

15.2 Key Concepts

Before presenting our avoidance model, we need to cover some key foundational concepts. The collision-avoidance system we describe here is *agent based*. This means that each animated character a user may encounter in the current scene, no matter how complex, is described by a simple abstract representation known as an agent. Each agent has a few variables that store the state of the corresponding animated character. The exact variables used will vary from different implementations, but common agent states include position, velocity, radius, and goal velocity.

Each agent is expected to update its state as part of a larger game loop. We assume that each agent has an individual goal velocity that represents its desired speed and direction of motion, typically set by external factors such as an AI planner or a player's input. Each time through the game loop, our task will be to compute collision-avoidance behaviors for each agent. The approaches we will discuss are anticipatory, updating the positions of each agent by finding new velocities that are free of all *upcoming* collisions. In the following, we detail each variable in the agent state and give complete code for quickly determining if two agents are on a collision course.

15.2.1 Agent State

Listing 15.1 provides the complete state of each agent. Each variable is stored as an array across all the agents.

```
x  = []    /* array of agent positions */
r  = []    /* array of agent radii */
v  = []    /* array of agent velocities */
gv = []    /* array of agent goal velocities */
```

- *Radius (float)*: We assume that the agent moves on a 2D plane and is modeled as a translating disc having a fixed radius. At any time, the center of the disc denotes the position of the agent, while the radius of the disc defines the area that is occupied by the agent and that other agents cannot step into. By choosing a larger disc than the one defined by the shoulder–shoulder distance of the animated character, we can allow larger separation distances between agents while they pass each other. In contrast, if the radius is smaller than the visualization radius, the animation engine should be able to account for such a difference (e.g., by rotating the upper body).
- *Position (2D float vector)*: A simple 2D vector of the agent's x and y position is needed to locate the agent.
- *Velocity (2D float vector)*: The agent moves across the virtual world with a certain velocity. In the absence of any other agents, this velocity is the same as the goal velocity. Otherwise, the agent may have to adapt its current velocity to ensure a collision-free navigation.
- *Goal velocity (2D float vector)*: At any time instant, the agent prefers to move toward a certain direction at a certain given speed. Together, these two components define the agent's goal velocity (for instance, a velocity directed toward the agent's goal having a unit length). In most games, the goal velocity is passed to the agent by a global navigation method or directly by the player.

15.2.2 Predicting Collisions (Time to Collision)

To exhibit intelligent avoidance behavior, an agent must be able to predict whether and when it is going to collide with its nearby agents so that it can adapt its velocity accordingly. We can use the concept of a time to collision (denoted τ) to reason about upcoming interactions. Specifically, a collision between two agents is said to occur at some time $\tau \geq 0$, if the corresponding discs of the agents intersect. Consequently, to estimate τ, we extrapolate the trajectories of the agents based on their current velocities. Then, the problem can be simplified into computing the distance between the extrapolated positions of the agents and comparing it against the sum of the combined radii of the agents.

More formally, given two agents A and B, a collision exists if

$$\left\| (x_B + v_B \tau) - (x_A + v_A \tau) \right\| = r_A + r_B. \tag{15.1}$$

Here, to estimate the extrapolated positions of the agents, we assume that the agents move at constant speed. Even though such an assumption does not always hold, it practically works very well for predicting and avoiding upcoming collisions, especially in the short run. Squaring and expanding (15.1) leads to the following quadratic equation for τ:

$$(v \cdot v)\tau^2 + 2(w \cdot v)\tau + w \cdot w - (r_A + r_B)^2 = 0 \tag{15.2}$$

where
$$w = x_B - x_A$$
$$v = v_B - v_A$$

For ease of notation, let $a = v \cdot v$, $b = 2(w \cdot v)$ and $c = w \cdot w - (r_A + r_B)^2$. Then, the aforementioned equation can be solved following the quadratic formula, allowing us to estimate the possible time to collision between the two agents: $\tau^\pm = \left(-b \pm \sqrt{b^2 - 4ac}\right)/(2a)$. Note that since b is a factor of 2, by setting $b = -w \cdot v = w \cdot (v_A - v_B)$, the solution can be simplified as $\tau^\pm = \left(b \pm \sqrt{b^2 - ac}\right)/a$, allowing us to save a couple of multiplications.

If there is no solution $(b^2 < ac)$ or only one (double) solution $(b^2 = ac)$, then no collision takes place and τ is undefined. Otherwise, two distinct solutions exist leading to three distinct cases:

1. If both solutions are negative, then no collision takes place and τ is undefined.
2. If one solution is negative and the other is nonnegative, then the agents are currently colliding, that is, $\tau = 0$.
3. If both solutions are nonnegative, then a collision occurs at $\tau = \min(\tau^+, \tau^-)$.

In practice, one does not need to explicitly account for all these cases. Assuming that the agents are not currently colliding, it suffices to test whether τ^- is nonnegative. Otherwise, τ is undefined. The code for computing the time to collision between two agents is given in Listing 15.2.

15.2.3 Time Horizon

It is typically not necessary (or realistic) for an agent to worry about collisions that are very far off in the future. To account for this, we can introduce the notion of a *time horizon* that represents the furthest out point in time after which we stop considering collisions. In theory, an agent can try to resolve all potential collisions with other agents that may happen in the future. However, such an approach is computationally expensive and unrealistic, since game-controlled avatars and NPCs can drastically change their behaviors well before the predicted collision happens. As such, given a certain time horizon t_H (e.g., 3 s), an agent will ignore any collisions that will happen more than t_H seconds from now. This not only reduces the running time but also leads to more convincing avoidance behavior.

Note that the time horizon can vary between agents, increasing the heterogeneity in their behaviors. An aggressive agent, for example, can be modeled with a very small time horizon (slightly larger than the time step of the simulation), whereas a large time horizon

Listing 15.2. Function to compute the time-to-collision (τ) between two agents i and j.

```
function ttc(i,j):
    r = r[i] + r[j]
    w = x[j] - x[i]
    c = dot(w, w) - r * r
    if (c < 0):      //agents are colliding
        return 0
    v = v[i] - v[j]
    a = dot(v, v)
    b = dot(w, v)
    discr = b*b - a*c
    if (discr <= 0):
        return INFTY
    tau = (b - sqrt(discr)) / a
    if (tau < 0):
        return INFTY
    return tau
```

can be assigned to an introvert or shy agent. Some examples of varying the time horizon are shown in the following section.

15.3 Prototype Implementation

Armed with the concepts of agent-based simulations, goal velocities, time horizons, and an efficient routine to compute the time to collision between two agents, we can now develop a full multiagent simulation algorithm, complete with anticipatory collision avoidance between agents. After providing method details, and code, we'll show some simple example simulations.

15.3.1 Agent Forces

At any given time, an agent's motion can be thought of as the result of competing forces. The two most important forces on an agent's path is a driving force, which pushes an agent to its goal, and a collision avoiding force, which resolves collision with neighboring agents in an anticipatory fashion. Typically, an agent's driving force is inferred from its goal velocity. If the agent is currently moving at its desired direction and speed, no new force is needed. However, if the agent is moving too fast, too slow, or in the wrong direction, we can provide a correcting force that gradually returns an agent back to its goal velocity with the following equation:

$$F_{goal} = k(v_g - v) \tag{15.3}$$

where
v_g is the agent's goal velocity
k is a tunable parameter that controls the strength of the goal force

If k is too low, agents lag behind changes in their goal velocity. If k is too high, the goal force may overwhelm the collision-avoidance force leading to collisions between agents.

In the examples later, we found that a k of 2 balances well between agents reaching their goal and avoiding collisions.

If an agent is on a collision course with any of its neighbors ($\tau \geq 0$), it will also experience a collision-avoidance force. The magnitude and direction of this avoidance force will depend on the predicted time until the collision and the expected point of impact, as detailed in the next section. The sum of all of the collision-avoidance forces from the agent's neighbors along with the goal-directed driving force will determine the agent's motion.

As part of the overall game loop, each agent performs a continuous cycle of sensing and acting with a time step, Δt. A time step begins with an agent computing the sum of all the forces exerted on it as outlined earlier. Given this new force, an agent's velocity, v, and position, x, can be updated as follows:

$$v\mathrel{+}= F * \Delta t$$

$$x\mathrel{+}= v * \Delta t$$

(15.4)

which is a simple application of Eulerian integration, with the current force updating the agent's velocity and the new velocity updating the agent's position. A small time step, Δt, can help lead to smoother motion; in the examples later, we use a Δt of 20 ms.

15.3.2 Avoidance Force

Each agent may experience a unique avoidance force from each of its neighboring agents. Because this force is anticipatory in nature, it is based on the expected future positions of the agents at the time of collision rather than on the agents' current positions. The avoidance force is computed in two steps with the direction of the avoidance force being computed separately from the magnitude.

15.3.2.1 Avoidance Force Direction

To compute the direction of the avoidance force, both agents are simulated forward at their current velocity for τ seconds. The direction of the avoidance force is chosen to push the agent's predicted position away from its neighbor's predicted position as illustrated by the gray arrows in Figure 15.2a. By extrapolating an agent along their current velocity, the avoidance direction that an agent A experiences from a neighboring agent B can be computed efficiently as follows:

$$dir = (x_A + v_A * \tau) - (x_B + v_B * \tau)$$

(15.5)

15.3.2.2 Avoidance Force Magnitude

The magnitude of the avoidance force is inferred from the time to collision τ between the two agents. When τ is small, a collision is imminent, and a very large avoidance force should be used to prevent the collision. When τ is large, the collision will take place far in the future, and the avoidance force should have a small magnitude, vanishing to a value of zero at the time horizon t_H. There are many functions with these two properties. Here, we propose the function $(t_H - \tau)/\tau$ that is fast to compute and

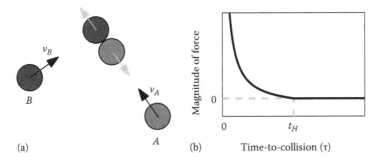

Figure 15.2

Computing the avoidance force. When agents are on a collision course ($\tau > 0$), an avoidance force is applied. (a) The *direction* of the force (gray arrows) depends on the relative positions at the moment of the predicted collision. (b) The *magnitude* of the force is based on how imminent the collision is (as measured by time to collision τ).

smoothly drops the force to zero as τ approaches t_H (see Figure 15.2b). This means the final avoidance force can be computed as

$$F_{avoid} = \frac{(t_H - \tau)}{\tau} * \frac{dir}{\|dir\|} \tag{15.6}$$

15.3.2.3 Corner Cases

If two agents are already colliding, the time to collision is zero, and the magnitude of the force is undefined. This condition can be quickly detected by comparing the distance between two agents to the sum of the radii. One option is to use a special nonanticipatory force to push colliding agents away from their current positions. In practice, we find the following simple trick to be sufficient: if two agents are colliding, shrink their radius for this one time step to just under half the distance between the agents. Most collisions between agents are quite small, and this will prevent the collision from getting any worse.

Additionally, agents who are very close and moving toward each other will have a very small time to collision. Following Equation 15.6, these agents will have very high (near infinite) avoidance forces that would dominate the response to all other neighbors. To avoid this, we can cap the maximum avoidance force to a reasonable value (we use 20 in the examples later).

15.3.2.4 Code

Listing 15.3 gives complete pseudocode implementing the collision-avoidance algorithm outlined in this section. The supplemental code corresponding to this chapter on the book's website (http://www.gameaipro.com) provides complete python code for this algorithm, including a simple scenario where agents move with heterogeneous velocities and directions on a 2D plane.

15.3.3 Runtime Performance

The aforementioned algorithm is fast to compute, and optimized implementations can compute avoidance forces for thousands of agents per frame on modest hardware. The main bottleneck in performance is actually determining an agent's neighbors. A naïve implementation might, for each agent, iterate over all other agents to see if they are on a collision course, resulting in quadratic runtime complexity. However, the pseudocode in Listing 15.3 illustrates a more efficient approach, pruning the search for nearest neighbors before computing any forces to only consider agents within a certain sensing radius (e.g., the distance that the agent can travel given its time horizon and maximum speed). The proximity computations in the pruning step can be accelerated using a spatial data structure for nearest neighbor queries, such as a k-d tree or a uniform grid. By selecting a fixed maximum number of neighbors for each agent, the runtime will be nearly linear in the number of agents.

15.3.4 Parameter Tuning

Any collision-avoidance method has tunable parameters that affect the behavior of the different agents. For example, agents with larger radii will move further away from their neighbors (perhaps looking more shy), and agents with a larger goal velocity will move faster

Listing 15.3. A time-to-collision-based avoidance algorithm.

```
//Precompute all neighbors for all agents (Section 15.3.3)
for each agent i:
    find all neighbors within sensing radius

for each agent i:
    F[i] = 2*(gv[i]-v[i]) //Compute goal force (Eqn. 15.3)

    for each neighboring agent j:
        //Compute time-to-collision (Section 15.2.2)
        t = ttc(i,j)

        //Compute collision avoidance force (Section 15.3.2)
        //Force Direction (Eqn. 15.5)
        FAvoid = x[i] + v[i]*t - x[j] - v[j]*t
        if (FAvoid[0] != 0 and FAvoid[1] != 0):
            FAvoid /= sqrt(FAvoid.dot(FAvoid))

        //Force Magnitude (Eqn. 15.6)
        mag = 0
        if (t >= 0 and t <= tH):
            mag = (tH-t)/(t + 0.001)
        if (mag > maxF): mag = maxF
        FAvoid *= mag

        F[i] += FAvoid

//Apply forces (Eqn. 15.4)
for each agent i:
    v[i] += F[i] * dt
    x[i] += v[i] * dt
```

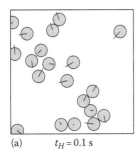 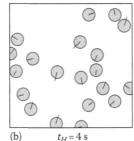 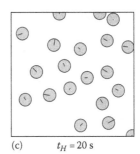

(a) $t_H = 0.1$ s   (b) $t_H = 4$ s   (c) $t_H = 20$ s

Figure 15.3

Effect of time horizon. Changing the time horizon, t_H, has a strong affect on an agent's behavior. (a) With a too small value of t_H, agents come very close and sometimes collide. (b) A moderate value of t_H produces high-quality anticipatory motions. (c) If t_H is too large, agents separate out in an unnatural way and may not reach their goals.

(looking more hurried or impatient). For an anticipatory method, one of the most important parameters to tune is the time horizon, as it has a strong affect on an agent's behavior.

Figure 15.3 shows the effect of varying the time horizon. In this scenario, every agent is given a goal velocity of moving in a random, predetermined direction at 1.5 m/s. With a very small time horizon of 0.1 s (Figure 15.3a), agents do not show any anticipation in their motion, do not avoid each other until collisions are imminent, and can even overlap. With too large a time horizon of 20 s (Figure 15.3c), agents avoid too many collisions and separate out much more than necessary, slowing the progress to their goals. Using a moderate time horizon of 4 s, the agents avoid all collisions while following their goals and show clear anticipatory motion (Figure 15.3b).

As mentioned before, the time horizon can be varied on a per-agent basis. Agents who are aggressive or impulsive can be given a smaller time horizon, and will perform many last minute avoidance maneuvers. Agents who are shy or tense can be given a larger time horizon and will react far in advance of any potential encounters.

15.4 Advanced Approaches

The collision-avoidance routine outlined earlier can provide robust, collision-free avoidance for many agents and works well in a wide variety of scenarios. However, recent work in crowd simulation and multiagent collision avoidance has gone beyond just modeling robust collision avoidance and focused on closely reproducing human behavior and providing rigorous guarantees on the quality of the motion.

15.4.1 Human Motion Simulation

Many assumptions we made in deriving the previous algorithm are unrealistic for modeling real humans. Our proposed model, for example, assumes that agents can see forever, know perfectly the radii and velocities of all of their neighbors, and are willing to come indefinitely close to any neighbors. Recent work such as the predictive avoidance method (PAM) provides some guidelines to making a more realistic model [Karamouzas 09].

15.4.1.1 Personal Space

Each agent in PAM has an additional safety distance that prefers to maintain from other agents in order to feel comfortable. This distance, along with the radius of the agent, defines the agent's personal space. When computing the time to collision to each of its nearest neighbors, an agent in PAM tests for intersections between its personal space and the radius of its neighbor. This creates a small buffer between agents when they pass each other.

15.4.1.2 Field of View

Agents in PAM are not allowed to react to all the other agents in the environment, but rather are given a limited field of view in which they can sense. Often, the exact orientation of an agent is unknown, but we can generally use the (filtered) current velocity as an estimate of an agent's facing direction. PAM agents use a field of view of $\pm100°$, corresponding to the angle of sight of a typical human, and discard any agents who fall outside of this angle.

15.4.1.3 Distance to Collision

In PAM, agents reason about how far away (in meters) the point of collision is—defining a distance-to-collision, rather than a time-to-collision, formulation. This distance to collision is used to control the magnitude of the avoidance force. If the predicted collision point between two agents is closer than is allowed by an agent's personal space ($d_{\min}$), the magnitude of the avoidance force rises steeply to help create an "impenetrable barrier" between agents. If the distance is further away than some maximum distance ($d_{\max}$), the avoidance force will be zero. Between $d_{\min}$ and $d_{\max}$, the magnitude is shaped to reduce jerky behavior.

15.4.1.4 Randomized Perturbation

In PAM, some perturbation is introduced in the collision-avoidance routine to account for the uncertainty that an agent has in sensing the velocities and radii of its nearby neighbors. Such perturbation is also needed to introduce irregularity among the agents and resolve artifacts that arise from perfectly symmetrical patterns (e.g., two agents on antipodal positions having exactly opposite directions). This perturbation can be expressed as a force that is added to the goal and collision-avoidance forces.

Figure 15.4a provides an illustration of the concept of an agent's personal space and limited field of view. Figure 15.4b shows how the magnitude of the avoidance force falls off as a function of distance to collision. Finally, a simulation of two PAM agents was used to create the anticipatory avoidance example shown in Figure 15.1b.

15.4.2 Guaranteed Collision Avoidance

Rather than trying to closely mimic the limitations of human sensing and planning, some researchers have focused on providing mathematically robust, guaranteed collision-free motion between multiple agents. The optimal reciprocal collision avoidance (ORCA) algorithm is one such approach, which is focused on decentralized, anticipatory collision avoidance between many agents [van den Berg 11].

The ORCA method works by defining a set of formal constraints on an agent's velocity. When all agents follow these constraints, the resulting motion is provably collision-free,

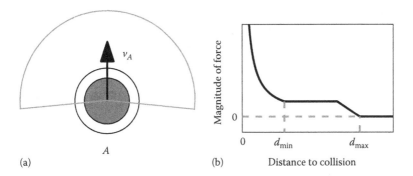

(a)   (b)   Distance to collision

Figure 15.4

PAM agents' parameters. (a) Here, agents have a limited field of view and an extended soft personal space past their radius (dashed circle). (b) The magnitude of the avoidance force is a function of the distance to collision that rises sharply when this distance is less than d_{min} (the radius of the personal space) and falls to zero at some user-defined distance threshold d_{max}.

even with no communication between agents. In games, this formal guarantee of collision avoidance can be important, because it allows a high degree of confidence that the method will work well in challenging scenarios with fast-moving characters, quick dynamic obstacles, and very high density situations that can cause issues for many other avoidance methods.

Unlike PAM and the time-to-collision-based approach, which both use forces to steer an agent, ORCA is a velocity-based approach directly choosing a new velocity for each agent, at each time step. The idea of a velocity space can help illustrate how ORCA works. Unlike normal world space (Figure 15.5a) where each 2D point represents a position, in velocity space, each 2D point represents an agent's (relative) velocity. So the origin in

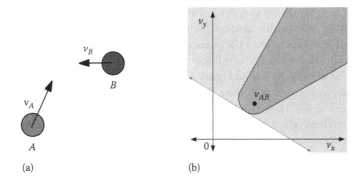

(a)   (b)

Figure 15.5

ORCA collision avoidance. (a) The world space shows the true position and velocities of two agents on a collision course. (b) Agent A's velocity space. The dark-shaded region shows the RVO (forbidden relative velocities), and the gray line shows a linear approximation of this space used by ORCA resulting in a larger forbidden region (both the light- and dark-shaded regions).

velocity space, for example, represents an agent moving at the same speed as its neighbor. We can now designate the set of all velocities that lead to a collision before a given time horizon as forbidden and prevent agents from choosing those velocities for the next time step. This set of forbidden velocities is commonly called a velocity obstacle (VO). Figure 15.5b illustrates an agent's velocity space and shades as gray the velocities that are forbidden. Because these forbidden velocities are based on future collisions, ORCA is a fundamentally anticipatory technique.

Conceptually, ORCA can be thought of as each agent on each time step, computing the VO for each of its neighbors and choosing a velocity outside the union of all VOs that is closest to its goal velocity. Unfortunately, directly implementing such an approach does not lead to great results. In practice, ORCA presents two important improvements to this simple approach in order to get efficient, stable motion. These changes derive from the key concepts of reciprocity and linearization.

In this context, *reciprocity* means the sharing of the collision-avoidance responsibility between two agents. Imagine Agents A and B on a collision course (as in Figure 15.5a). If A chooses a velocity outside of the VO, that means it has resolved the collision completely on its own and B does not need to respond anymore. Likewise, if B avoids the entire collision, A should do nothing. Both agents choosing velocities outside the VOs will overly avoid the collision resulting in inefficient motion and can ultimately lead to distracting oscillations in an agent's velocity. ORCA resolves this issue through the use of reciprocity, allowing each agent to avoid only part of the collision with the knowledge that the neighboring agent will resolve the reminder of the collision (a simple solution is to split the work 50–50 between the two agents). This modified set of forbidden velocities, which only avoid half of the collision, is known as a reciprocal velocity obstacle (RVO), which is illustrated as the dark-shaded region in Figure 15.5b.

When there are multiple neighbors to avoid, each neighbor will cast a separate RVO onto the agent's velocity. The agent should choose a new velocity outside the union of all these RVOs that is as close as possible to its goal velocity. Unfortunately, this is a complex, nonconvex space making it difficult to find an optimal noncolliding velocity. Potential approaches include randomly sampling velocities (as is implemented in the original RVO library) or testing all possible critical points that may be optimal (as implemented in ClearPath and HRVO [Gamma 14]). In contrast, ORCA avoids this issue by approximating each RVO with a single line. This linear approximation is called an ORCA constraint and is illustrated as the gray line in Figure 15.5b. The result is an overapproximation with many new velocities now considered forbidden (i.e., both the dark- and the light-gray regions in Figure 15.5b). However, the linearization is chosen to minimize approximation error near the current velocity, allowing ORCA to work well in practice. Because the union of a set of line constraints is convex, using only linear constraints greatly simplifies the optimization computation resulting in an order of magnitude speedup and allows some important guarantees of collision-freeness to be formally proved [van den Berg 11].

In some cases, the ORCA constraints may overconstrain an agent's velocity leaving no valid velocity choice for this time step. In these cases, one option is to drop constraints from far away agents until a solution can be found. When constraints are dropped in this manner, the resulting motion is no longer guaranteed to be collision-free for that agent, for that time step. However, in practice, this typically results in only minor, fleeting collisions.

A complete C++ implementation of the ORCA algorithm is available online as part of the RVO2 collision-avoidance library (http://gamma.cs.unc.edu/RVO2/). This implementation is highly optimized, using a geometric approach to quickly compute both the RVOs and the ORCA constraints for every agent. The library then uses a randomized linear programming approach to efficiently find a velocity near the goal velocity that satisfies all the ORCA constraints. Using this optimized approach, ORCA can update agents' states nearly as quickly as force-based methods, while still providing avoidance guarantees.

15.4.3 Herd'Em!

ORCA, and methods using similar geometric principles, has been integrated into many different computer games, both free and commercial. One freely available game that makes use of the library is *Herd'Em!* (http://gamma.cs.unc.edu/HERDEM/) [Curtis 10]. *Herd'Em!* simulates a flock of sheep and allows the user to control a sheepdog in an attempt to herd the sheep into the pen on the left side of the screen (Figure 15.6). The game uses a simple boids-like approach with one force pulling agents toward each other, one force encouraging some separation, and another force aligning the agents toward the same velocity. The new velocity as a result of these three forces is used to provide a goal velocity to ORCA. The ORCA simulation is set with a small time horizon, so that the flocking behavior is only modified when a collision is very imminent. This allows agents to flock nicely, while still guaranteeing collision avoidance.

The guaranteed avoidance behavior is very important once a user is added in the loop. In *Herd'Em!*, every sheep feels an additional repulsive force away from the direction of the dog. As the user controls the dog by dragging it quickly around the screen, the dog can have a very high velocity. It is also common for users to try to stress the system by steering

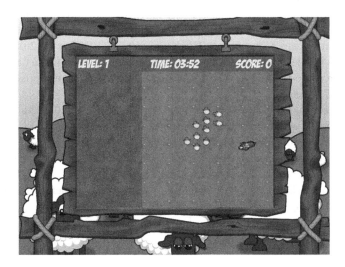

Figure 15.6

ORCA in practice. The game *Herd'Em!* combines a simple flocking method with ORCA to provide guaranteed collision avoidance of the characters under a wide variety of user inputs. (Courtesy of Dinesh Manocha, © 2012 University of North Carolina, Wilmington, NC. Used with permission.)

as many sheep as possible into a small corner. In both cases, the guaranteed avoidance of ORCA allows the simulation to remain collision-free despite the challenging conditions.

15.5 Conclusion

While anticipation in an agent's motion is a wide-ranging topic, this chapter has covered many of the most important concepts to get started understanding the many exciting new developments in this area. Agent-based modeling, force-based versus velocity-space computations, time-to-collision calculations, time horizons, and goal velocities are all concepts that are central to a wide variety of character planning and navigation topics. While the code in Listing 15.3 provides good collision-avoidance behaviors in many situations, there is still room for improvement and exploration.

One exciting area of recent interest has been applying anticipatory collision-avoidance techniques to robots [Hennes 12]. An important consideration here is to robustly account for the uncertainty caused by imperfect sensing and actuation. Other interesting challenges include incorporating an agent's anticipation into its character animation or adapting techniques such as ORCA to account for stress, cooperation, and other social factors. We hope the concepts and algorithm we have detailed in this chapter provide readers with a solid starting point for their own experimentations.

References

[Curtis 10] Curtis, S., Guy, S. J., Krajcevski, P., Snape, J., and D. Manocha. 2010. HerdEm. University of North Carolina, Wilmington, NC. http://gamma.cs.unc.edu/HERDEM/. (accessed January 10, 2015).

[Gamma 14] Manocha, D., Lin, M. et al. 2014. UNC GAMMA group's collision avoidance libraries, University of North Carolina, Wilmington, NC. http://gamma.cs.unc.edu/CA/and http://gamma.cs.unc.edu/HRVO (accessed September 10, 2014).

[Guy 15] Guy S. J. and Karamouzas, I. 2015. Python implementation of the time-to-collision based force model. Game AI Pro Website. http://www.gameaipro.com (accessed February 7, 2015).

[Hennes 12] Hennes, D., Claes, D., Meeussen W., and K. Tuyls. 2012. Multi-robot collision avoidance with localization uncertainty. In *Proceedings of the 11th International Conference on Autonomous Agents and Multiagent Systems*, pp. 147–154.

[Karamouzas 09] Karamouzas, I., Heil, P., van Beek, P., and M. H. Overmars. 2009. A predictive collision avoidance model for pedestrian simulation. In *Motion in Games, Lecture Notes in Computer Science 5884*, eds. A. Egges, R. Geraerts, and M. Overmars, pp. 41–52. Springer-Verlag, Berlin, Germany.

[Snook 00] Snook, G. 2000. Simplified 3D movement and pathfinding using navigation meshes. In *Game Programming Gems*, ed. M. DeLoura, pp. 288–304. Charles River Media, Hingham, MA.

[Stout 00] Stout, B. 2000. The basics of A* for path planning. In *Game Programming Gems*, ed. M. DeLoura, pp. 254–263. Charles River Media, Hingham, MA.

[van den Berg 11] van den Berg, J., Guy, S. J., Lin, M., and D. Manocha. 2011. Reciprocal n-body collision avoidance. In *Springer Tracts in Advanced Robotics*, Vol. 70, eds. C. Pradalier, R. Siegwart, and G. Hirzinger, pp. 3–19. Springer-Verlag, Berlin, Germany.

16

Hierarchical Architecture for Group Navigation Behaviors

Clodéric Mars and Jérémy Chanut

16.1 Introduction

It is now fairly common to find autonomous human-like characters that are able to navigate in 3D environments, finding paths and avoiding collisions while exhibiting convincing navigation behavior. In the past few years, several major publications have been applied successfully to games: we now have well-tested recipes to generate navigation meshes (nav meshes), compute paths, have pedestrians follow them, and avoid collisions in a convincing way.

However, we still fall short when it comes to group navigation. Like real groups, we want virtual humans to be able to walk down roads with their group of friends. Like real ones, virtual soldiers should be able to patrol while staying in formation. And like real ones, virtual tourists should be able to enjoy a tour of the Mont Saint-Michel following their guide's umbrella.

The aim of this chapter is to provide a base recipe to implement a group navigation system. The first two sections form an introduction, presenting the different kinds of group navigation and the basics of navigation behaviors. The next section presents our proposed hierarchical architecture, and the following sections present different aspects of its design.

16.2 Group Navigation

Taxonomy can be a daunting word, but classification can help establish a common understanding. Reading the navigation simulation literature, three main categories of approaches can be found: flocks, formations, and small "social" groups.

16.2.1 Flocks

A flock is, by definition, a group of birds traveling together. Flocking strategies for navigation can be applied for other animal species as well as humans (e.g., school children crossing the street to the swimming pool).

Entities in a flock travel at roughly the same speed and form a cohesive group without strict arrangement. Figure 16.1 showcases such a flock; you can notice that entities are not facing in the same direction and are not evenly distributed. Generally, an entity in a flock will follow independent local rules to stay in the group. While the term is primarily associated with a large number of entities, the same kind of strategy can be used for groups of only a few members.

Reynolds popularized flocking simulation in what must be the two most cited articles in the field, making their implementation a well-known subject [Reynolds 87, Reynolds 99].

16.2.2 Formations

While flocks emerge from a set of individual rules enforcing the general cohesion of the group, formations are a kind of group arrangement where members enforce a set of strict top-down rules. The first and most important one is the formation's spatial arrangement, that is, the relative positions of members; it is designed for tactical, aesthetic, or other specific purposes. Most of the time, a formation gets much of its usefulness from allocated fields of fire and sight, which is why orientation is also enforced [Dawson 02].

Figure 16.1

A flock of navigating entities.

Figure 16.2

A formation of navigating entities.

The last rule is to assign entities having the right role to the right slot: archers at the back, foot soldiers facing the enemy.

Figure 16.2 showcases a formation of nine entities in three layers dedicated each to a specific role, represented by the entities' colors. As formations are important for real-time strategy games, interesting and working solutions have been known for some time: Dave Pottinger, who worked on the *Age of Empire* series, presented his in a Game Developer Magazine article, which is now available for free at Gamasutra.com [Pottinger 99].

16.2.3 Social Groups

Beyond amorphous flocks and rigid formations, groups that are more common in our everyday lives are small and their spatial configuration is the result of social factors and crowd density.

In two different surveys focusing on those small social groups, the authors showed that there are more groups than single pedestrians in urban crowds and that groups of more than four are very rare [Peters 09, Moussaïd 10].

Furthermore, it appears that the formation assumed by the observed groups is influenced both by the lateral clearance to nearby obstacles and by the need of social interaction between members of the group.

These two surveys show that social groups tend to follow three preferred formations depending on the density of the crowd. When motion is not constrained (i.e., when obstacles are far and the crowd density is low), a group tends to adopt an abreast formation that facilitates dialog between its members (leftmost formation on Figure 16.3).

When facing navigation constraints, the group compacts the formation to reduce its frontal width. And, when the lateral space between members becomes too thin, that is, when members are shoulder to shoulder, the formation is staggered. The bending of the

Figure 16.3

Social navigation formations, from left to right: abreast, V-like, lane.

group is, most of the time, forward (V-like formation—in the middle in Figure 16.3) to maintain good communication. A backward bending (inverted-V-like or wedge formation) would be more flexible moving against an opposite flow but seems to be less usual. As the crowd density increases, groups tend to form a tight lane (rightmost formation of Figure 16.3).

Another observation found in these studies is that groups tend to avoid collisions with other pedestrians or with obstacles while remaining together, but if needed, they are able to split and merge back afterward.

In the following section, we introduce a way to efficiently include the group navigation process into a software architecture.

16.3 Navigation Pipeline Architecture

Before delving into topics specific to group behaviors, in this section, we will give a quick overview of what we call *navigation behavior* and the *navigation pipeline* that makes it possible to combine them.

16.3.1 Navigation Behaviors

Typically, a navigation behavior is responsible for computing velocity changes from

- Higher-level individual orders
- Other entities (e.g., neighbors to take into account for collision avoidance)
- And, generally, the state of the world (nav mesh, scene geometry, etc.)

As illustrated in Figure 16.4, this input is usually a path to follow. Paths are computed to reach a target, which is selected by some decision-making code. It then outputs orders driving a locomotion engine that actually makes the entity move.

This architecture supports partial updates. For example, the navigation behavior and the following components can be updated on their own by reusing the previous navigation orders. This allows a compromise between costly components that do not require high reactivity (such as decision making or path finding) and cheaper ones that benefit from a high update frequency (e.g., physics or animation) [Mononen 10, RecastDetour 14].

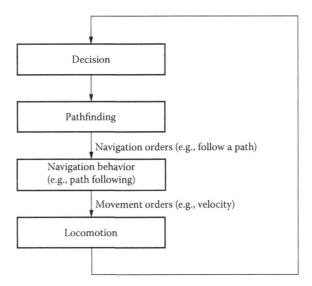

Figure 16.4

Typical character update loop involving navigation.

16.3.2 Navigation Pipeline

In real-life scenarios, entities exhibit different navigation properties and are able to handle several types of orders and constraints:

- An entity can reach a target
- Wounded and thus not walking straight
- While it is avoiding obstacles

In order to model this kind of complex behavior, we use a *navigation pipeline*: a sequence of navigation behaviors.

At runtime, the behaviors are updated sequentially, each considering the state of the entity as well as the orders output by its predecessor in the pipeline. In practice, each behavior "corrects" the orders of the previous one.

Consider the "wounded" behavior in the pipeline of Figure 16.5. The previous behavior computes a velocity that makes the entity follow a path. The "wounded" behavior will use this desired velocity as an input and compute a new one that is close to it by applying some noise function. In turn, the "collision avoidance" behavior will correct the orders to avoid future collisions. As the last behavior in the pipeline, it has the last word on the actual decision.

This architecture comes with two great benefits: modularity and reusability. In the case of groups, member entities behaviors need to take into account both the collective goals, for example, flock or stay in formation, and the individual goals, for example, avoid collisions early or minimize deviation from initial trajectory. Modeling these as navigation behaviors and using the navigation pipeline architecture gives us a flexible framework to fulfill these requirements.

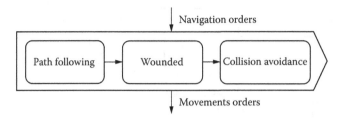

Figure 16.5

A navigation pipeline using three navigation behaviors.

In the following sections, we'll see how the navigation pipeline can be used to model the described group navigation behaviors.

16.4 Group to Members Relationship Model

While some behaviors might be decentralized, in order to manage groups in a context where we need to make them go from A to B, top-down decision making is needed [Musse 01]. A group-level process will be able to make the group move while each of its members follows. Two very different approaches can be used:

1. Make one of the group members the leader.
2. Introduce a virtual entity representing the group itself.

The two following sections will describe the two approaches through their use in the technical literature; the third will describe how we propose to implement an entity hierarchy.

16.4.1 Leader

When trying to enforce a strict equivalence between simulated entities and actual characters, many approaches rely on a leader–followers approach. With such an approach, one member of the group is the leader and the others are the followers. The leader takes responsibility for the whole group's navigation [Loscos 03, Qiu 10].
Implementation using a navigation engine for independent entities is straightforward:

- The leader is similar to any entity.
- The followers maintain a reference to their leader and follow its decisions.

However, the leader cannot reuse the exact same navigation process as an independent entity. Its navigation must take into account the bulk of the whole group as well as the different locomotion constraints of its followers. It is also better to differentiate the leader's own attributes (position, orientation and velocity) from the group's [Millington 06]. Taking all these constraints into account makes the decision-making process of the leader very different from those of the other members.

16.4.2 Virtual Group Entity

Noting that the leader-based approach has several flaws, a growing proportion of architectures chose to move the group "anchor" from the leader to a virtual group entity [Karamouzas 10, Schuerman 10, Silveira 08]. This virtual entity is similar to any other simulated entity but does not have a visual or physical representation. In such an architecture, the group members are identical to one another. The group entity creates a one-level-deep hierarchy of entities. This approach can be taken a step further to create groups of groups and so on [Millington 06, Schuerman 10], allowing a more structured crowd.

Such hierarchical separation of responsibility leads to a cleaner software architecture as well as arguably simpler behaviors, but it is also slightly more complex to implement. In the following section, we'll describe the design choices we made when doing this.

16.4.3 Hierarchical Entity Architecture

In our architecture, we build upon the virtual group entity approach to create a hierarchy of entities (see Figure 16.6). Everything is an entity and is handled in the same way in our navigation loop; groups are composites of entities.

This hierarchy allows us to differentiate the group from the individual. An individual is the most basic entity we can have in our simulation. Groups, on the other hand, are entities containing other entities. It is a fairly standard implementation of a composite pattern.

Navigation behavior algorithms need information about the entity they are working on (position, velocity, orientation, etc.). They could take these from the entity, but the situation is more complicated when working with groups, because a group's properties depend on its entities. The way to define this relationship can be tricky to get right; here are the key ideas:

- The group's position can be computed from the members as their barycenter.
- Its bulk can also be computed either as a radius or as an oriented bounding box.
- Its orientation is tricky to define from the members; the best course of action is to tie it to the group's velocity or to have specific navigation behaviors handle the group's rotation [Millington 06].
- Its maximum speed, acceleration, and other movement limits need to be computed from the entities so that they are able to follow the group. For instance, the maximum speed of the group should be below the smallest of the members' maximum speeds. It is also important to consider that the maximum rotation rate of the group needs to take into account the maximum speed of its members and the width of the group.
- Finally, its velocity is independent, as we want the entities to "follow" the group.

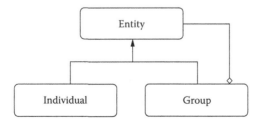

Figure 16.6

Entity hierarchy.

As we mentioned, a navigation behavior only relies on its "orders," the state of the world, and the state of the following entities:

- The one it is working on
- Its parent and/or children, used, for example, by formation slots assignment (discussed later)
- Its geometrical neighbors, used, for example, by collision avoidance

This means that it is easy to make the entities' navigation processes completely independent from one another by keeping the previous simulation update state as a read-only input. Thus, allowing easy multithreading.

One drawback is that the entity hierarchy has to be static from the point of view of the navigation behaviors. In other words, a navigation behavior cannot split or merge groups. The preferred approach to control groups' creation and membership changes is to treat the group hierarchy as an external parameter akin to a path planning target. A higher-level control layer is in charge of organizing groups; the navigation behavior should be resilient to these changes when they occur between updates.

This architecture can be used to create hierarchies with more than one level. This allows a complex structure and choreography for groups of entities with no actual additional cost.

One pitfall can be observed in deep hierarchies, however. Group members only take into account orders computed by the group during the previous simulation update, thus introducing a tiny delay. When adding layers of hierarchy, the delay grows linearly with its depth. We believe that this is not a real-world problem as a deep hierarchy does not have many use cases.

16.5 Pathfinding

One of the reasons to introduce group navigation is to factorize a costly aspect of navigation: pathfinding. As the members of a group are expected to follow the same high-level path through the environment, a single query should be sufficient for the whole group.

The most important aspect of group-level path planning is to choose how to take the bulk of the group into account. Contrary to a single entity where its bulk is static and thus is a hard constraint, a group may be able to reconfigure itself in order to pass through narrower corridors.

Therefore, the query has to be tuned in order to

- Prefer paths on which the group, in its current spatial configuration, can navigate
- Allow the use of narrower passages, for which the group can be reconfigured, if necessary

This means that the cost of falling back to a narrower spatial configuration needs to be comparable to the cost of taking a longer path [Bayazit 03, Kamphuis 04, Pottinger 99].

Once the path is computed, the path-following process provides local steering orders resulting in the entity following the path. In some works, the group-level path-following computation is also responsible for environment-aware formation adaptation, allowing the formation to change when the clearance to obstacles changes [Bayazit 03, Pottinger 99].

16.6 Emergent Group Structure

In most modern navigation engines, the simulated entities are autonomous, with their behavior relying on local "perception" to take action, not on an external choreographer. With this approach in mind, it is possible to design decentralized navigation behaviors to comply with group constraints.

16.6.1 Boids and Derivatives

At the core of Reynolds' work [Reynolds 87, Reynolds 99], three steering forces allow entities to flock. For a given entity in the group, separation makes it move away from close neighbors, alignment makes it go in the same direction as other members, and cohesion makes it move toward the group's anchor. The combination of these simple forces allows the emergence of a simple flocking behavior.

Given the nature of this model, it is simple to add new forces or to change the relative importance of forces (e.g., more or less repulsion) to better control the structure of the group. One example of such adaptation is the addition of a force modeling the desire for members of small social groups to keep all group members in their field of view for communication purposes [Moussaïd 10]. Another example is the modulation of members' attractivity to better take into account social relations [Qiu 10].

16.6.2 "Local" Formations

With the same strictly decentralized approach and by taking inspiration from molecular crystals, some formation control can be applied using an attachment site method. Each entity defines several attachment sites indicating, relatively, where its neighbors are supposed to be. When navigating, group members locate the nearest available site among their neighbors' and steer toward it.

The resulting formation arrangement is a direct result of the attachment sites position and it can scale to any number of group members. But, as the attachment rules are local, no control on the overall shape is possible; it is a good fit, though, for modeling social groups [Balch 00].

16.6.3 Implementing an Emergent Group

To get an idea of how such an emergent group structure can be implemented using our hierarchical architecture (see Figure 16.7), let us consider Boids' flocking behavior. In the by-the-book approach, given an initial velocity, the group will move cohesively in some direction. But, an adaptation is needed to control the group's movement.

Usually, a special entity is added: orders are given (e.g., a path to follow) to this leader, who "drags" the rest of the group around. Using our approach, no physical leader is needed. The group entity is the high-level order recipient and executor, and the group members use its position and velocity as an input for their cohesion and alignment behaviors.

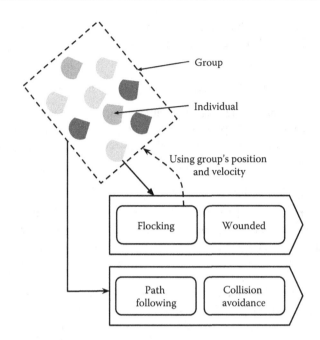

Figure 16.7

Flock architecture in our hierarchical group architecture.

The algorithm unfolds as follows during each update (the order of these is not important):

- The group updates its position and current velocity based on its members and then computes a new velocity based on a given path.
- Group members compute their new velocity based on the group's position (cohesion), the group's velocity (alignment), and the other members' relative positions (separation).

16.7 Choreographed Formations

While groups whose members are implementing local rules can exhibit convincing behavior, they cannot take into account the group as a whole and thus are not fully controllable. If exact group arrangement is needed, some of the behavior must be delegated to a higher level of control [Musse 01]. In this section, we will study the three steps needed to make a group stay in a given formation: formation design, slot assignment, and formation following.

16.7.1 Formation Design

In the context of navigation, a formation is the specification of the spatial arrangement of the members of a group. As we focus on pedestrians walking on the ground, each slot of the specification has a 2D position; two properties might be added, an orientation and a role (i.e., which kind of entity should be assigned to each slot). The slots are defined relative to the group's own position and orientation. The slots specification can come from different sources for different use cases, such as military doctrine, artistic choices, or even survey results.

The number of slots should match the number of entities in the group. If not, simple techniques can be used to select the used slots or create needed slots [Silveira 08].

16.7.2 Slots Assignment

Before our entities can navigate as a group, each of them must be assigned slot. This might seem trivial but should be implemented with care to avoid congestion between members of the same group; this will affect the credibility of the simulation. The greedy approach of each member being assigned the closest slot doesn't always work: the entities might have to cross each other's paths and the last entities might have to circle around the group to get to their slots [Dawson 02, Millington 06].

The best solution would be to globally minimize the distance the entities are covering to get to their slots but its implementation would lead to an $O(n!)$ complexity as every permutation would have to be tested.

One solution works well when no specialized slots are defined: The general idea is to sort the slots spatially then sort the members in the same way and assign the ith entity to the ith slot [Mars 14].

16.7.3 "Blind" Formation Following

The most basic approach to formation following is to have members no longer be responsible for their steering: members are placed on relative coordinates around the group's position [Pottinger 99]. This solution is fine if the group steering is robust.

Implementing this approach using our architecture is straightforward:

- The group updates its position and current velocity based on its members and then computes a new velocity based, for example, on a given path. Finally, it assigns a slot to each group member. It is also possible and often desirable to extend the group's navigation behavior with collision avoidance.
- Group members retrieve their slots and set their position accordingly.

One potential evolution of this approach is to assign group members a simple behavior that can compute and apply the necessary velocities for reaching their slot's position.

This makes it possible to customize the velocity application phase, taking into account characteristics such as maximum speed or acceleration or delegating it to an external system (e.g., locomotion).

When using this strategy, it is important to extrapolate the slot position to make it nonreachable in a single simulation update. This will contribute to avoid motion jolts [Karamouzas 10, Schuerman 10]. In practice, a simple extrapolation of the slot position using the group velocity over a time period greater than the frame duration is enough. This computation also handles gracefully nonmoving groups, as their velocity is null.

Additionally, the extrapolation time period can be controlled to define the "cohesion" of the formation, a small value for a tight formation a larger one for a very "loose" formation. The farther the target is, the less it will impact the member velocity.

16.7.4 Autonomous Formation Following

In most instances, members of a formation do not follow orders blindly. Instead, they have an autonomous strategy to stay in formation. This is especially true when simulating small social groups, where the formation is more of an emergent feature than a strict rule. Furthermore, it allows entities to break formation to pass through tight corridors and around small obstacles [Silveira 08].

This use case is where our architecture shines. The same strategy as before can be applied and, to enhance the individuality of the members, their behavior can be extended with (as shown in Figure 16.8)

- Collision avoidance, so that groups do not have to micromanage everything to avoid collisions between their members
- Specific behaviors, allowing entities to have "subgoals," for example, attraction to store fronts
- Specific velocity noise functions, to give them "personality"

While the same collision avoidance behaviors can be used by the entities whether they are part of a group or not, they must be adapted. As a matter of fact, collision avoidance algorithms, such as Reciprocal Velocity Obstacle [van den Berg 08], try to enforce a safe distance to obstacles and other entities that might forbid close formations [Schuerman 10].

To mitigate this issue, a member's behavior needs to either differentiate between its peers (other members of the group) and the other entities or to be adapted when it is part of a group by, for example, only considering imminent collisions.

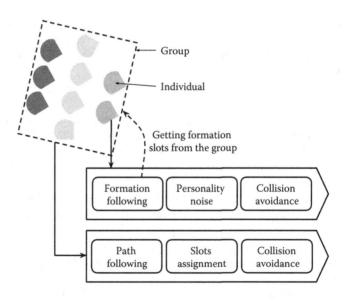

Figure 16.8

Autonomous formation following.

16.8 Group Collision Avoidance

In real life, groups tend to stay coherent when navigating between obstacles and among other pedestrians, which is why it is interesting to use group-level collision avoidance. Many existing algorithms for entities can be applied directly or adapted for group-level collision avoidance. As we noted earlier, the main difference between groups and single entities is that their bulk is not a hard constraint. The spatial configuration of a group can be adapted to occupy less frontal space, less longitudinal space, or both.

16.8.1 Velocity Correction

Existing collision algorithms such as RVO can be applied by considering the bulk of the group as a disc. The resulting collision avoidance is very conservative as the disc is, most of time, greatly overestimating the real footprint of the group [Schuerman 10, van den Berg 08].

To get better results, navigation behaviors of this family can be adapted to reason on the group's oriented bounding box [Karamouzas 04, Karamouzas 10, Peters 09].

16.8.2 Formation Adaptation

As discussed for path following, groups can spatially reconfigure themselves to change their bulk; this idea can be applied for better collision avoidance.

Consider a couple, walking side by side in a corridor: a simple formation. When another pedestrian arrives in the opposite direction, the couple will form a lane, reducing their frontal bulk, allowing the crossing. This is an instance of formation adaptation.

In RVO-like collision avoidance algorithms, several candidate velocities are computed around the current velocity, the ones leading to future collisions are pruned and the remaining one closest to the desired velocity is kept. The same approach can be used for formation adaptation [Karamouzas 10]:

- Define a set of formations the group can use and its preferred one (cf. Section 16.2.3 for social groups).
- At each time step, interpolate a number of candidate formations from the group's current state to the formations of the initial set.
- For each candidate formation, do an RVO-like evaluation outputting its "best" velocity and time to collision.
- Compute a cost for each candidate that take into account those values and the distance to the preferred formation.
- Take the lowest cost.

It is important to limit the number of candidate formations to preserve the performance of the algorithm. The original work uses a set of five formations and interpolates three candidates to each one of them, thus evaluating 15 in total.

Those group-level navigation methods allow the group to take responsibility for a part of the collision avoidance and more easily preserve the group cohesion. They can be easily implemented in our architecture as group behaviors and combined with finer granularity entity level steering.

16.9 Conclusion

In this chapter, we introduced a hierarchical architecture for group navigation, and we have shown how it can be used to fulfill different use cases, flocks, formations, and social groups, leveraging existing work. We proposed a generic framework to design and implement group navigation. A similar architecture was already implemented as a part of the Golaem SDK [GolaemSDK 14] and it is our plan to implement it in the open source navigation engine Recast/Detour [RecastDetour 14].

Externalizing some of the tricky collaborative decision making to a virtual group entity is one of the major design choices we made. Such "choreographer" entities are also a good pattern to apply when a high degree of control is needed over a group of individuals: traffic management around a door, group discussions, tactical synchronization, combat pacing, etc. Moreover, as we have shown in the context of navigation, this centralized decision-making method does not come at the cost of the individuality of each entity's behaviors.

References

[Balch 00] Balch, T. and Hybinette, M. 2000. Social potentials for scalable multi-robot formations. In *IEEE International Conference on Robotics and Automation*, San Francisco, CA, pp. 73–80.

[Bayazit 03] Bayazit, O., Lien, J., and Amato, N. 2003. Better group behaviors in complex environments using global roadmaps. In *Eighth International Conference on Artificial Life*, Department of Computer Science, Texas A&M University, College Station, TX, pp. 362–370.

[Dawson 02] Dawson, C. 2002. Formations. In *AI Game Programming Wisdom*, ed. Rabin, S., pp. 272–282. Charles River Media, Hingham, MA.

[GolaemSDK 14] Golaem SDK. 2014. Available from: http://golaem.com/ (accessed July 10, 2014).

[Kamphuis 04] Kamphuis, A. and Overmars, M.H. 2004. Finding paths for coherent groups using clearance. In *ACM SIGGRAPH/Eurographics Symposium on Computer Animation*, Copenhagen, Denmark, pp. 19–28.

[Karamouzas 04] Karamouzas, I. and Overmars, M. 2004. Simulating human collision avoidance using a velocity-based approach. In *VRI-PHYS 10: Seventh Workshop on Virtual Reality Interactions and Physical Simulations*, Eurographics Association, Copenhagen, Denmark, pp. 125–134.

[Karamouzas 10] Karamouzas, I. and Overmars, M. 2010. Simulating the local behaviour of small pedestrian groups. In *17th ACM Symposium on Virtual Reality Software and Technology*, Hong Kong, China. Center for Advanced Gaming and Simulation, Utrecht University, Utrecht, the Netherlands, pp. 183–190.

[Loscos 03] Loscos, C., Marchal, D., and Meyer, A. 2003. Intuitive crowd behaviour in dense urban environments using local laws. In *Proceedings of the Theory and Practice of Computer Graphics*, Manchester, U.K., p. 122.

[Mars 14] Mars, C. 2014. Simple formation assignment. *GDC 2014 AI Summit*, San Francisco, CA.

[Millington 06] Millington, I. 2006. *Artificial Intelligence for Games*, pp. 41–202. Morgan Kaufmann, San Francisco, CA.

[Mononen 10] Mononen, M. 2010. Navigation loop. In *Paris Game/AI Conference 2010*, Paris, France.

[Moussaïd 10] Moussaïd, M., Perozo, N., Garnier, S., Helbing, D., and Theraulaz, G. April 2010. The walking behaviour of pedestrian social groups and its impact on crowd dynamics. *PLoS ONE*, 5(4):e10047.

[Musse 01] Musse, S. and Thalmann, D. 2001. Hierarchical model for real time simulation of virtual human crowds. *Transactions on Visualization and Computer Graphics*, 7(2):152–164.

[Peters 09] Peters, C., Ennis, C., and O'Sullivan, C. 2009. Modeling groups of plausible virtual pedestrians. *IEEE Computer Graphics and Applications*, 29(4):54–63.

[Pottinger 99] Pottinger, D. January 1999. Implementing coordinated movement. Available from: http://www.gamasutra.com/view/feature/3314/implementing_coordinated_movement.php?print=1 (accessed May 21, 2014).

[Qiu 10] Qiu, F. and Hu, X. 2010. Modeling dynamic groups for agent-based pedestrian crowd simulations. In *IEEE/WIC/ACM International Conference on Web Intelligence and Intelligent Agent Technology*, Toronto, Canada, pp. 461–464.

[RecastDetour 14] Recast/Detour. 2014. Available from: https://github.com/memononen/recastnavigation (accessed July 10, 2014) and https://github.com/masagroup/recastdetour (accessed July 10, 2014).

[Reynolds 87] Reynolds, C. 1987. Flocks, herds and schools: A distributed behavioral model. In *ACM SIGGRAPH '87 Conference Proceedings,* Anaheim, CA, pp. 25–34.

[Reynolds 99] Reynolds, C. 1999. Steering behaviors for autonomous characters. In *Proceedings of Game Developers Conference.* Miller Freeman Game Group, San Francisco, CA, pp. 763–782.

[Schuerman 10] Schuerman, M., Singh, S., Kapadia, M., and Faloutsos, P. 2010. Situation agents: Agent-based externalized steering logic. In *International Conference on Computer Animation and Social Agents*, University of California, Los Angeles, CA.

[Silveira 08] Silveira, R., Prestes, E., and Nedel, L. 2008. Managing coherent groups. *Computer Animation and Virtual Worlds*, 19(3–4):295–305.

[van den Berg 08] van den Berg, J., Lin, M., and Manocha, D. 2008. Reciprocal velocity obstacles for real-time multi-agent navigation. In *International Conference on Robotics and Automation*, Pasadena, CA, pp. 1928–1935.

17

Dynamic Obstacle Navigation in *Fuse*

Jan Müller

17.1 Introduction

Climbing over obstacles like walls, ledges, or ladders plays a supporting role in video games: they are not usually central to the experience, but they stand out when done poorly or omitted entirely. There are, of course, exceptions to the rule, games like *Mirror's Edge* [EA 08] or *Tomb Raider* [CD 14] that make the climbing sections, so called *traversal*, the core gameplay element. Traversal makes the AI navigation more complicated: it requires additional markup and programming for the AI to understand how to mount a ladder or jump over a wall, not to mention special animation states to control their location as they jump, vault, climb, or swim. As a result, video games with very complex or varied AI characters tend to avoid climbing altogether. Instead, AI navigation [Snook 00] is usually limited to finding paths on a continuous mesh [Mononen 12], where the actors can walk or run everywhere they need to go.

Traversal is hard enough if we have consistency between obstacles, that is, if all jumps are the same length and all walls the same height, so that there is a single solution to any locomotion problem. What if it is more complicated? What if there are hundreds of different volumes placed by either a designer or a content creation tool, each with different attributes and the AI has to decide which ones to consider based on the real time context? In the game *Fuse* [IG 13], from Insomniac Games, four hero agents with different abilities fight cooperatively. Of those four actors, up to three can be under AI control at any given time. Furthermore, we had a complex and highly varied environment, making locomotion more challenging. In contrast to many games with cooperative NPCs, we wanted to make our AI characters follow the same rules as a human player. They aren't tougher to kill, can't teleport to keep up with the player, and need to be able to follow the same gameplay mechanics with regard to activities like climbing a ladder or manning a turret. It is crucial for the game balance that the AI plays as well as a human—not better or worse. The rule we ended up with is "50/50," meaning that half of the total damage is dealt by human players and the other half should be dealt by the AI (assuming that at least two of the four heroes are AI controlled, of course).

To make things even more challenging for the AI, *Fuse* features the *leap* ability, which allows human players to switch from their current character to any of the other heroes that isn't already being controlled by another human player. The game does not restrict leaps to any specific time or place; you can leap in the middle of combat just as easily as during a traversal section. Furthermore, players can drop in or out of the game at any time, and all of this has to work in a peer-to-peer online environment.

The result of all of this is that there can be no cheating. Whatever the human player is capable of doing, the AI has to be able to do it too. Whatever situation the human player is in, he or she can leap to another character (or drop out of the game), leaving the AI to deal with it. This circumstance leads to volatile AI characters that must be able to function smoothly when they initialize halfway through a nontrivial traversal section. Imagine waking up to find yourself hanging one-handed from a ledge 50 ft above the ground, while your enemies are firing semiautomatic rifles at you and a teammate is in need of medical attention down at the bottom. In such a context, the AI cannot rely on markup alone, but needs to evaluate dynamically changing traversal paths at runtime.

17.2 Fuse Traversal Setups

Fuse has numerous, wide-ranging traversal sections. To give players a break between fights, the protagonists will often have to climb obstacles like a mountain side or sewage pipes below a medieval castle in India. These setups usually have three or four possible ascents, which intersect at various points. In addition to the complexity of the ascent itself, there are often enemy bots or turrets that can shoot at you during the climb. When a character is hit, he or she can fall down to the ground and become incapacitated. If that happens to the player, the AI has to be able to find a path down to revive him.

On the content-authoring side, these traversal setups are represented as a group of volumes with different markup options. The most common types of such volumes are vertical pipes and horizontal ledges, as well as variations of those such as ladders. Depending on their attributes and the situation, you can perform different climb animations. For example, you might hang from a ledge and traverse with your hands or mount it to stand on top of it. Connections between volumes may be explicitly marked in the places where they intersect or overlap, or they are implicitly allowed through jump and drop thresholds. To determine whether an actor, be it human or AI controlled, can jump from one ledge to the next, we match their attributes and then perform distance and collision tests between the two points closest to each other. Additionally, we place custom clues that connect the navigation mesh between the start and end of the traversal section. These elements

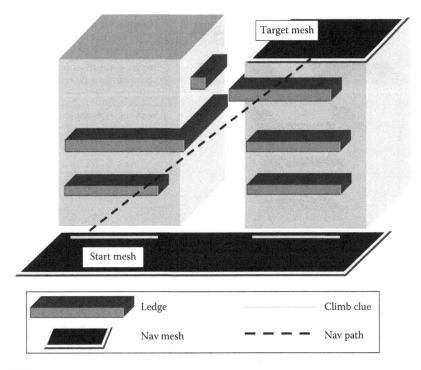

Figure 17.1

A traversal section with ledge markup and navigation path between two meshes.

together provide enough information for the AI to parse the traversal and generate a climb path procedurally. For a typical traversal section in *Fuse*, refer to Figure 17.1. For simplicity's sake, we exclude vertical elements, like pipes or ladders. However, their connections within the climb mesh work the same way as the horizontal elements.

The navigation path in Figure 17.1 connects two disjoint navigation meshes. It creates a link between the start and the end point of the traversal. The path is a straight line between these two climb clues, since the navigation system has no further information about the connecting climb.

17.3 Climb Mesh Generation

The first step of the procedural traversal system is to generate the climb mesh. It collects all possible traversal elements from a group of traversal volumes and creates connections between them. Each connection can link to multiple other traversal elements, but the most common case is that there are no more than one or two connections per node. The system first considers touching or overlapping volumes, which explicitly link two elements together. If two elements touch each other at their end points, they share one merged node in the climb mesh and create explicit connections. For example, if a ledge touches a pipe at a cross section, they share a node at their intersection that forms edges to the start and

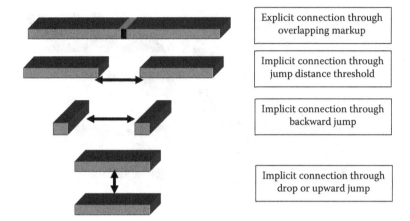

	Explicit connection through overlapping markup
	Implicit connection through jump distance threshold
	Implicit connection through backward jump
	Implicit connection through drop or upward jump

Figure 17.2

Possible connections between two ledge elements in the climb mesh.

end of the ledge as well as the pipe element. If two ledges intersect at their end points, they form an explicit connection between them. Examples of two ledges generating links between each other can be seen in Figure 17.2.

Once all explicit connections have been generated, the system searches for implicit links like jumps or drops. Players can jump between two elements at any time, as long as certain distance and angle thresholds are not exceeded. For simplicity's sake, the *Fuse* AI considers such transitions in the climb mesh only from the end points and between the center points of the volume markup, although other transitions would be possible. Thus, for every traversal element, the algorithm tests three nodes for implicit links to nearby elements. Alternately, you can generate these links at fixed intervals, for example, one per meter, but that has an impact on both the mesh complexity and the parsing resolution. We discuss those implications in the section on generating a virtual controller input (VCI).

The node connections are stored in the climb mesh. Cyclic connections are allowed and are resolved in the path generation step by marking already visited nodes. At this level of abstraction, the actual animation that moves a character from one climb element to the next does not matter. That means a connection between two elements could result in a jump animation for one character and in a swing animation for another. Only the type and distance of the connection, as well as line of sight tests between its elements, are considered. Figure 17.3 illustrates the climb mesh that the example in Figure 17.1 would generate, including all of its nodes and connections.

17.3.1 Path Following on Climb Meshes

As mentioned before, the climb meshes are independent from our navigation system, which only knows about the existence of the traversal, not its layout. When an actor needs to pass through a traversal section, the navigation system returns a path that includes two special clue edges that connect the start and end points of the climb. The clue edges are placed by the level designer and represent the traversal section within the navigation system.

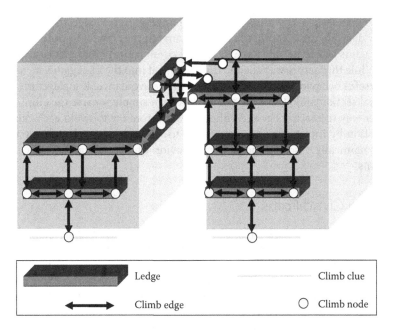

Ledge	Climb clue
Climb edge	○ Climb node

Figure 17.3

The fully generated climb mesh with all possible transition edges.

It does not store any further information about the climb elements or connections. The navigation system only knows the distance between two climb clues and that a climb has to happen to move the character from edge A to B and continue the path from there.

Within the climb mesh, the closest point from the climbing actor on the custom clue is added as the initial climb node. From there, the traversal system triggers a secondary path query that follows the traversal nodes between the start and end clues. Path following on climb meshes utilizes a standard A* search. It searches from the initial climb node and iterates through the neighboring edges, starting with the least-cost candidate, meaning the closest to the target node. Each step of the pathfinding parses the links from the current node to connected nodes in the climb mesh, marking those it already visited as closed. When a path to the target node is reached, then all nodes of that path are returned as a set of 3D vectors. The result is the shortest path on the climb mesh that connects two custom clues on the navigation mesh.

17.3.2 Caveats of the Climb Path Generation

The traversal system in *Fuse* does not consider different costs per traversal element and does not store how long specific animations take to play back. The edge costs are generally normalized within the climb mesh and increased only if other bots use the same climb elements on their path. This means that the shortest path does not necessarily take the least amount of time. However, since there are usually only a few routes to choose from in *Fuse*, avoiding other characters is of higher importance than finding the shortest-time path.

At one point during development, there was a plan to support combat during climbing. This involved shooting from climb elements as well as being incapacitated by hits. If this were to happen to the player while he or she was hanging from a ledge, the character would hang on for dear life until another teammate came to the rescue. In order to allow this, the AI characters had to be able to parse partial climb paths to and from any location on the mesh. While the feature was cut and didn't make it into the final game, it enabled us to add other useful behaviors such as dynamic obstacle avoidance. If a player turns around on a traversal section and blocks the path, the AI can simply reparse the climb mesh and find another way to reach its goal. Without it, AI actors try to avoid each other during path generation by increasing the costs of the used climb edges. But the system is not updating dynamically based on the player's behavior, which can lead to traffic jams along blocked paths.

17.4 Parsing Climb Paths

The second part of the procedural traversal system is the climb parser. The hero AI in *Fuse* shares about half of its implementation with the player controlled characters. This is possible by splitting hero character states into drivers and processors: drivers are responsible for the state input and transition logic. For human players, this means interpreting controller inputs and context into animation parameters. For AI actors, these transitions are controlled by their behaviors and VCI. While drivers are fundamentally different between human and AI characters, the state processors can be shared. The state processor interprets driver updates and communicates with the animation tree of the character. The reuse of hero state processors means that the hero AI automatically inherits all traversal animations from the player characters.

The climb parser generates the VCI for AI-controlled characters. The state transition logic then compares the input data against animation thresholds to determine when, for example, a ledge climb animation can transition into a jump to a nearby pipe. Once the first traversal state has been initialized, the AI behavior strictly follows the VCI and the current state's transition logic. Thus, during the traversal, there is no decision making in place beyond following the VCI, adhering to the state transitions thresholds (including terminating states like the death of the character), and checking against collision with geometry and other characters.

17.4.1 Generating Virtual Controller Input

To generate VCI, the climb parser first resolves the climb path as a Bézier spline curve [DeBoor 78, Farin 97]. Curves in Bézier form are defined as a set of four control points that span a curve between each other. A Bézier spline is a continuous set of such curves that form a smooth, higher-order shape. Such splines can be straight lines, only spanning between two points, but also complex curves with dozens or hundreds of control points. Using the path points as input data for a Bézier curve automatically interpolates the path and creates better results than the raw input data with 90° turns. The reason for this is that the additional curve points add angular momentum to the path. A simple example is a 180° turn around 2 corners: in its raw form, the path is only as long as the total length of its three sides and incorporates two sharp, 90° turns. A spline following the same control points however will extrude the curve to avoid sharp angles, which adds length and curvature to the path.

This is important because the system projects the VCI target on that curve at a fixed distance of 2.8 m ahead of the AI actor from its current position on the spline curve. A traversal move resolution of 2 m gave the best results for the climb animations in *Fuse* but might differ in other games. Many transitional animations move the character by roughly this distance and need to trigger ahead of a directional change to look smooth. The projection distance is the length of the diagonal of a 2×2 m^2 square, which is roughly 2.8 m. That also means that the climb parser is not accurate if there are multiple intersections within a 2 m radius (plus a certain margin for error) and generally speaking chooses the closest one. For example, if there were two vertical pipes intersecting a ledge 1 m apart, the parser would pick the closest one (based on the approach direction). This occurs because the Bézier curve doesn't follow the raw path data precisely, so when two elements are close together, the algorithm can't tell which one was originally on the A*-generated path. Regardless, this doesn't necessarily impact the result. When this happens in *Fuse*, it always appears correct if the parser chooses the closest element.

The 3D vector between the current actor position on the spline curve and the projected VCI target is the VCI vector as depicted in Figure 17.4. The parser generates input strength values for all three axes relative to the character. Those input values are then tested against thresholds for different transitions. A transition in this sense does not necessarily mean jumping or climbing to another element but also transitioning from an idle animation to a climb animation on the existing one. Each climb state has individual thresholds in its transition functions that define the points where characters can switch from one state

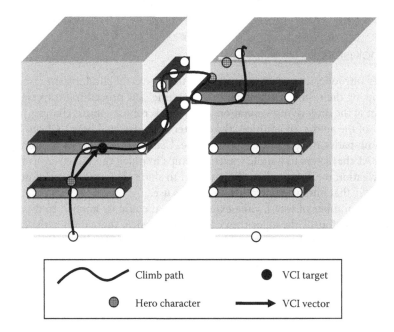

Figure 17.4

The VCI generates a 3D vector between the current actor position and the immediate, projected target position.

to another. For example, if the input vector mostly points to the relative right of the character while he or she is hanging from a ledge, he or she will start climbing to the right. If the character gets into the proximity of a pipe element and the input vector points to the right and top, he or she will transition to the vertical climb animation, attach to the pipe, and start climbing upward. This sequence of traversal animations ends when a terminating state is reached. Examples for such states are mounting the top of a wall or dropping from a ledge back onto the navigation mesh. The system also supports depth transitions such as jumping backward between two parallel ledges on opposing walls or flipping over the top of a flat wall.

There are a limited number of entry states for traversal sections, such as mounting a ladder or jumping up to a ledge above the initial climb node. This makes the transition from walking or running to climbing relatively predictable. The most common case has the VCI vector pointing up or down at the traversal start. In that case, the climb could start by attaching to a ladder or jumping up or down to a ledge. Once the traversal state has been initialized, the VCI target is projected forward on the climb path as described. The state treats the VCI data the same way it would interpret human controller input and matches the values against transition thresholds. In the example in Figure 17.4, the initial jump-up state would transition to a ledge hang state, which would be followed by another jump, since the VCI mostly points upward. Once the character reaches the second ledge, the VCI would point to the relative right side of the character, which leads to a ledge move animation. The character would follow the climb path until eventually reaching the final ledge and playing a mount animation at the top of the traversal section. That state would terminate the climb so that we can return the AI to the navigation mesh.

17.5 Conclusion

This chapter introduced an approach to generating traversal climb meshes from markup and to following the resulting climb paths at runtime. The procedural traversal system is independent of the underlying animation states and is robust against changes in the locomotion sets of the actors. In addition, the chapter demonstrated how VCI can be utilized to parse climb paths along a Bézier spline curve. Using climb paths in combination with VCI allows AI characters to handle traversal setups in much the same way as they would normal navigation meshes. It also allows the AI to share the same traversal markup and transition logic that human-controlled characters use.

There are a number of worthwhile extensions that could be applied to this approach: as mentioned previously, the algorithm can be modified so that climb paths can be generated between any two locations within the climb mesh. This allows dynamic obstacle avoidance and path replanning. Games with mid-climb combat elements would especially benefit from those features.

Furthermore, using Euclidean distance as the edge cost worked well for *Fuse*, but might not be accurate enough for more complex climbing setups. If this approach is implemented for a game with very long or complex traversal segments, then the climb path generation should consider animation playback times to accurately detect the shortest path.

References

[CD 14] Crystal Dynamics. 2014. *Tomb Raider* [PC, Xbox 360, PS3]. Redwood City, CA.

[DeBoor 78] de Boor, C. 1978. *A Practical Guide to Splines*. Springer Verlag, New York.

[EA 08] Electronic Arts DICE. 2008. *Mirror's Edge* [Xbox 360]. Stockholm, Sweden.

[Farin 97], Farin, G. 1997. *Curves and Surfaces for Computer Aided Geometric Design*, 4th edn. Academic Press, San Diego, CA.

[IG 13] Insomniac Games. 2013. *Fuse* [Xbox 360, PS3]. Burbank, CA.

[Mononen 12], Mononen, M. 2012. Recast and Detour, a navigation mesh construction toolset for games. http://code.google.com/p/recastnavigation/ (accessed July 21, 2014).

[Snook 00] Snook, G. 2000. Simplified 3D movement and pathfinding using navigation meshes. In *Game Programming Gems*, pp. 288–304. Charles River Media, Newton, MA.

18

Steering against Complex Vehicles in *Assassin's Creed Syndicate*

Eric Martel

18.1 Introduction

The different worlds in which videogames exist are becoming more and more complex with each passing day. One of the principal reasons NPCs appear intelligent is their ability to properly understand their environments and adjust their behaviors accordingly. On *Assassin's Creed Syndicate*, part of the mandate for the AI team was to support horse-drawn carriages at every level for the NPCs. For this reason, we adapted the NPCs' steering behaviors to navigate around a convex hull representing the vehicles instead of using a traditional radius-based avoidance. We succeeded in building general-purpose object avoidance behavior for virtually any obstacle shape.

A real-time JavaScript implementation of this material is available at http://steering.ericmartel.com should you wish to experiment with the solution as you progress throughout the article.

18.2 Challenges and Initial Approaches

Most object avoidance steering behaviors are implemented by avoiding circles or ellipses (Reynolds 1999, Buckland 2005). In our case, the vehicles were elongated to such an extent that even by building the tightest possible ellipse encompassing the entire bounding box of the vehicle, we ended up with unrealistic paths from our NPC agents. They would venture far away from the sides of the vehicle despite having a straight clear path to their destination. We wanted NPCs to be able to walk right next to a vehicle like a person in real life would. Note that the solution provided here was only for the navigation of humanoids. Steering behaviors for the vehicles themselves are handled differently and will not be described here.

18.2.1 Navigation Mesh Patching

From the very beginning, we decided that the NPCs should reject a path request if it is physically impossible for them to pass when a vehicle is blocking their way. This implies that, in these situations, changes needed to be made to the navigation mesh. Considering that many vehicles can stop at the same time, each forcing the navigation mesh to be recomputed, we decided to time slice the process. In other words, several frames might be required before the pathfinder properly handles all the stopping vehicles. To avoid having NPCs run against them, a signal system is used to turn on the vehicle in the obstacle avoidance system as soon as it moves and then turn it off as soon as the navigation mesh underneath it is updated. Unfortunately, the steering technique described here will not identify situations where vehicles will completely block a path. The algorithms could be adapted, if required, to test the intersection with the navigation mesh outside edges.

18.2.2 Obstacle Avoidance

Classical obstacle avoidance provides an agent with a lateral pushing force and a braking force, allowing the agent to reorient itself and clear obstacles without bumping into them, as shown in Figure 18.1. Given circular or even spherical obstacles, this is pretty straightforward.

18.2.3 Representation Comparison

Starting off with our existing technology, we experimented with various representations. The first implementation used a circle-based avoidance, increasing the diameter of the circle to encompass the entire vehicle. Although this worked, it did not look realistic enough; agents would walk far away from the sides of a vehicle to avoid it, as is shown in Figure 18.2.

To mitigate the wide avoidance paths, we considered modifying the circular obstacles into ellipses. Ellipses are slightly more complicated to use for obstacle avoidance, as their orientation needs to be taken into account when calculating the lateral push and the breaking factor. Unfortunately, as seen in Figure 18.3, even without implementing them, we knew we would not get the kind of results needed, as the sides were still too wide. Another solution had to be created.

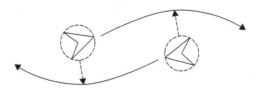

Figure 18.1

Circle-based obstacle avoidance between two agents.

18. Steering against Complex Vehicles in *Assassin's Creed Syndicate*

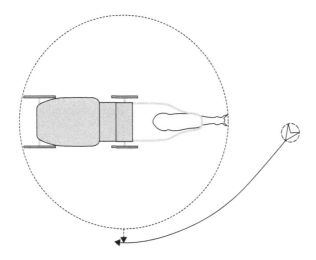

Figure 18.2

Circle-based representation of an elongated obstacle.

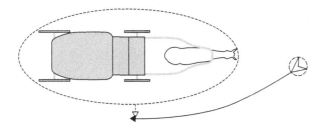

Figure 18.3

Ellipse-based representation of an elongated obstacle.

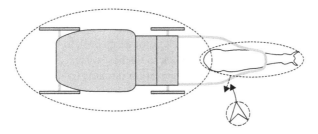

Figure 18.4

Multiple ellipses representing an elongated obstacle.

We considered representing each portion of the vehicle as an ellipse, as it would allow us to represent our collision volumes more accurately. The problem with this representation, as depicted in Figure 18.4, is that by using multiple ellipses, a nook is created between the horse and the carriage. Without handling multiple obstacles at the same time, one risks having the agent oscillate between both parts and then get stuck in the middle.

18.3 Convex Hull Generation

The best representation of the vehicle we could conceive was a convex hull, as it could wrap around all of the subparts of the vehicle without creating any concave sections. This would allow the NPC to steer against the horse-drawn carriage as if it were a single uniform obstacle.

Our obstacles are made out of multiple rigid bodies, each representing a subpart of the vehicle. Some carriages have two horses, others a single one, and after firefights or accidents, a carriage can be left with no horse at all.

18.3.1 Rigid Body Simplification

In order to reduce the number of elements in our data structures, we simplified the representation of our rigid bodies to 2D object-oriented bounding boxes (OOBB). Since our NPCs are not able to fly, we could forgo the complexity of 3D avoidance. By flattening down the 3D OOBB encompassing the rigid bodies provided by our physics engine, we managed to have an accurate representation of our vehicle from top view. In the following examples, we have omitted adding yaw or roll to the subparts (Figure 18.5).

When computing circle-based avoidance, it is easy to simply add the radius of the agent to the repulsion vector, thus making sure it clears the obstacle completely. In our case, we simply grew the shapes of our OOBB of half the width of the characters, making sure that any position outside that shape could accommodate an NPC without resulting in a collision. From that point on, NPCs are navigating as a single point against the expanded geometry of the vehicles.

18.3.2 Cases to Solve

We identified three main situations that need to be handled, pictured in Figure 18.6, ordered from most to least frequent. The most interesting case is the one where shapes are partially overlapping (Figure 18.6a). The algorithm to solve this case is provided in Section 18.3.4.

Two shapes are disconnected when all of the vertices of the first shape are explored finding that none of its edge segments intersect with the second shape, and that none of the vertices of either shape lie inside the other. When shapes are disconnected, we decided to simply merge the two closest edges. In our example from Figure 18.6b, the edges "AD" and "BC" would be removed. Starting from the first vertex of the bottom shape, we iterate on the shape until we reach vertex "A," then switch shape from vertex "B." The process continues until we reach vertex "C" at which point we go back to the initial shape from "D." The operation is complete once we loop back to the first vertex. As long as our vertices are kept in clockwise order, performing this operation remains trivial.

A case that we did not tackle in our implementation is demonstrated in Figure 18.7, where the shapes loop, creating two contours. Given the shape of our entities, this is simply

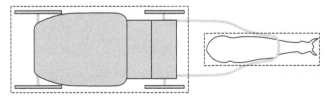

Figure 18.5

Object-oriented bounding boxes representing the obstacle subparts.

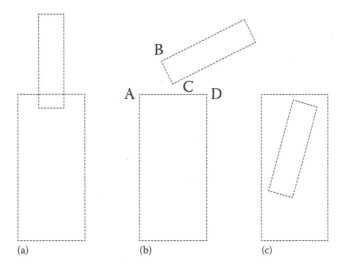

B
A C D

(a)   (b)   (c)

Figure 18.6

The various cases that need to be supported when joining shapes, from left to right:
(a) partial overlap, (b) disconnection, and (c) complete overlap.

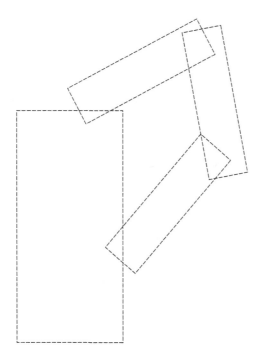

Figure 18.7

Additional case. When enough subparts are present or when the subparts themselves are
concave polygons, multiple contours have to be handled.

not required. It would be easy to adapt the algorithm to support multiple contours with a single convex hull built around the outer contour.

18.3.3 Building the Contour

Before diving into the construction of the contour, the following algorithms were chosen in order to keep things simple, understandable, and to make most of the intermediate data Vuseful. There might be specialized algorithms that are more efficient in your case, feel free to replace them.

First, let us take a look at a useful function, as shown in Listing 18.1, that will be used on multiple occasions in the code. This method simply moves an index left or right of a current value, while wrapping around when either ends of the list are reached. This will allow us to avoid having to include modulo operations everywhere in the code. Although adding `listSize` to `currentValue` might look atypical at first, it allows us to handle negative increment values which in turn make it possible to iterate left and right in the list.

Listing 18.1. Pseudocode to handle index movement in a circular list of items.

```
uint circularIncr(uint currentValue,
                  int increment,
                  uint listSize)
{
    return (currentValue + listSize + increment) % listSize;
}
```

What follows next is an example of how the algorithm merges and constructs intersecting shapes. As pictured in Figure 18.8, we start from a vertex outside of the second shape, and we iterate in a clockwise fashion as long as we are not intersecting with any edge of the second shape. When finding an intersection, we simply insert the intersection point and swap both shapes as we are now exploring the second shape looking for intersections until we loop around.

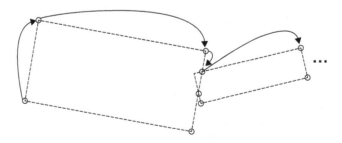

Figure 18.8

Algorithm for intersecting shapes. Merging the shapes by iterating over them, creating vertices on intersections.

The code in Listing 18.2 merges shapes one at a time. Instead of handling the complexity of merging n shapes at the same time, shapes are added to a contour that grows with every subpart added.

Listing 18.2. Pseudocode to merge shapes into a contour.

```
currVtx = newShapeToAdd;
altVtx = existingContour;

firstOutsideIndex = firstOutsideVtx(currVtx, altVtx);
nextVtx = currVtx[firstOutsideIndex];
nextIdx = circularIncr(firstOutsideIndex, 1, currVtx.size());

mergedContour.push(nextVtx);

while(!looped)

{
    intersections = collectIntersections(nextVtx,
                                         currVtx[nextIdx],
                                         altVtx);
    if(intersections.empty())
    {
        nextVtx = currVtx[nextIdx];
        nextIdx = circularIncr(nextIdx, 1, currVtx.size());
    }
    else
    {
        intersectionIdx =
            findClosest(nextVtx, intersections);
        nextVtx = intersections[intersectionIdx];
        // since we're clockwise, the intersection can store
        // the next vertex id
        nextIdx = intersections[intersectionIdx].endIdx;

        swap(currVtx, altVtx);
    }
    if(mergedContour[0].equalsWithEpsilon(nextVtx))
        looped = true;
    else
        mergedContour.push(nextVtx);
}
```

For the full source code, please visit the article's website listed in Section 18.1. Consider that `firstOutsideVtx` could fail if all the vertices of `currVtx` are inside `altVtx` as seen in Figure 18.6c. If the while loop completes and `mergedContour` is the same size as `currVtx`, either no intersections happened or all the vertices of `currVtx` are inside `altVtx`, which is easy to test.

18.3.4 Expanding the Convex Hull

At this point, we now have a list of vertices ordered clockwise that might, or might not, represent the convex hull. For the polygon to represent a convex hull, all of its interior angles need to be lower or equal to 180°. If an angle is greater than 180, it is easily solved by removing the vertex and letting its two neighbors connect to one another. Removing it from the array corrects this because of the use of ordered list of vertices. Listing 18.3 describes how this can be accomplished with a few lines of code by using the Z value of the cross product to determine on which side the angle is heading. It is important to always step back one vertex after the removal operation, as there is no guarantee that the newly created angle is not greater than 180° as well.

Listing 18.3. Pseudocode to create a convex hull out of a contour.

```
convexHull = contour.copy();
for(index = convexHull.size(); index >= 0; --index)
{
    leftIndex = circularIncr (index, -1, convexHull.size());
    rightIndex = circularIncr (index, 1, convexHull.size());

    goingLeft = convexHull[leftIndex] - convexHull[index];
    goingRight = convexHull[rightIndex] - convexHull[index];

    if(zCross(goingLeft, goingRight) < 0)
    {
        convexHull.removeAtIndex(index);
        index = min(convexHull.size() - 1, index + 1);
    }
}
```

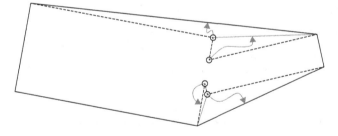

Figure 18.9

Removing vertices that make the polygon concave.

As can be seen in Figure 18.9, it is as if we are folding out the pointy ends of the polygon until we end up with a convex hull.

18.4 Obstacle Avoidance

Now that the geometry is constructed, we can go about shaping the NPCs' behavior around it. This implies that we must first find out if our current position or our destination is inside the convex hull. Any position between the vehicle's OOBB and the convex hull is actually a walkable area. If neither position is located inside the convex hull, we must then check if there is a potential collision between the NPC and the obstacle.

18.4.1 Obstacle Detection

Most steering behavior systems use a feeler system to detect potential incoming obstacles. In our case, to accelerate and parallelize the system, we utilize axis-aligned bounding boxes that are sent to the physics system. The physics system then matches pairs that are intersecting and allows us to easily know, from the gameplay code, which other entities to test for avoidance.

Once we know we have a potential collision, we can determine if either the start or end positions are inside the convex hull. Using a method similar to Listing 18.4, that is by counting the number of intersections between a segment starting at the tested position and ending at an arbitrary position outside of the polygon and with the polygon itself, we can determine whether or not we are located outside of the shape. An odd number of intersections signals that the position is inside. Otherwise it is outside, as our segment went in and out of the shape an even number of times.

Listing 18.4. Pseudocode to validate if a position is inside an arbitrary polygon.

```
// add small offset
testedXValue = findMaxXValue(vertices) + 5;

intersections = collectIntersections(point.x,

                                     point.y,
                                     testedXValue,
                                     point.y,
                                     vertices);

return intersections.size() % 2;
```

For an example of `collectIntersections` or how to check for intersections between segments, feel free to refer to the website listed in the introduction.

18.4.2 Movement around the Convex Hull

When we know that both our current position and destination are outside of the convex hull, a simple intersection check using a segment between both of these positions and the convex hull can confirm whether or not the NPCs are clearing the shape. Having expanded the shape by the radius of the agent guarantees us that if there is no intersection; the NPC is free to go in straight line and will not collide with the obstacle. If the agents have different radii, it is also possible to simply offset the intersection check by the radius of the agent, either on its right or left vector, depending on the relative side of the obstacle.

If an intersection is detected, the NPC must avoid the obstacle. Depending on the relative velocities, you might want to control on which side the avoidance occurs. For the purpose of demonstration, we define that our objective is to minimize the angle between our avoidance vector and our current intended heading.

From the intersection detection, we can extract the vertex information from both ends of the segment with which we intersect. As the vertices are in clockwise order, we know that we can explore their neighbors by decreasing the index of the start vertex to go on

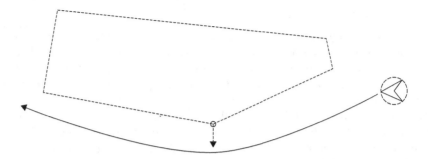

Figure 18.10

Obstacle avoidance when both the start and end points are outside of the obstacle.

the right, and increase the index of the end vertex to go on the left. We are looking for the furthest vertex to which we can draw a straight line without intersecting with the other segments of the convex hull, which also minimizes the angle difference with the intended direction. In Figure 18.10, the end vertex of the intersected segment happened to be the best vertex matching this criterion, as its next neighbor would cause an intersection with the convex hull, and the exploration on the right leads to a greater angle difference.

18.4.3 Movement into the Convex Hull

In the game, NPCs are able to interact with vehicles even while in movement. For this reason, it can happen that their interaction point lies inside the convex hull. In this case, two situations can occur: either the segment between the character and its destination intersects with the contour, or it does not. The convex hull being only a virtual shell around the vehicle does not prevent the agent from going through it, so if no intersection is found with the contour, the NPC can simply walk in straight line to its destination, as shown in Figure 18.11.

The real challenge when an intersection is detected is to find the right direction to send the NPC, since if it walks around the obstacle, it will eventually clear the contour and enter the convex hull. A solution for this problem is to find the edge of the convex hull that is closest to the destination. Doing this, we have two vertices that represent an entry point to the convex hull. By reusing part of the solution in Section 18.4.2, we iterate over the convex hull from our initial intersection toward the two vertices we found earlier. We are trying to find the closest vertex to us that minimizes the distance between it and one of the two vertices without

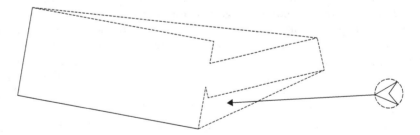

Figure 18.11

Obstacle avoidance when the destination is inside the convex hull.

18. Steering against Complex Vehicles in *Assassin's Creed Syndicate*

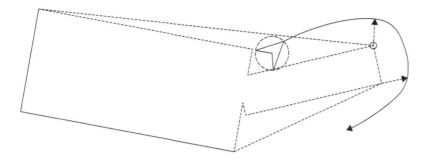

Figure 18.12

Obstacle avoidance when the agent is inside the convex hull.

intersecting with the contour. This distance can be calculated by summing the length of the edges of the convex hull as we are moving in either direction. As we progress, the edge of the convex hull that connects with space where the destination lies will be reached.

At this point, we know the destination is in a polygon, and we are about to enter it. Unfortunately, it is possible that the shape between the contour and the convex hull is a concave polygon. No trivial solution is available, but two well-known options are available to you. Either the NPC "hugs the walls" of the contour by following its neighbor edge until it gets a straight line between itself and the destination or the space is triangulated allowing the algorithm to perform a local path planning request, which will be described in Section 18.5.1.

18.4.4 Movement Out of the Convex Hull

When the agent lies inside the hull, we can deduce the way to exit the shape by reversing the operations of those proposed in Section 18.4.3. We first make the NPC navigate out of the polygon representing the difference between the contour and the convex hull. Once outside, the methods described in Sections 18.4.2 and 18.4.3 should be applied, as the destination will either be inside or outside of the convex hull (Figure 18.12).

18.5 Pushing It Further

The following suggestions are not required to make steering against arbitrary shapes work, but it could improve the quality of your results.

18.5.1 Triangulation from Convex Hull Data

When taking a closer look at Figure 18.9, one might notice that as we removed the vertices, we were actually adding triangles to the contour to push it outward and create the convex hull. As pictured in Figure 18.13, a simple adjustment to the algorithm can push the triangle data as the vertices are popped in order to create a simple local navigation mesh. Local path planning can be used to guide the obstacle avoidance going in and out, generate optimal paths, and simplify the logic required when positions are inside the convex hull.

18.5.2 Velocity Prediction

Given that the state of these obstacles are volatile, we did not spend the time to model the velocity of the subparts of the vehicle but only the obstacle's velocity. If you were to model

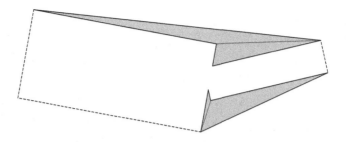

Figure 18.13

Adapting the convex hull generation algorithm to produce a navigation mesh inside the convex hull.

a giant robotic space snake, then allowing NPCs to predict where the tail will be ahead of time may be required, but it comes at the expense of computing the position of the subparts in advance.

In most cases, mimicking what humans would do gives the best results. In the case of our game, an agent crossing a moving vehicle will often try to go behind it. Modeling whether the agent is going roughly in the same direction, in opposite direction, or in a perpendicular direction will allow you to give more diversity in which vertex from the convex hull you want to target and how much you want to modulate the braking factor.

18.6 Conclusion

Converting obstacles' shapes to a convex hull really improved the quality of the navigation of our NPCs around them. This solution is also generic enough to be applied to any rigid body, from vehicles to destructible environments. Performance wise, by lazily evaluating the shape of the rigid body and caching the results for all surrounding characters, we managed to get the best of both worlds.

References

Buckland, M. 2005. *Programming Game AI by Example*. Plano, TX: Wordware Publishing.
Reynolds, C. W. 1999. Steering behaviors for autonomous characters, in *The Proceedings of Game Developers Conference 1999*, San Jose, CA. San Francisco, CA: Miller Freeman Game Group, pp. 763–782.

19

Predictive Animation Control Using Simulations and Fitted Models

Ingimar Hólm Guðmundsson, Hendrik Skubch,
Fabien Gravot, and Youichiro Miyake

19.1 Introduction

In the move toward more believable realism in games, animation and AI continue to play an important role. For *FINAL FANTASY XV's* diverse world, one of the challenges was the large amount of different types of characters and monsters. The need for a well-informed steering solution and total freedom for each team to implement animation state graphs that suited their needs called for an unconventional solution to the problem of accurate steering and path following. Our solution treats the game as a black-box system, learning the character's movement parameters to later build an independent motion model that informs steering. In the following sections, the steps taken to fulfill this aim are described, along with the unexpected side effects that came from simulating almost every character type in the *FINAL FANTASY XV.*

19.2 Getting Actors to Hit Their Marks

Games share one thing in common with theatre and cinema: actors must hit their marks. When the AI has no control over the actor's root motion, this problem quickly devolves from interpolating along a curve into begging the animators to stop changing the stop animations and blends. This can affect various aspects of gameplay such as in-engine cut-scenes as well as physical combat, where game actors will overstep their mark or worse, never reach it and the cut-scene will not progress.

Although this simple example is not the only challenge in steering actors, it is a good one to start with as it will highlight all the moving parts in the actor's update as it approaches its mark. In a typical game engine (Gregory 2009), the update order is something like:

Begin frame $\Rightarrow$ AI $\Rightarrow$ Steering $\Rightarrow$ Animation $\Rightarrow$ Physics $\Rightarrow$ End frame.

In each frame, we want to approach our goal and not fall off the mesh or bump into collision unless absolutely necessary. In the first frame, AI will decide that it wants to go to a specific goal point $\vec{p}$ and does the necessary pathfinding and informs steering of the path. Steering will have some model of the actor's motion capabilities, such as

- Min speed, v_{min}
- Max speed, v_{max}
- Acceleration, a

When steering starts to accelerate with its desired velocity vector along the path, animation will receive information about the desired velocity and will trigger an animation clip to play (using its internal representation of locomotion), and physics will ensure that the character does not pass through walls or the floor. In this setup, animation receives only two inputs from AI, the speed and the desired direction; it then outputs a transform to reflect the character motion. In some games, this might be the end of it; the transform is applied to the actor, and it reaches his or her target and everyone is happy. Now let us break down all the different ways this might break, and the actor will not reach his or her goal.

1. *Animation is lying just a tiny bit to steering*: In some cases, there could be a variant in one of the animation clips that might have a different acceleration or even exceed the min/max speeds.
2. *Other parts of the game interfere*: For either a single character or a range of characters, it may have been discovered that the animations needed some slight nudge here or there, and a brave programmer took it upon himself to add bespoke code that slightly modifies the movement.
3. *The environment is too restrictive*: For very sharp turns, an actor running at the AI's desired velocity will not necessarily know that it needs to slow down or else it will slam into a wall or fall off a ledge instead of smoothly following his or her path.
4. *The character's playback rate and/or size are being dynamically modified in the runtime*: It is clear that an actor that has been scaled up to double its size will have also doubled its speed, which if unchecked will wreak havoc when the actor tries to follow its path.

Each and every one of these problems can be addressed with a number of solutions, one being motion graphs (Ciupinski 2013). In the case of *FINAL FANTASY XV*, the solution was to assume that all the errors exist at all times and apply a form of machine learning to model the motion capabilities of actors, therefore solving all the problems with a single approach.

19. Predictive Animation Control Using Simulations and Fitted Models

19.3 Simulations to the Rescue

Our desire is to be able to construct an arbitrarily complex motion model that steering can use to accurately control actors at any given desired velocity or angle, moving an actor to the goal without ever accidentally leaving the navigation mesh. This means running simulations and, from the observed motion, building a set of parameters that approximate the actor's motion *accurately enough*. As described in Section 19.2, our update loop was something as shown in Figure 19.1.

In an update loop that is only built for offline simulations, we no longer need any AI or steering, as we want to control the actor in a different way. Furthermore, we are no longer interested in using the output from the actor to inform our future velocity; we only measure it. The new loop can be seen in Figure 19.2.

In this simulation loop, we replace the AI with a simulation controller that drives the movement space exploration. This is perfectly reasonable, as we are not interested in pathfinding or avoidance, only the velocity we feed to the animation and the effect it has on the actor.

19.3.1 Simulation Controller

The simulation controller is the piece of the update that manages the exploration of the motion range. As each game has a different way to initialize its actors, the only aim for the simulation controller is to interfere as little as possible with the *normal* way of spawning, initializing, and updating an actor.

There are a couple of requirements though

- We must ensure that the actor is of unit-scale size and playback rate.
- We must spawn the actor close to the origin and move it back when it strays too far, as floating point precision issues may affect the measurements.

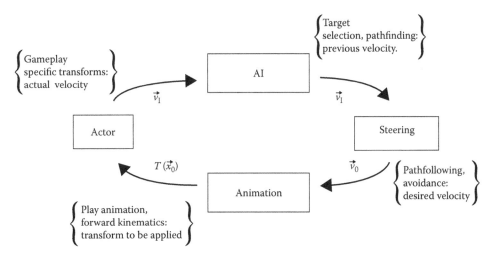

Figure 19.1

A typical game loop.

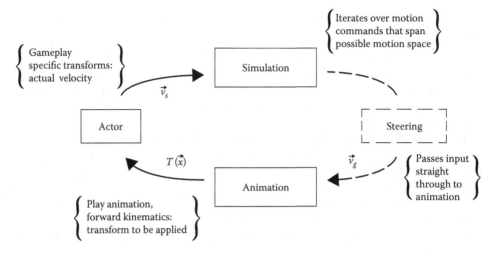

Figure 19.2

The simulation loop.

We expect the game to provide rough estimates of each actor's motion capabilities, such as its approximate minimum and maximum speed. This range will form the basis of the motion range to explore.

Once the actor has been initialized, a series of movement commands are issued to the actor. It is recommended that the actor be given a deterministic set of movement commands and that each command perform some sampling, so some measure of variance can be calculated, as well as noise can be filtered out in the analysis stages. Having a deterministic set of movement commands helps greatly in catching rare bugs, for example, a float overflow in the animation system.

Each simulation command C_s is a point on an interpolation over a range, such as $(v,\theta)_n \to (0,\theta)_n$, signifying the exploration of the motion from speed v to stopping, over n intervals between v and 0 with a constant facing θ. The set of simulation commands might differ slightly depending on the animation capabilities of the game, but generally, quantities such as speed, turn motion, and so on should be explored.

A command C_s is considered finished once the measurement has reached a stable output. For example, starting at speed v and wanting to reach speed v_g, the command is considered complete once the measured output v_s is stable.

19.3.2 Measurement Output

At the end of every command, the observed motion parameters are logged. Below the quantities measured are described with an attached notation set in Table 19.1.

We declare the rotational speed to be $\partial\theta/\partial t = \dot\theta$ for time t. The raw measurements are therefore a set of trajectories where each data point T_i on the trajectory is defined as the tuple:

$$T_i = \left(t, \vec{p}, \theta_s, \dot\theta_s, v_s\right)$$

19. Predictive Animation Control Using Simulations and Fitted Models

Table 19.1 Measurement Variables and Notation

Name	Notation	Description
Goal speed	v_g	The speed at which the actor should travel
Simulated speed	v_s	The speed that the actor actually traveled at
Desired angle	θ_g	The direction to which the actor should travel
Simulated angle	θ_s	The direction in which the actor traveled

with $\vec{p}$ as the position on the trajectory. From the trajectories T_i, other quantities can then be derived, such as variance of speed and rotation, distance travelled, and so on.

19.4 Building an Accurate Movement Model

Once the measurement phase is complete, the construction of the movement model that accurately describes the actor begins. The following sections will address different parts of an actor's motion and will give a rough overview of how the model parameters are formed.

19.4.1 Speed

The first constraint to determine is the speed range of an actor, as it will go on to inform the rest of the model construction. Our goal is to find the largest speed range in which the error between the goal speed v_g and the stable simulated speed v_s will not exceed a given minimum error. We determine the valid speed range using only data points where the actor is moving straight forward, that is, with $\dot{\theta} = 0$ and at a stable speed $\dot{v} = 0$. Figure 19.3 depicts the stable speeds obtained from fixed input speeds in these data (for a dog character). The error in this graph is the deviation between the resulting speed and the goal

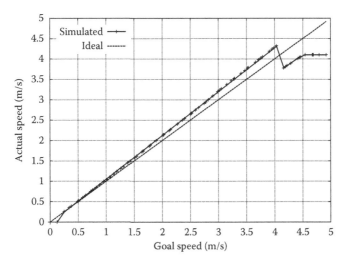

Figure 19.3

Speed measurements.

speed $\varepsilon = |v_g - v_s| / v_s$. We look for the largest interval of speeds in which ε does not exceed a fixed bound. Minimum and maximum speed then simply equate to the bounds of this interval.

If no speed range can be determined in this way, or if the speed range is significantly smaller than expected, the simulation is marked as a failure and no model is extracted, such as in Figure 19.3 where a drop in v_g occurs at around 4 m/s.

19.4.2 Stopping

Given the real speed range of the actor, the next part of the motion model can be constructed. As was mentioned in the introduction, stopping on the mark can be a difficult problem both in the real world as in the virtual one. We analyze trajectories where the actor moves at a stable speed in a straight line and stops due to receiving a goal speed of zero.

Since at runtime, we need to answer questions such as when to issue a stopping signal such that an actor will come to a halt at a predetermined goal position; we cast these data as a function of distance mapping onto velocity. In other words, given an available distance d, the function maps to the velocity at which the actor would take exactly a distance of d in order to come to a complete halt. Figure 19.4 shows an example of this curve. It clearly shows data points generated from different stopping animations, that is, stop-from-walking and stop-from-running. After manually analyzing a varied set of characters, we concluded that most data behaved in a piece-wise linear fashion, as shown in Figure 19.4.

19.4.3 Deceleration

Generalizing from stopping, we arrive at deceleration. Having accurate information about how long it takes to decelerate a given amount of speed allows the actors to fluidly decelerate before taking a turn and to confidently accelerate again afterward.

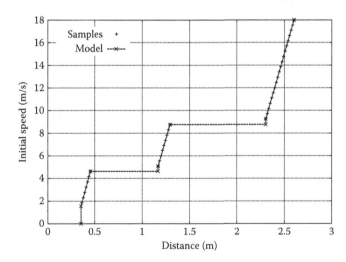

Figure 19.4

Stopping measurements.

19. Predictive Animation Control Using Simulations and Fitted Models

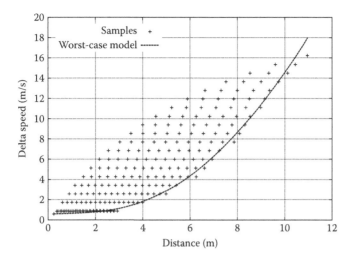

Figure 19.5

Deceleration measurements.

Figure 19.5 shows a typical result when recording the distance necessary to decelerate by a certain delta speed. Note the large spread for medium delta speeds. This is because the actual relationship depends on the absolute speed, not just the relative speed. The faster an actor travels, the larger a distance is necessary to decelerate by 1 m/s.

Instead of representing the full 3D relationship, we opted to project the data into 2D and use a worst-case estimate:

$$\Delta v(d) = ad^2 + bd + c\sqrt{d} \tag{19.1}$$

With only three parameters, this is a very compact representation that is easily regressed by using sequential least squares programming. The increase in fidelity when using a 3D representation was deemed too small to warrant the additional memory investment necessary.

19.4.4 Overshoot

Overshoot is a measurement for how much space a character requires to turn. More specifically, it is the distance between the trajectory that a character would follow if it would follow the control input perfectly and the actual trajectory measured after a change in direction has been completed. Figure 19.6 shows the measured distance between ideal and performed trajectory.

This overshoot distance can be represented as a function of velocity and angle.

Figure 19.7 shows the overshoot of a monster in *FINAL FANTASY XV*. We represent these data as a velocity function over distance and turn angle. The approximation is done as a set of piece-wise linear functions, uniformly distributed over angles between $0°$ and $180°$.

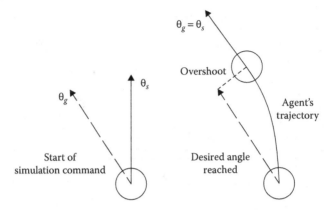

Figure 19.6

Overshoot definition.

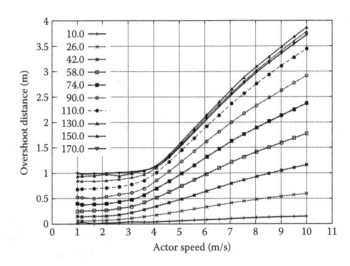

Figure 19.7

Actor speed versus overshoot distance.

19.4.5 Rotation Radius

We record the rotation radius of a character as a function of speed by letting the character run in a circle at a constant linear speed, as shown in Figure 19.8. Thus, we measure the character's rotational speed. We represent the rotation radius as a piece-wise linear function of speed. Thereby, we assume a constant maximum rotation speed for large proportions of the speed range. At runtime, this information is used to interrupt a movement command early and avoid characters getting stuck on a circular path around their goal position.

19. Predictive Animation Control Using Simulations and Fitted Models

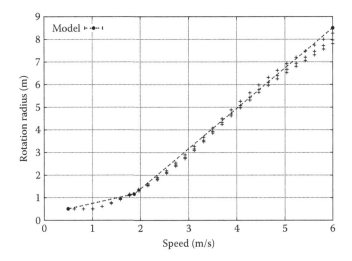

Figure 19.8

Rotation radius measurements.

19.5 Runtime

The extracted motion model is made available to inform steering decisions at runtime.

First and foremost, minimal and maximal speeds are used to limit the range of selectable speeds. The remainder of the data is used to improve control precision. Steering control and animation form a loop in which steering commands are sent to animation, which changes the physical state of the agent, which in turn is observed by steering.

The deceleration function informs the runtime of how much space is needed to achieve a certain negative Δv. Consequently, it is used to calculate the current control speed given a future goal speed. For example, if an agent is supposed to move at 2 m/s at a distance of 3 m, its current speed is capped by the deceleration function to 4 m/s for example. This is used in all cases where a future goal speed is anticipated, such as when charging for an attack and thus arriving with a certain speed at a target or following a path with a tight turn.

Collision avoidance, however, asserts the necessity to stop within a certain distance. The special case of stopping is handled by a stopping function. Deceleration is typically achieved by a combination of a blend and changes to the playback speed. In contrast, stopping typically is achieved by a separate animation altogether. Playing this animation does not fit the simple deceleration model we introduced in Section 19.4.3.

Whenever an agent is required to stop within a certain distance, be it in order to hit its mark, or avoid a collision, an upper limit for the control velocity is looked up in the stopping function. In addition, whenever the current physical velocity of the agent exceeds this limit, the control velocity is immediately pulled down to zero, thereby triggering a transition to a stopping animation. In order to avoid accidentally triggering this stopping maneuver due to noisy velocity measurements, the maximum control velocity is actually capped at 95% of this limit.

The overshoot function is used to calculate the maximum speed while taking a turn and when anticipating a future turn in a path currently followed. In addition, for characters without a turn-in-place animation, such as some larger monsters, it is also used to judge whether to turn left or right when aligning with a path. In case of an anticipated turn, an upper bound of future speed is simply a look up using the sine of the anticipated turn angle; the resulting velocity then serves as an input for the deceleration function to obtain an upper bound for the control speed as described above. In *FINAL FANTASY XV*, path information is imperfect, meaning that a path may only be part of the surrounding free space. Moreover, the path does not take moving obstacles into account. Thus, for immediate turns, both due to path following and due to collision avoidance, the available distance as given by collision avoidance sampling is used to look up a limit to the control speed in the overshoot function.

Finally, the rotation function is used to avoid circling around a target indefinitely by increasing the arrival radius, given an actor's current physical velocity and angle to its target.

19.6 Pipeline

All of this work can be wrapped up in a nice little continuous integration loop, as can be seen in Figure 19.9, containing the following steps:

1. Create a valid movement model for steering.
2. Provide the developers a view for an actor's movement model for the whole period of development.
3. Alert the developer when there is a problematic movement model that needs addressing.

Due to the fact that the simulation of an actor takes more time than to build the animation data per actor, the pipeline structure tries to reduce the lag as much as possible by running constantly. The choice of the next actor to simulate is made by a simple

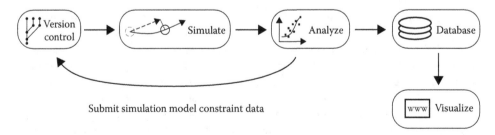

Figure 19.9

Continuous simulation pipeline.

19. Predictive Animation Control Using Simulations and Fitted Models

heuristic of the time since last simulation and whether the actor has been just added to the repository. Failures are logged to a database, and stakeholders are automatically notified.

19.7 Scaling Up

There are two scale issues to take into account when building the simulation pipeline.

19.7.1 Size and Playback

A game might want to scale the size of actors and expect the motion constraint model to still apply. Similarly, the animation playback rate might vary on a frame-to-frame basis. Both factors must be applied to the motion model and, depending on the different parts in the model, both size and/or time scales must be applied. As an example, the deceleration function (Equation 19.1 in Section 19.4.3) with respect to size scaling u and playback rate scale p becomes:

$$\Delta v(d,u,p) = p\left(\frac{ad^2}{u} + bd + c\sqrt{ud}\right)$$

The rest of the overall model is either multiplied by u, p, or both.

19.7.2 Content

When the need arises to scale up the number of entities via the use of prefabs, the simulation pipeline does not suffer as much from the time delay between authoring data and exporting constraints. However, there is still a possibility that the prefabs have an element in either some part of their unique-data setup or in code that will differentiate their motion, and there is no easy way to test this without simulating all users of the prefab and doing a similarity test between the results.

19.8 Benefits

The biggest benefit of this methodology is how well it scales to differences in characters and changes to the data and code throughout the development cycle. Precision is also increased with this methodology. As an example, the stopping distance is normally the distance of some "to-stop" animation plus whatever may be done to the animation in the runtime. This overall distance can be hard to parameterize at the authoring time, but the simulation can easily extract the worst case from the observed movement.

Issues, such as a nonmonotonic speed function, can be easily identified from a graph, instead of through loading the game. This is seen in an example of a *FINAL FANTASY XV* cat speed graph found in Figure 19.10.

When comparing the speed graphs of cats (Figure 19.10) and dogs (Figure 19.3), it is clear from the simulated data that cats are indeed more independent than dogs with respect to speed, at least in *FINAL FANTASY XV*.

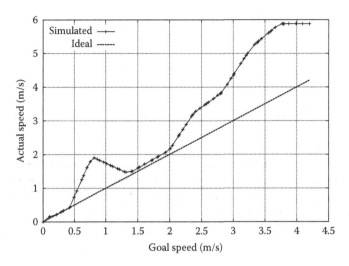

Figure 19.10

Speed measurements of a cat.

19.9 Conclusion

We have presented a way of significantly decoupling dependencies between AI and animation. This approach treats animation as the dominant party in this relationship of motion and shows a way of gaining benefit from such an approach.

Although significant work was invested in setting up and maintaining the pipeline, the work needed to identify and fix issues has dramatically decreased. Typically, it amounts to analyzing graphs on a web server and determining from there what the fault is. Common bugs include the gait being exported from the raw animation, so the actor does not have a fixed acceleration or a genuine code bug that has been introduced, which can be found by looking at the graphs by date and revision to determine what revision introduced the code bug.

Overall, the usage of simulations to improve steering control of an animation-driven agent has proved to be a success. It is not particularly expensive at runtime, as the models are mostly sets of piece wise linear functions and one nonlinear function. Furthermore, scaling of size, playback rate, or both are easily supported.

References

Ciupinski, J. 2013. Animation-driven locomotion with locomotion planning. In *Game AI Pro: Collected Wisdom of Game AI Professionals*, ed. S. Rabin. Natick, MA: A. K. Peters, Ltd, pp. 325–334.

Gregory, J. 2009. *Game Engine Architecture*. Wellesley, MA: A. K. Peters, Ltd.

19. Predictive Animation Control Using Simulations and Fitted Models

20

Fast Cars, Big City
The AI of Driver San Francisco

Chris Jenner and Sergio Ocio Barriales

20.1 Introduction

Driver San Francisco was an open-world driving game set in a fictionalized version of the city of San Francisco. The game's version of the city was very large, and in some areas had very dense traffic.

The player was given different missions that involved navigating through traffic at high speeds interacting with other mission-critical NPC vehicles, which also had to move quickly through the traffic. NPC vehicles might be chasing another vehicle, evading a vehicle, racing around a set course or trying to get to a particular point in the city. Also, at any point, the player could switch vehicles and start controlling any other car in the city; when this happened, it was the job of the AI to take over control of the player's vehicle, continue driving, and try to achieve the player's mission objective.

An important part of the game design was to produce dramatic, cinematic car chase sequences. Due to this, the AI-controlled vehicles as well as the player vehicle were often the centers of attention, being closely watched by the game camera. To create the most impressive visuals, it was a requirement that the AI code could control a vehicle simulated by the same system that was used for the player vehicle. We were not allowed to cheat by giving the AI vehicles more power or tighter grip between the tires and the road.

We also had to perform at a level that was similar to the best human players, so the cars had to be capable of coming close to the limits of friction when cornering, without pushing too far and skidding out of control.

The game was designed to run at 60 frames per second. This put a significant restriction on the amount of work we could do in any single frame. For this reason, the AI system was designed to be asynchronous and multithreaded. Individual tasks to update the state of a particular AI were designed to run independently and to update the state of the AI when the task was finished. Even if the task was finished after several frames, the AI would be able to continue intelligently while waiting for the result.

Planning a path for the AI vehicles in this environment posed several problems:

- The vehicles' main interactions were with other vehicles, so the path planning had to deal with moving obstacles. This meant that we had to look ahead in time as well as space and plan to find gaps in traffic that would exist at the time we got to them.
- Valid paths for vehicles must take into account parameters of the physical vehicle simulation, such as acceleration, turn rates, and tire grip if they are to be feasible for a vehicle to drive.

Classical path planning algorithms such as A* work well for static environments of limited dimension, but trying to search through a state space including time, velocity, and orientation would be impractical.

In this chapter, we present the path planning solution *Driver San Francisco* used: a three-tier path optimization approach that provided locally optimal paths. The three stages of the process—route finding, mid-level path planning, and low-level path optimization—will be detailed in the subsequent sections.

20.2 Active Life AI

Driver San Francisco had two distinct types of AI to control his or her vehicles: *Civilian Traffic AI* and *Active Life AI*. Civilian vehicles were part of a deterministic traffic system that simply moved vehicles around a set of looping splines throughout the city. Each spline had been defined to ensure that it did not interact with any other spline. Each civilian vehicle would follow a point around the spline, knowing that there was no chance of colliding with other civilian vehicles. Nontraffic vehicles were controlled by the more complex Active Life AI system. These vehicles perform much more complex actions than simply blending in with traffic, such as racing, chasing, or escaping from other vehicles. The Active Life AI system performed much more complex path generation.

Driver San Francisco's most important gameplay mechanic, *shift*, allowed players to switch cars at any point. When the player activated *shift*, the vehicle the player left was taken over by an Active Life AI, which would start running the appropriate behavior to replace the player. For example, if the player *shifted* out of a cop car chasing a suspect, the AI would give a "chase target" behavior to the cop car, which would continue what the player was doing before the switch. If the player had been driving a civilian vehicle with no particular objective, the AI would select the closest free slot on the traffic splines and try to rejoin traffic; as soon as this happened, the driver was downgraded to a regular civilian vehicle.

20.2.1 Vehicle Paths

As any car could transition from civilian to Active Life and vice-versa at any moment, it was important to keep an unified system to define what vehicles were trying to do, so each one owned a *vehicle path*. These paths represented the predicted movement of the vehicle for the next couple of seconds, and the AI system was constantly updating them—actually, path updating happened approximately every second. Paths were updated appending new segments at their end before they were completely used. So, from the vehicle's perspective, the path was continuous. Updating paths this way allowed us to run costly calculations in parallel over multiple frames. Even the player's vehicle had a path!

The way vehicle paths were generated depended on the system that was controlling them. For player vehicles, physics and dead reckoning generated this path; traffic splines generated paths for civilians. For Active Life AIs, we used different levels of detail, based on range to the AI. We had three levels of detail (LODs):

- AIs using the lowest level of detail generated their paths using only their route information. A route, as we will talk about later, is a list of roads that can take us from point A to B. These roads are defined as splines, and these splines are connected by junction pieces. Routes were basically very long splines. Low-LOD vehicle paths were a portion of the route's spline with an offset to simulate that they were driving in a certain lane on the road.
- The next level of detail used mid-level paths to generate vehicle paths. A mid-level path is a first approximation of a good path for a vehicle. It uses the route information plus some extra details, such as lane information (we prefer maintaining our current lane if possible), some rough dynamic obstacle avoidance, and some speed limit data. Mid-level path generation is described in detail in a subsequent section.
- Finally, the highest level of detail was used for vehicles around the player that were in camera and needed to be fully simulated and as polished as possible. They used the full three-tier path generation (route finding, mid-level path planning, and low-level path optimization).

The vehicle paths also supported another significant optimization in the game's simulation code. The large number of vehicles being simulated in the world at any one time would be very costly in terms of physics and vehicle handling. For this reason, there was a system of simulation level of detail acting at the same time as, but independently of the AI LOD. When vehicles were close to the player, they would be fully simulated by the physics and handling system, and they would follow their paths using the AI path-following system to calculate driving input into the handling system. When vehicles were distant from the player, they could be removed from the physics engine and vehicle-handling code, and simply placed at the position defined by their path for that particular time.

20.2.2 Driver Personalities

In the game, AIs had different goals, but also different driving styles or *personalities*. AIs had a set of different traits that defined their characters. Some examples of these traits were:

- Likeliness to drive in the oncoming traffic.
- Likeliness to drive on sidewalks.
- Preferred driving speed.
- How desirable highways, alleyways, or dirt roads were?
- How strongly hitting other vehicles should be avoided?

Personality traits affected every stage of the path planning, as we will see in later sections.

20.3 Road Network

Our virtual San Francisco was, in the eyes of the AI, a network of interconnected roads. For each of these roads, the game exposed the following information, as shown in Figure 20.1:

- A spline that represents the road.
- Each road had a start and an end extremity. For each extremity, we had:
- A list of roads that were connected to the extremity.
- Cross-section information: This defines the number of lanes at the extremity, as well as the width and the type of each of these lanes.

In the example, our road has two directions. We call the lanes that travel from the *start* to the *end* extremity as "with traffic" lanes, and the ones traveling in the opposite direction are called "oncoming." The example road presents two "with traffic" and two "oncoming" lanes; it also has a sidewalk on the oncoming side (the left-most lane on the cross section) and a sidewalk on the right side of the road that disappears at the end of the spline.

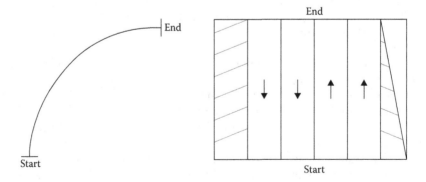

Figure 20.1

An example road spline with its cross section information.

20.4 Route Finding

The path generation process for Active Life AIs started by selecting the roads that these vehicles would use to reach their destination. The goal was to generate a list of connected roads, a *route*, which allowed cars to drive to their destination. For this, we used the connectivity information in the road network.

Depending on the goal or behavior of a vehicle, we used one of the following two methods to generate a route:

- A traditional A* search on the road network was used when we knew what our destination road was.
- A dynamic, adaptive route generator was used by the AI when its objective was to get away from a pursuer. For more details on this system, readers can refer to Ocio (2012).

Due to the size of the map and the strict performance requirements the AI systems had to meet (*Driver San Francisco* runs at 60 FPS on Xbox 360, PS3 and PC), we split the map in three different areas, which are connected by bridges, and used a hierarchical A* solution. If two points, A and B, were in different areas, we would first find a path to the closest bridge that connected both areas, and then find a path from the bridge to position B on the second area.

The path planning system itself imposed extra requirements. For instance, we always needed to have "enough road length" ahead of our vehicle, so sometimes an artificial node was appended at the end of the route. This was very often the case when an AI was following another vehicle, and both cars were pretty close to each other. This extra road allowed vehicles to predict where they should be moving to next and helped them maintain their speed. This will be explained in the following sections. During a high-speed chase, approaching junctions required a constant reevaluation of the intentions of the vehicle being chased. The goal was to predict which way the chased car was trying to go. We achieved this by making use of our simplified physics model that provided us with a good estimation of what a car was capable of doing based on its current state and capabilities. Figure 20.2 depicts the problem.

Route finding was also affected by the personality of the driver. The cost of exploring nodes varied based on the specific traits of the AI, and this could produce very different results. For example, civilian-like drivers could follow longer but safer routes to try and avoid a dirt road, whereas a racer would not care. Finally, AIs would, in some situations, try to avoid specific roads. For instance, a getaway driver would try to not use roads with cops.

20.5 Mid-Level Path Planning

Driver San Francisco's path planning solution did not look for optimal paths, as a more traditional A*-based approach would normally do. Instead, we were trying to generate locally optimal paths by optimizing some promising coarser options that we called *mid-level paths*. Mid-level path planning was the second stage of our three-tier process that happened after a route had been calculated.

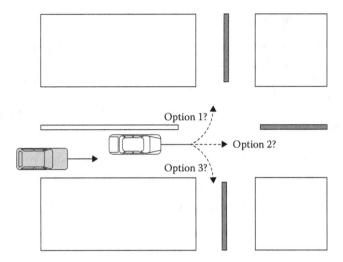

Figure 20.2

When chasing another vehicle, our AIs needed to decide which road the chased car was going to take at every intersection.

The route was defined in terms of the splines describing the center lines of the roads we wanted to follow, but it contained no information about which road lane we should drive down. The mid-level path allowed us to specify where on the road the vehicle should drive. The mid-level path was generated by searching for a path between a set of possible path nodes spread out in a grid over the road in front of the vehicle. The search space began at the current position of the vehicle and extended forward down the road far enough that the path would be valid for several seconds. The search space would typically be about 100 m in length. We placed sets of nodes at regular intervals over this part of the spline. With regard to width, one node was placed in each traffic lane. We show an example search space in Figure 20.3.

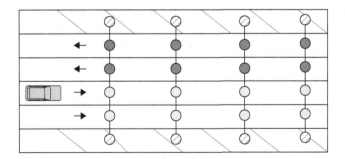

Figure 20.3

Node sets placed every few meters along the roads in the route constitute our search space for the midlevel path planning.

Once the search space was defined, we generated all the possible paths from the vehicle to each node on the last set, scoring them, and then selecting the five best options, which became the seeds for the optimizer. Evaluating a path meant giving each node used a numeric value; the final cost would be the sum of all the individual values. The game used costs for paths, which meant the higher the number, the less ideal the path was. The criteria used to generate these costs were:

- Nodes near dynamic obstacles (i.e., other vehicles) were given some penalty; if the obstacle was static (e.g., a building), the node could not be used.
- We always preferred driving in a straight line, so part of the score came from the angle difference between the vehicle's facing vector and the path segment.
- Depending on the driver AI's personality, some nodes could be more favorable. For example, a car trying to obey traffic rules will receive big penalties from driving on sidewalks or in the oncoming lane, whereas a reckless driver would not differentiate between lane types.

Figure 20.4 shows a couple of example mid-level paths and their costs.

In the example, the cost calculation has been simplified for this chapter, but the essence of the process remains. Moving in a straight line costs 1 unit and switching lanes costs 2 units. Driving close to another car costs an additional point, so does driving in the oncoming lane. With these rules, we calculated a cost of 5 for the first path and 11 for the second one.

Although in Figure 20.4, we treated other vehicles as static when we calculated the cost of driving next to an obstacle, in the real game, these calculations were made taking into account current vehicle speeds and predicting the positions of the obstacles (by accessing their *vehicle paths*). So path 2 could potentially have been scored even higher in a couple of locations. For example, the first node, which got a cost of 4, could have produced a bigger cost if the car driving in the opposite direction was moving. Path 1 could have even just been a completely straight line, if the vehicles we are trying to avoid in the example were moving fast enough, so they were not real obstacles for our AI!

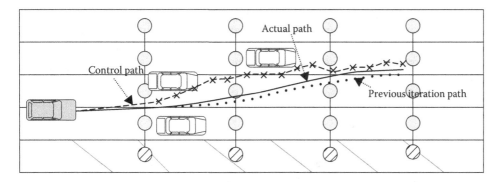

Figure 20.4

Two possible midlevel paths found for the given search space; path 1 has a lower cost, so it would be the preferred option.

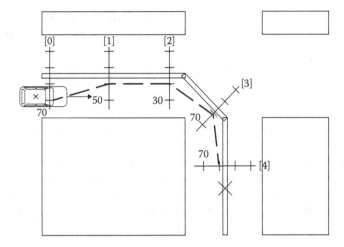

Figure 20.5

Midlevel paths contained information about the maximum speed the vehicle could travel at each of their nodes.

Another piece of information we could get out of mid-level was speed information and, particularly, speed limitations, or how fast a corner can be taken without overshooting. Starting from the last node set backward, we calculated the maximum speed at certain nodes based on the angle that the path turned through at that node. This speed was then propagated backward down the path based on the maximum acceleration/deceleration, so the path contained some information the vehicle could use to start slowing down before taking a corner. Figure 20.5 shows an example mid-level path with speed limits.

In the example, calculations would start at node set 4. The maximum speed at that node is the maximum desired speed for our vehicle (let us use 70 mph for this). Traveling from node 3 to node 4 is almost a straight line, so the vehicle can travel at maximum speed. However, moving from node 2 will require a sharp turn. Let us say that, by using the actual capabilities of our car, we determined the maximum speed at that point should be 30 mph. Now, we need to propagate this backward, so node 1 knows the maximum speed at the next node set is 30. Based on how fast our vehicle can decelerate, the new speed at node 1 is 50 mph. We do the same thing for the very first node, and we have our speeds calculated. Path speeds also took part in the path cost calculation; we tried to favor those paths that took us to the last set of nodes faster than others.

20.6 Low-Level Path Optimizer

Mid-level paths represented a reasonable approximation of a path that could be driven by a vehicle, but this was not good enough for our needs. Although the velocity of the path has been calculated with an idea of the capabilities of the vehicle, the turns have no representation of the momentum of the vehicle or the limits of friction at the wheels. These problems are resolved by the low-level path optimizer.

The low-level optimizer uses a simplified model of the physics of the vehicle, controlled by an AI path-following module, to refine the path provided by the mid-level into a form that a vehicle could actually drive. When the constraints on the motion of the vehicle are applied to the mid-level path, it is likely to reduce the quality of the path—perhaps the vehicle will hit other cars or skid out of control on a tight corner. These problems are fixed by an iterative path optimization process.

To choose a good path, it was necessary to have a method of identifying the quality of a particular path. This was done by creating a scoring system for paths that could take a trajectory through the world and assign it a single score representing the desirability of the path. Good paths should move through the world making forward progress toward our goal as close as possible to a desired speed while avoiding collisions with other objects. The aim of the optimization process is to find a path with the best possible score.

The environment through which the vehicles were moving is complex, with both static and dynamic obstacles to avoid, and a range of different target locations that could be considered to be making progress toward a final goal. To simplify the work of the optimizer, the environment is initially processed into a single data structure representing where we want the vehicle to move. This structure is a potential field, in which every location in the area around the vehicle is assigned a "potential" value. Low-potential areas are where we want the vehicle to be, and high-potential areas are where we want the vehicle to move from. Good paths can then be found by following the gradient of the potential field downward toward our goal.

The various different systems that came together to form the low-level path optimizer are described in the following sections.

20.6.1 Search Area

Before the optimizer could start generating paths, it needed to prepare data to use during its calculations. The first piece of data we prepared was a small chunk of the world where the path planning process would take place, the *search area*.

A rectangle was used to delimit the search area. This rectangle was wide enough to encompass the widest road in the network, and it was long enough to allow the vehicle to travel at full speed for a couple of seconds (remember mid-level paths were generated for this length). The area was almost centered on the AI vehicle, but not quite; while the car was indeed centered horizontally, it was placed about ¼ along the rectangle's length. Also, the area was not axis aligned. Instead, we would use the vehicle's route to select a position in the future and align the rectangle toward this point. Figure 20.6 shows an example rectangle.

After the rectangle was positioned, we detected the edges of the roads and used them to calculate inaccessible areas. Vehicles in *Driver San Francisco* were only able to drive on roads and some special *open areas*, designer-placed zones attached to a road spline that we wanted to consider as a drivable area. Likewise, we had *closed* areas or zones that we wanted to block, such as a static obstacle. Figure 20.7 shows the previous search zone, now annotated with some example areas.

In this example, the lower left building was cut by an open area, and a road separator (closed area) was added to the first road in the route.

The search area was used to define the limits within which we calculated a potential field, where the potential of a particular area represents the desirability of that location for our AI.

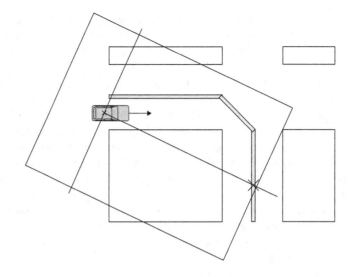

Figure 20.6

The search area is a rectangular zone that encompasses the surroundings of the AI vehicle.

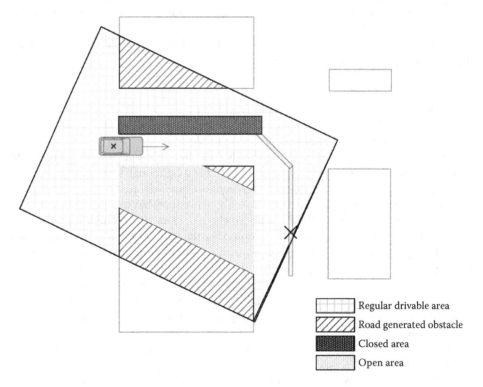

	Regular drivable area
	Road generated obstacle
	Closed area
	Open area

Figure 20.7

The search area's static obstacles were calculated from the road information and from some special areas placed by designers on the map to open or close certain zones.

20. Fast Cars, Big City

Movements through the potential field toward our target should always result in a lowering of the potential value. Areas that were inaccessible because of static or dynamic obstacles needed to have high potential values. As the path planning algorithm was trying to find a path that was valid for several seconds into the future, and other vehicles could move a significant distance during the time that the path was valid, it was important that we could represent the movement of obstacles within the potential field. For this reason, we calculated both a static potential field and a dynamic potential field. By querying the static potential field for a particular location, querying the dynamic potential field at the same location for a particular time, and then summing the results, we could find the potential for a location at a particular time. Similarly, we could find the potential gradient at a location at a particular time by summing the potential gradient value from both fields.

20.6.2 Static Potential Field

With the search area defined, the next data calculated were a static potential field. This was used to help us define how movement should flow—in what direction while avoiding obstacles. It worked almost as water flowing down a river. This potential field was created using the fast marching method (Sethian 1996). The search area triangle was split into a grid, so we could do discrete calculations. We set a row of goal positions at the end part of the search area rectangle and calculated the values for each cell in the grid.

For the algorithm, we needed to define the propagation speed at each cell, and this came mainly from the type of lane below the cell's center position and the personality of the AI driver. For a civilian driver, for example, a cell on the oncoming late should be costlier to use, which means the gradient of the field on those cells will be pointing away from them. Figure 20.8 shows what the field's gradient would look like in our example.

In this example, we set two goal cells for the potential field. With a civilian personality, oncoming lanes should normally be avoided, and sidewalks should be avoided at all costs. This produced a nice gradient that helps navigate toward the goals. If we dropped a ball on any cell and move it following the arrows, we will end up at the objective cell.

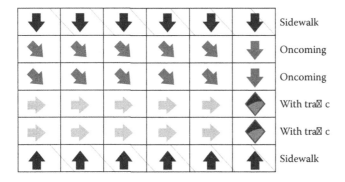

Figure 20.8

The search area was split into cells, and a potential field was generated to show how movement should flow to avoid static obstacles.

20.6.3 Dynamic Potential Field

AIs in *Driver San Francisco* had to deal with static obstacles but mostly with dynamic, moving ones. Although the static potential field was necessary to avoid walls, we needed a way to produce some extra forces to avoid surrounding vehicles. The approach taken in *Driver San Francisco* was to apply these forces as an extra layer on top of the static field.

The dynamic potential field could be queried at any point for any particular time. If we visualized it overtime, we were able to see forces produced around vehicles, pushing things out of the obstacle. Clusters of vehicles could produce gaps between them or forces to go around the whole cluster, depending on how far apart the different vehicles were. Figure 20.9 shows an example.

20.6.4 Simple Physics Model

The vehicle motion in the game was modeled using a complex physics engine with 3D motion, and collisions between dynamics and with the world. Vehicle dynamics were calculated using a wheel collision system and modeling of the suspension extension, which gave information about tire contacts with the world feeding into a model of tire friction. The wheels were powered by a model of a vehicle drive train applying a torque to the wheels.

This model was computationally expensive, but we needed to get some information about what constraints this model applied to the motion of the vehicle into our path planning algorithm, in order to create paths that the vehicle was capable of driving.

The fundamental aspects of vehicle behavior come from the torque applied by the engine and the tire forces on road, and this part of the vehicle simulation can be calculated relatively quickly. We implemented a simple 2D physics simulation for a single vehicle, driven by the same inputs as the game vehicle. This simulation shared the engine and drive-train model and the tire friction calculations from our main game vehicle-handling code but made simplifying assumptions about how the orientation of the vehicle changed as it was driving. Parameters of the handling model were used to ensure the simulation of vehicle was as close to the full game simulation as possible. The results of collisions were not modeled accurately; this was not a significant problem as the aim of the optimization process was to avoid collisions, so any paths that lead to collisions were likely to be rejected by the optimization process.

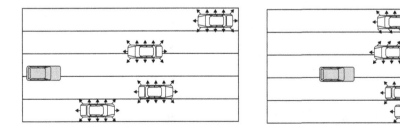

Figure 20.9

The dynamic potential field dealt with moving obstacles, generating forces around them so they could be avoided.

20.6.5 AI Path Following

To control the vehicle in the simple physics simulation, a simple AI path-following module was used. This module was exactly the same as the AI that was used to follow paths in the real game. The AI was fed with information about the current dynamic state of the vehicle and details of the path it was expected to follow. The module calculated controller input based on these data that were sent to the vehicle simulation. The action of the AI in any frame is based on the desired position and orientation of the vehicle, as defined in the path it is following, at a time in the future.

Internally, the AI used a simple finite-state machine to define the type of maneuver that was being attempted. Each state had some heuristics that allowed the control values to be calculated based on the differences between the current heading and velocity and the target position and orientation of the vehicle.

20.6.6 Simulating and Scoring a Path

The physics simulation and AI code could be used together to simulate the progress of a vehicle following a path. The physics simulation could be initialized with the current dynamic state of the vehicle, and then it could be stepped forward in time using the AI module to generate control inputs designed to follow a particular control path.

The output of this simulation was the position and orientation of the vehicle at each step of the simulation. We will refer to this series of position/orientation pairs as an actual path for a vehicle. This path generated for a particular control path is the trajectory we would expect the vehicle to follow if the control path was used to control the full game simulation representation of the vehicle. It is worth noting that we expect the actual path to deviate from the control path to some extent, but that the deviation should be small if the control path represents a reasonable path for the vehicle to take, given its handling capabilities.

The score for a particular control path is calculated by considering the actual path that the vehicle follows when given that control path. The total score is calculated by summing a score for the movement of the vehicle at each step of the physics simulation. In our case, we chose to assign low scores for desirable motion and high scores for undesirable motion, which leads to us trying to select the path that has the lowest total score. The main aim of the scoring system was to promote paths that moved toward our goal positions, avoided collisions, and kept the speed of the vehicle close to a desired speed. To promote these aims, the score for a particular frame of movement was calculated by summing three different terms:

- Term 1 was calculated from the direction of the movement vector of the vehicle over that frame, compared with the gradient of the potential field at the vehicle's location and the time of the frame. The value of the dot product between the two vectors was scaled and offset to add a penalty to movements that went toward higher potential.
- Term 2 was calculated by considering the current speed of the vehicle and the desired speed. The absolute value of any difference between the two was added to the score.
- Term 3 was calculated based on collisions. If the physics engine had found any collisions for the vehicle on that frame, a large penalty was added to the score.

The three terms were scaled by factors we arrived at empirically to give the best results.

20.6.7 Optimizing a Path

A single mid-level path can be converted to a path that is suitable for the capabilities of the vehicle that has to drive it. Initially, the mid-level path is converted into control path by sampling points from it at regular time intervals, corresponding to the frame times for the simplified vehicle simulation. This control path is then scored by passing it through the simplified simulation system as described in Section 20.6.6, which generates an actual path for the vehicle. This is shown in Figure 20.10.

This actual path can then be compared with the potential field and used to generate an optimized control path that we expect to have a lower score. First, the actual path is converted to a control path by using the positions of the vehicle at each frame to represent the positions in the control path. These positions are then adjusted based on the gradient of the potential field at those points. This process will push the path away from areas of high potential—that is, obstacles and parts of the world where we would prefer the vehicle not to drive. Figure 20.11 shows the results of this first iteration of the optimization process.

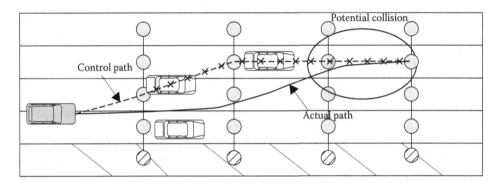

Figure 20.10

The first control path is created from the midlevel path we used as a seed and can still present problems, such as potential collisions.

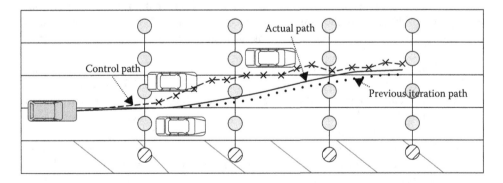

Figure 20.11

Vehicle positions along the first actual path are modified by the potential field; we use this as our second control path, which generates an optimized version of the original actual path.

This optimized control path is then ready for evaluation by the scoring algorithm and can be optimized again in an iterative process while the score continues to decline. The paths that we are dealing with only last for a few seconds, and over that time, the motion of the vehicle is initially dominated by its momentum. The control input can only have a limited effect on the trajectory of the vehicle through the world. Due to this, we found that three or four iterations of the optimization loop were enough to approach a local minimum in scoring for a particular mid-level path starting point.

20.6.8 Selecting the Best Path

The optimization process begins with a set of five potential paths from the mid-level planner and ends up with a single best path that is well suited to the capabilities of the vehicle that is expected to follow the path. Each mid-level path was optimized in turn, iterating until it reached a local minimum of score. The path that leads to the lowest score overall is selected as the final path and returned to the vehicle to be used for the next few seconds.

20.7 Conclusion

Driver San Francisco's AI used state-of-the-art driving AI techniques that allowed the game to run a simulation with thousands of vehicles that could navigate the game's version of the city with a very high level of quality, as our path generation and following used the same physics model as any player-driven vehicle. The system was composed of multiple levels of detail, each of which updated vehicle paths only when required to do so. This allowed the updates to be spread asynchronously across many threads and many frames, meaning the game could run smoothly at 60 FPS. Path optimization allowed the system to deal efficiently with a world composed of highly dynamic obstacles, a world which would have been too costly to analyse using more traditional A*-based searching.

References

Ocio, S. 2012. Adapting AI behaviors to players in driver San Francisco: Hinted-execution behavior trees. In *Proceedings of the Eighth AAAI Conference on Artificial Intelligence and Interactive Digital Entertainment (AIIDE 12)*, October 10–12, 2012, Stanford, CA.

Sethian, J. A. 1996. A fast marching level set method for monotonically advancing fronts. *Proceedings of the National Academy of Sciences* 93(4), 1591–1595.

21

A Unified Theory of Locomotion

Graham Pentheny

21.1 Introduction

AI character movement in games is a complex problem with many disparate solutions. Character movement techniques must account for many considerations and constraints. Different movement solutions for games address different aspects of the problem, necessitating a combination of complementary solutions for robust character movement. Often, combining multiple movement systems results in complex, intricate, and brittle logic that is both difficult to debug and reuse.

The unified theory of locomotion is a common language by which all movement systems can be defined. Common systems such as velocity obstacle collision avoidance, steering behaviors, and PID controllers can be viewed as specific applications of this theory, with their own individual strengths. Viewing movement systems in this way can help solve many issues faced in aggregating multiple movement systems together. The unified theory of locomotion is a common language for movement that can provide a basis for improving AI movement systems to be more robust to design changes, debugging, and experimentation.

21.2 Unified Theory of Locomotion

Character movement in games can be viewed as a series of steps, each answering a different question about the desired behavior. First and most fundamentally, the character must have a goal location. This is often determined by domain-specific high-level reasoning. Once a destination is established, the character must figure out the best way to move through the world to the destination. Path-planning algorithms are designed to solve this problem, breaking a larger positional goal into a series of shorter subgoals. Next, the character must determine what dynamic obstacles, if any, exist that would prevent them from getting to their next subgoal. These obstacles must be avoided, while maintaining a course toward the character's current subgoal. Finally, the character must move itself through the world, holding as close as possible to an ideal velocity.

The unified theory of locomotion breaks down movement solutions into the component values of motion that they influence and the type of influence they impart on each value. Movement systems are categorized as affecting one or more of the character's position, velocity, or acceleration values. Additionally, each system is categorized as either restricting or directing each value they influence. In this way, we can describe systems with terms like "velocity restrictor" and "acceleration director."

Systems that are defined as a value restrictor remove allowed values from the possible range of outputs. For example, a velocity restrictor generates a set of velocity vectors that the agent is not allowed to follow. A value director, conversely, determines a specific desired value for a movement attribute. Steering behaviors, for example, are generally "velocity directors," each outputting a single, ideal velocity value. By categorizing behaviors by the attributes they affect, and whether they direct or restrict them, we can easily compare two or more movement systems objectively.

21.3 Positional Restrictors and Directors

The simplest influencer on a character's movement is the environment that they move within. A simplified representation of the walkable area is usually generated in the form of a navmesh (Tozour 2004). A navmesh dictates which areas the character is able to move in and thus restricts the positions that a character can have in an environment. Because it is narrowing the infinite domain of positional values to a small subset, it is considered a "positional restrictor."

Conversely, path planning takes a goal location and directs the movement of a character though the environment toward that goal. Path planning determines a sequence of positional subgoals, defining the ideal movement direction and position of the character. Because it provides a specific position, or sequence of positions, it is considered a "positional director."

21.4 Velocity Restrictors and Directors

Reciprocal velocity obstacles (RVO) (van den Berg et al. 2011) are a common approach to local collision avoidance. This technique avoids localized collisions with obstacles and other characters by disallowing velocities that would result in a collision with another character or obstacle. As velocity obstacle approaches directly limit the allowed velocity values, velocity obstacles are an ideal example of a "velocity restrictor."

PID controllers (Melder and Tomlinson 2014) are a signal feedback control mechanism that is often used to control character velocity in games. PID controllers modify a character's velocity incrementally, attempting to smoothly match it to a goal velocity. Often, a character's ideal velocity will be computed as their fastest move speed along the direction of the path to their goal. PID controllers augment the character's velocity incrementally to match this ideal computed velocity. As PID controllers output a single velocity that respects the current set of velocity restrictions, PID controllers are considered a type of "velocity director."

21.5 Cascading Value Dependencies

An important aspect of the unified theory of locomotion is the relationship between restrictors and directors across physical values. Effects on lower level movement attributes indirectly affect higher level derived values. For example, positional restrictors also indirectly affect the velocities that the character is allowed to follow. Velocities that move the character into a disallowed position should also be disallowed. In a similar way, velocity restrictors also indirectly affect the domain of allowed accelerations.

The opposite, however, does not hold true. Velocity value restrictions should not affect the positions a character can reach. For example, certain types of characters may not be able to move backward very quickly. Although this characteristic imparts a restriction on the set of allowed velocities, it does not affect the positions where the character is allowed to be. Additionally, a character might have certain restrictions on the magnitude that it is capable of accelerating in a given direction. This should not affect what velocities the character is able to reach, just the steps necessary to achieve their desired velocity. This assertion, however, does not hold if the character is only able to accelerate in a single direction. This is a rare case that would necessitate special consideration and will not be addressed.

21.6 Combining Movement Systems

Often, combining multiple movement systems is difficult because each system is designed and tested in isolation. Combining multiple systems is greatly simplified by applying the unified theory of locomotion as a context for viewing movement systems. In this context, combining multiple systems simply consists of separately combining the restrictions and directions that each system imparts on each movement value. For example, context steering (Fray 2015) generates a map of velocity values and weights the benefit of each according to a set of rules. RVO performs a similar action, restricting sets of velocities that would result in a collision with an obstacle. As RVO and context steering are both velocity restrictors, we can compute the union of their velocity domain restrictions to combine their effects. This combination reaps the benefits of both systems; however, it simplifies them to a single result.

21.7 Value Arbitration and Combination

Combining multiple movement systems necessitates combining the restrictions and directions that each system imparts on each physical value. Combining restrictors simply involves generating the union of the sets of restrictions they impart on a physical value.

The process of combining value directors, however, is more involved. It consists of combining individually computed physical values, while respecting the limitations imparted by the restrictors. The director combination process can be broken down into two steps: high-level arbitration between directors and low-level combination of the resulting values.

High-level director arbitration determines which director techniques are combined to drive a character. High-level arbitration observes the character, its position, and its relationship to the other characters and the environment and makes a judgment about which value directors should affect the character and with what precedence. For example, a character with many neighbors might prefer a collision avoidance director over a formation-following director, as avoiding collisions is considered more important than maintaining formation. High-level arbitration is a subtle, domain-specific process that has a significant impact on the resulting character behavior. Designing an arbitration system involves understanding the behavioral considerations of a character, and how different systems address those considerations.

Low-level combinators are systems that combine the results of multiple value directors. Different techniques exist for combining value directors, and like high-level arbitrators, designing effective combinators involves understanding the problem domain and the character's desired behavior. A common low-level combinator approach is to prioritize each value director and combine their resulting values in priority order until a threshold of total influence is met. This ensures that important behaviors are more impactful on character behavior than others. This straightforward approach is often utilized successfully in the context of steering behaviors (Reynolds 1987).

In addition to prioritized summation, value directors can additionally be weighted, artificially amplifying their output. The result of each director is scaled by a specific, corresponding value before being combined. This approach gives control over how sensitive a specific system should be on a character and can be used to create unique movement styles or personalities.

21.8 Conclusion

The unified theory of locomotion provides a context for viewing and reasoning about character movement. It provides a common language that can describe the behavior of different movement systems. Each system can be broken down into either directing or restricting one of the physical movement values of a character. These directors and restrictors on low-level movement values also indirectly affect derived values.

Applying the unified theory of locomotion helps simplify and direct the combination of multiple movement systems. Value restrictors are combined by taking the logical union of their results, while combining directors are broken into high-level arbitration and low-level combination. High-level arbitration determines which value directors affect a character and in what precedence. Low-level combination aggregates the resulting values in a way that prioritizes more important behaviors while giving AI designers the ability to control the characteristics of a character's movement behavior.

References

Fray, A. 2015. Context steering: Behavior-driven steering at the macro scale. In *Game AI Pro 2*, ed. S. Rabin. Boca Raton, FL: CRC Media, pp. 173–181.

Melder, N., and S. Tomlinson. 2014. Racing vehicle control systems using PID controllers. In *Game AI Pro*, ed. S. Rabin. Boca Raton, FL: CRC Media, pp. 491–500.

Reynolds, C. 1987. Flocks, herds and schools: A distributed behavioral model. *International Conference and Exhibition on Computer Graphics and Interactive Techniques*, Anaheim, CA: Association for Computing Machinery, pp. 25–34.

Tozour, P. 2004. Search space representations. In *AI Game Programming Wisdom 2*, ed. S. Rabin. Hingham, MA: Charles River Media, pp. 85–102.

van den Berg, J., S. J. Guy, M. Lin, and D. Manocha. 2011. Reciprocal n-body collision avoidance. *Springer Tracts in Advanced Robotics*, 70: 3–19.

22

RVO and ORCA
How They Really Work

Ben Sunshine-Hill

22.1 Introduction

The reciprocal velocity obstacles (RVO) algorithm and its descendants, such as hybrid reciprocal velocity obstacles (HRVO) and optimal reciprocal collision avoidance (ORCA), have in recent years become the standard for collision avoidance in video games. That is a remarkable achievement: Game AI does not readily adopt new techniques so quickly or broadly, particularly ones pulled straight from academic literature. But RVO addresses a problem that previously had no broadly acceptable solution. Moreover, it is easy to understand (because of its simple geometric reasoning), easy to learn (because its creators eschewed the traditional opaqueness of academic writing, and wrote about it clearly and well), and easy to implement (because those same creators made reference source code available for free). Velocity obstacle methods, at least for the moment, are the deserving rulers of the kingdom of collision avoidance.

Which is why it is a little ironic that very few people actually understand how VO methods work. Not how the papers and tutorials and videos describe them as working, but how they *really* work. It's a lot weirder, more complicated, and cooler than you suppose.

There are four stages to really *getting* RVO:

1. Understanding the assumptions that RVO makes, and the guarantees it provides.
2. Realizing that those assumptions and those guarantees are, in practice, constantly violated.
3. Figuring out why, then, RVO still seems to work.
4. Tweaking it to work even better.

In the remainder of this chapter, we will take you through these stages. Our goal is not to present you with a perfect collision avoidance system but to walk you through the nuances of VO methods and to help you iteratively develop a collision avoidance system that works well for your game. First, though, a brief history of RVO, and VO methods in general. We promise it's important.

22.2 History

The velocity obstacle method originally targeted mobile robots—that is to say, real physical robots in the real world, moving around without hitting each other. Compared to previous approaches to robot steering, velocity obstacles were intended to be:

- Decentralized, with each robot making its own decisions rather than all robots being slaved to a central controller.
- Independent, with decisions based solely on each robot's observation of other robots' positions and velocities.

These features are not of much use to game developers, but they are important to understanding the strengths and weaknesses of VO methods. VO agents do not explicitly communicate or coordinate with each other. Cooperation between them is an emergent effect of their observations, decisions, and actions over time. VO methods spare us the morass that is multiagent planning, focusing on the behavior of individual agents. But the lack of coordination means that agents can make mistakes when predicting what other agents are going to do, thus failing to cooperate properly.

The original VO method was hilariously prone to such failures, with two agents almost guaranteed to start oscillating back and forth when they encountered each other, as in Figure 22.1. Each expected the other to be a mindless blob traveling at a constant velocity, and each was repeatedly surprised when the other instead changed direction and ruined its plan.

22.2.1 Introducing RVO

Those oscillations motivated the design of RVO (van den Berg et al. 2008). The idea was to come up with a decision process for the agent, which assumed that the other agent was *also* using that decision process. Each agent would move only halfway out of the way of a collision, anticipating that the other agent would do its part as well by moving halfway in the other direction. The paper proved that this would eliminate incorrect predictions, and set agents on optimal noncolliding paths in a single step once they came into view. This is shown in Figure 22.2.

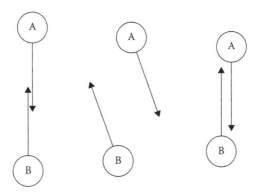

Figure 22.1

The original velocity obstacles method causes oscillation between two agents attempting to avoid each other.

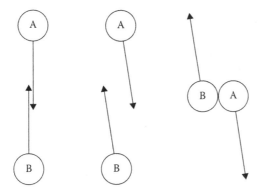

Figure 22.2

The reciprocal velocity obstacles resolve an upcoming collision between two agents in a single frame, putting them on optimal noncolliding trajectories.

22.3 Examining RVO's Guarantees

The proof of collision-free movement only holds for a world containing two agents (and no obstacles). With only two agents, each one is free to choose the perfect reciprocating velocity, without having to also dodge something else. Moreover, with nothing else in the world, each agent can assume that the current velocity of the other agent is also their preferred velocity.

Let us throw a third agent into the mix and see what happens in Figure 22.3. A and B are moving south side-by-side, when they see C coming toward them. A dodges a bit west, assuming that C will dodge a bit east. B dodges a bit east, assuming that C will dodge a bit west. Obviously C cannot do both of these. In fact it does neither, instead dodging west in order to pass to the west of both A and B. (It would be equally valid for C to dodge east instead, but let's say it breaks ties by going west.)

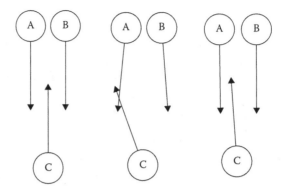

Figure 22.3

Three RVO agents attempting to resolve an upcoming collision.

All three agents are unhappy now. A and C are on a collision course, having both dodged west. B is not going to hit anything, but it has dodged for no good reason, straying from its preferred velocity. For C, it makes the most sense to move to a nearly northward trajectory; its deviation back east, it thinks, will be reciprocated by A deviating west, and even after B's reciprocation will graze by B. A decides to return to a due south trajectory, which it likes doing better and which it expects C to reciprocate by going even further west than he or she was already. B also returns to due south, reasoning that C is going so far west now that B does not have to worry about a collision.

In short, after two frames, we are back to the original problem. The oscillation that RVO solved for two agents still occurs for three. RVO, in other words, is not guaranteed to avoid collisions in situations such as the above because of an inconsistent view of possible velocities and preferred velocities between agents.

Except… it does avoid collisions. Set up that situation in a real RVO implementation, and C will get past A and B just fine. We have seen that the noncollision guarantee does not hold here, so what is really going on?

Well, after two frames, we aren't *really* back to the original problem. Over the two frames, A and B have moved slightly apart from each other. C has moved slightly west and is now traveling slightly west of north. In future frames, these displacements become more pronounced affecting later decisions. While there is a great deal of "flickering" going on with the velocities initially, the three eventually manage to cooperate.

In fact, you could argue that that's what *real* cooperation should look like, with each agent not only guessing each other's plans but reacting when those guesses don't work out. Eventually the three make simultaneous decisions that are entirely compatible, and then they stick to them until they are safely past.

So reciprocation—perfect avoidance through perfect prediction—has failed. Has RVO, then, gained us anything over original VO? As it turns out, yes. Run the scenario with VO avoidance, and the three will oscillate for much longer. It is easy to construct scenarios where RVO will avoid collisions and VO will not. There's something more to RVO, beyond the possibility of getting it right the first time.

In Figure 22.4, let's look at a scenario where A is going south toward B. But, let's also say that B is malfunctioning, and at a standstill rather than performing proper avoidance.

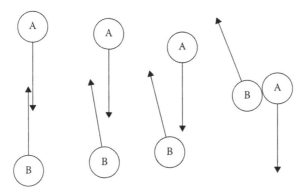

Figure 22.4

An RVO agent steers around a malfunctioning agent.

This is a perfect scenario for A to be using VO, and you might expect RVO to fail entirely, expecting a reciprocation that never comes. Surprisingly, though, RVO still works pretty well! On the first frame, A only dodges half as much as it should... but on the second frame, seeing that a collision is still imminent, dodges half of the remaining half... and then a half of that on the third frame... and so on, asymptotically avoiding the collision. (More or less.) A really *expected* B to dodge, but when it did not, A could deal with that too.

The magic in RVO, then, is that it strikes a balance between eager collision avoidance and a cagey wait-and-see attitude. An RVO agent faced with a collision dodges *some*, but not all, of the way. It is less likely than VO to dodge too much, overshooting the optimal velocity and requiring corrections. Moreover, if it has dodged too little, it's still set up to make up the difference on future frames. This magic is not unique to RVO: so-called *gradient methods*, such as the gradient descent algorithm for finding minima of functions, and similar techniques, use a multiplier to avoid overshooting the goal.

22.4 States, Solutions, and Sidedness

The goal of any gradient method is to converge to a locally optimal state, where no further improvements can be made. For collision avoidance, that generally looks like agents on trajectories which *just* squeeze past each other. Any closer and they would collide; any further and they would be wasting time.

RVO isn't exactly a gradient method, though. In a normal gradient method, you have as many steps as you want to converge onto an optimum; you are only limited by processing time. But in standard VO methods, after every iteration, the agents move along their chosen velocities. So while the "state" of an RVO simulation is the momentary positions and velocities of all agents, the "solution" is the full trajectories of the agents over time.

There is a more obvious—and, in my opinion, more useful—way to think about the "solution" to an avoidance problem, though: Sidedness. Two agents heading toward each other can each dodge left or each can dodge right; either way is a potential solution. If the two are not on perfect head-on trajectories, one may be a better solution, in the sense that they will get to their goals sooner; but both are *stable*: Once on one of those trajectories, they will not change their minds unless the situation changes.

There are three closely related ways to define sidedness. All involve the point of closest approach. Consider two agents whose trajectories are currently bringing them closer together. Determine the time at which A and B are predicted to be closest together (allowing penetration between them), and compute the vector from A's center to B's center.

The first notion of sidedness is an absolute one: If that vector is (say) eastward, then A is projected to pass to the west of B, and B is projected to pass to the east of A. Sidedness computed in this way is always symmetric between A's calculations and B's calculations.

The second notion is relative to current velocity: If the closest approach vector winds left of A's velocity relative to B, then A is projected to pass B on the left, and similarly if the vector winds right, A is projected to pass B on the right. This calculation is likewise symmetric: Both will project passing left, or both will project passing right.

The third notion is relative to A's desired velocity, wound against the closest approach vector. This formulation most closely aligns with our intuitive sense of "passing side." However, it can be inconsistent between A and B in situations where their current velocities diverge from their desired velocities. As a result, "sidedness" as a tool for coordination generally uses one of the first two formulations.

22.5 ORCA

The ORCA algorithm (van den Berg et al. 2011), which succeeded the original RVO algorithm (the reference library implementing ORCA is called RVO2) had this sidedness concept as its central insight. ORCA was less concerned with stability, though, and more concerned with optimality. Looking back at the three-agent avoidance scenario in Figure 22.3, a central problem was the agents' inconsistent intentions regarding passing sides. If one agent plans to pass on the left, and the other intends to pass on the right, a collision is inevitable. Since ORCA maintained the independent, decentralized design of other VO methods, it was not possible to centrally settle on a set of passing sides. Instead, ORCA forces agents to maintain their current passing sides. Two agents that are not on an *exact* collision course have consistently defined passing sides, even if they do not have enough separation in their trajectories to avoid the collision. ORCA picks trajectories that maintain those passing sides while expanding the separation to prevent the collision.

An implicit assumption behind ORCA is that the "original" passing sides, as of whenever the agents first encountered each other, just so happen to be reasonable ones. Remarkably, this assumption is usually true, particularly in situations without static obstacles. When ORCA's solver succeeds, it reliably produces reasonably optimal trajectories, and it absolutely eliminates velocity flicker from inconsistent passing sides.

The problem is that ORCA's solver often does not succeed. Although the set of illegal velocities generated by one RVO agent is an infinite cone (ruling out a significant percentage of potential velocities), the set of illegal velocities generated by one ORCA agent is an infinite half-space (ruling out about half of them). It is easy for a small number of nearby agents to completely rule out all velocities. In fact, the three-agent problem from Figure 22.3 does that. C is passing A on the right and B on the left; A's obstacle prohibits it from going left, B's obstacle prohibits it from going right, and both prohibit it from going straight, or even from stopping or going backward. ORCA satisfies this by linearly relaxing all constraints. This produces a velocity that maximizes the minimum passing distance.

Like RVO's partial dodging, ORCA's constraint relaxation has the effect of resolving complex avoidance scenarios over several frames. Although A must resort to a "least-worst" solution, B and C have legal velocities that have the effect of making more room for A. In fact, ORCA resolves this scenario in a single frame, as A's "least-worst" velocity is actually due north. More generally, when two rows of agents heading in different directions encounter each other, ORCA has the effect of expanding the rows, starting with the outer ranks. RVO does this too, but ORCA prohibits the middle ranks from taking extreme dodging action while it is happening, thereby leading to cleaner and more optimal solutions by maintaining the original set of passing sides.

22.6 Cornering

ORCA exhibits a more serious problem in real-world scenarios. In most articles on VO methods, there is an assumption that each agent has a preferred direction of travel, either constant or directly toward a fixed goal point. But in most game situations, the direction of travel is generated by following a path toward a goal, which winds around corners.

VO methods can adapt to occasional changes in heading without much issue. But while rounding a corner, an agent's preferred direction of travel will change every frame. This violates the assumption mentioned earlier that each agent's velocity from the previous frame is their preferred velocity for the current frame. RVO agents can exhibit unusual trajectories when rounding corners or when reacting to a nearby agent rounding a corner, that is, there is a characteristic "snap" turn as the agents change their passing sides.

But ORCA does not allow that snap. As mentioned earlier, the original passing sides are generally a good approximation of ideal passing sides, but that is not the case for cornering. ORCA agents at corners will often travel far, far from their desired trajectories to maintain passing sides, or simply become stuck at the corner, unwilling to cross paths and unable to make progress otherwise (as shown in Figure 22.5). This behavior is sometimes

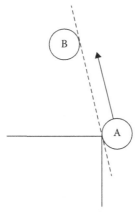

Figure 22.5

ORCA agent A is unable to continue turning around the corner without violating the sidedness constraint against B.

acceptable when all agents are traveling toward the same goal, as the front agents can still make progress but in general leads to frequent deadlocks.

22.7 Gradient Methods Revisited

What we want from collision avoidance is for agents to find a consistent set of passing sides quickly, and ideally for that solution not to be *too* far from the optimum. When the situation changes—when a new agent arrives, or when existing agents change their minds about which way to go—we would like the system to adapt and find a new solution quickly, and for that new solution to look as much like the old one as possible. The key to that is weights.

22.7.1 Modifying Weights

In the original RVO paper, agents can be "weighted" with respect to each other—one agent can dodge by a larger or smaller percentage of the total required dodge than the other, as long as the two weights add up to 1 and the agents agree on what those weights are. But if we view RVO as a gradient method, as opposed to an instant, perfect collision solver, then it is clear that nothing forces that constraint. For instance, you could set both weights to 0.1, making agents slowly move out of each other's way over many frames, but reliably settling into a stable configuration. Or you could set both weights to 0.9, causing agents to dodge sharply and exhibit the reciprocal oscillations that RVO was designed to avoid. (In fact, original-recipe VOs are simply a special case of RVO, with all weights set to 1.)

As mentioned, RVO is not quite a gradient method, because agents move after each iteration. In addition, if an upcoming collision has not yet been resolved, it just got a bit closer, and the problem just got a bit harder. If two agents are on a collision course, and the weights between them sum to anything less than 1.0, then their decisions each frame are guaranteed *not* to fully resolve the collision, and eventually they are guaranteed to veer off sharply and collide. If an algorithm can be said to "panic," that's what it looks like when an algorithm panics.

Low weights have their advantages, though. They tend to result in better solutions in the sidedness sense, particularly with large numbers of agents. But we need a way to cope with their tendency to fail asymptotically.

22.7.2 Substepping

Recall that as an algorithm for robot control, RVO relies on a cycle of steering, moving, and observing. One robot cannot react to another until that other robot has actually turned and started moving in another direction. But we have the benefit of knowing all agents' velocities immediately after each steering step, even without moving the agents. We can use this knowledge to cheat, running multiple iterations of RVO between each movement step. The velocity outputs of one RVO substep become the velocity inputs of the next substep, and the positions remain unchanged.

This has a number of advantages. When groups of agents come upon each other, there is likely to be a number of frames of velocity flicker, as in the earlier example. Substepping allows that flicker to die down before velocities are presented to the animation system, giving the illusion that all agents made consistent choices the first time around.

Substepping also gives you more flexibility with your weights. Weightings that sum to less than 1.0 failed to resolve collisions, but they were good at finding the seeds of efficient solutions. During a step consisting of many substeps, you can start the weights low to smoothly hint toward an efficient solution, then ramp the weights up to 0.5 to fully settle into that solution along noncolliding trajectories.

If you're familiar with stochastic optimization methods, you may find that sort of schedule, moving from the conservative to the abrupt, to be counterintuitive and backward. The goal here, though, is to converge reliably to a constraint-satisfying local optimum, rather than to converge reliably to the global optimum while maintaining constraints.

22.7.3 Time Horizons

ORCA's cornering problem (getting stuck rather than changing passing side) is one example of a larger class of problems exhibited by VO methods when the assumption of constant preferred velocity is violated. Another, simpler form can be demonstrated with a single VO agent traveling north toward a goal point with a wall behind it. All northward velocities are blocked by the wall's static velocity obstacle, so the agent can never reach the goal.

The original RVO reference library does not exhibit this problem, because it diverges from the paper and ignores collisions with static obstacles if they are further than the maximum stopping distance of the agent. Other RVO implementations address the problem by defining a maximum time-to-collision (TTC) beyond which projected collisions are ignored, causing the agent to slow as it approaches the obstacle, keeping its TTC above the threshold. The first approach assumes that the future policy is to come to a stop; the second approach assumes that the trajectory past the maximum TTC is too unpredictable to take into account. Both approaches are reasonable, but both are fairly arbitrary and can lead to collisions when agents end up squeezed between static obstacles and other agents.

In both cornering and approaching a goal in front of a wall, the basic issue is that agents are attempting to avoid a collision at a point that they would never reach. The cornering agent would veer off before getting to the collision point; the goal-approaching agent would stop first.

A more formal approach, then, would be to calculate the time at which the agent planned to stop at their goal, or to turn a corner, and to avoid collisions that would occur later than that time. The time horizon is specific to a given velocity candidate.

Time horizons are a little tricky to apply to cornering, because the agent does not plan to *disappear* after that but merely to turn a little bit. An agent currently rounding a corner has a time horizon approaching zero, yet should not ignore collisions entirely. Instead, one can construct a plane, perpendicular to the agent's postcornering direction, which the agent never plans to cross. Collisions past that plane can safely be discarded, as shown in Figure 22.6.

This is not a perfect solution, as agents still fail to consider collisions that *will* occur *after* cornering. And it is not necessarily true that an agent will never cross their cornering plane: On occasion they may do so to avoid a collision right next to the corner. A better solution would involve predicting collisions along a space defined by the agent's path, rather than world space. But because each agent has its own path, doing this in a way which would ensure proper reciprocation is, as far as we know, intractable in the general case.

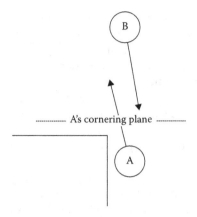

Figure 22.6

While A and B are on a colliding trajectory, the collision can be ignored as it would occur after A turns the corner.

22.8 Progress and Penalties

Original VO methods treated the duty to avoid collisions as absolute. Making progress in their preferred directions was a secondary concern, only coming into play when choosing among a set of noncolliding and therefore valid trajectories. But as we have seen, avoiding far-off collisions is not always necessary or reasonable: Between the current step and the projected collision, a lot can happen, particularly when many agents are involved.

The RVO algorithm softens VO constraints, treating projected collisions as only one aspect when "scoring" a velocity candidate, making it a utility method. (ORCA does not soften its constraints in the same way: Its constraint relaxation is to produce at least one admissible velocity, not to allow colliding velocities when noncolliding velocities are available.) The base utility of a velocity candidate is calculated as the distance between the preferred velocity and the velocity candidate. Predicted collisions are treated as penalty terms reducing the utility of a velocity candidate, with the penalty term increasing as the collision becomes more imminent. If a velocity candidate is predicted to result in multiple collisions, the soonest collision can be used to determine the penalty, or each collision can generate a separate penalty term; the latter approach tends to push agents away from crowds decreasing congestion.

An additive formulation like this is motivated by practicality, not theory: It makes no guarantees of collision avoidance and increases the number of user-specified parameters, making tuning more difficult. Nevertheless, in practice, it is more effective than "absolute" VO methods at clearing congestion, as it discounts distant collisions, making it more reactive to closer ones.

22.8.1 Putting Sidedness Back In

The additive formulation does not automatically maintain sidedness (though substepping with low weights helps). However, nothing is stopping us from adding it as an additional penalty term. Simply calculate, for each velocity candidate, how many agents it changes the sidedness of; then add a penalty for each. Sidedness-change penalty terms should be scaled similarly to collision penalty terms; since they sometimes need to be applied to agents without projected collisions, though, the time to closest approach can be used instead of the TTC.

22.8.2 Progress and Energy Minimization

In the additive formulation above, the base utility of a velocity candidate is calculated as the distance from preferred velocity. This is not the only option: Another is rate of progress. In this formulation, the main metric is how fast an agent is making progress toward their goal, computed as the dot product of the velocity candidate with the unit-length preferred direction of travel. Compared to the distance metric, rate of progress encourages sideways dodging over slowing and tends to get agents to their goals sooner.

Rate of progress is an unrealistic utility from the point of view of actual human behavior. Consider that when moving from place to place, humans have the option of sprinting, yet generally move at a walking speed. Biomechanics researchers have explained this as a tendency toward energy minimization: A normal walking gait allows a human to reach their goal with the minimum expenditure of energy by maximizing the ratio of speed to power output. A rough approximation to the energy wasted by traveling at a nonpreferred velocity may be calculated as the squared distance between the preferred velocity (at preferred speed) and the velocity candidate; the squared term differentiates it from RVO's approach. Agents using this utility calculation exhibit human-like trajectories, often slowing slightly to avoid a collision rather than turning left or right.

22.9 Putting It All Together: How to Develop a Practical Collision Avoidance System

Having a thorough knowledge of all the nuances and decisions and parameters involved in a VO-based collision avoidance system does not automatically give you the ability to make a perfect one. We are convinced that there is no perfect collision avoidance system, only one that works well with your scenarios, your needs, and your animation system. Developing such a system, like developing game systems in general, is an iterative process. There is a few important things you can do to increase the effectiveness of the process:

- Build up a library of collision avoidance scenarios, covering a variety of situations that your system will need to deal with. These should include all the factors you are likely to encounter in your game: static obstacles, cornering, multiple groups of agents, and so on. As you encounter problems with your system, make new scenarios that you can use to reproduce the problems, and test whether changes to your system have resolved them.
- Build up a library of collision avoidance algorithms too! As you make changes— either to the basic algorithms in use or the values you use for their parameters— keep the old algorithms around, not merely in source control but in active code. This will allow you to assess how well your iterative changes have improved collision avoidance quality, and it will allow you to test multiple approaches to resolving particular problems. Often later tweaks to a system will render earlier tweaks unnecessary, and keeping earlier versions around can help you recognize this and remove them, keeping your system as simple as possible.

- Put together a framework to automatically test each collision avoidance algorithm against each collision avoidance scenario. This isn't quite as easy as it sounds: It is difficult to formulate criteria to determine whether a particular algorithm "passes" a particular test. As a first pass, you can simply check whether an algorithm succeeds in eventually bringing all agents to their goals without collisions along the way. You can compare two algorithms to determine which one gets agents to their goals sooner, but keep in mind that a difference of a few fractions of a second is not significant in a game scenario. It is important not to test collision avoidance in isolation: If your collision avoidance feeds into your animation system, rather than directly controlling agent positions, then you have to make your animation system part of the test rig in order to ensure accurate results. An automated testing rig is primarily useful for quickly checking for significant regressions in one or more test scenarios. It can also be used to quickly determine the optimal values for a set of control parameters.
- Don't rely too heavily on your automated testing rig without doing frequent eyes-on testing of the results it is producing. Some collision avoidance algorithms can exhibit artifacts, which do not significantly impact the objective optimality of the results but which nevertheless look unrealistic to the player; velocity flicker is a prime example. You can try to come up with tests for this, but there's no substitute for subjective evaluation.

22.10 Conclusion

Much of the popularity of VO methods can be traced to the ease of understanding them as prohibited shapes in velocity space. RVO in particular is seductively elegant in sharing the burden of collision avoidance between agents. But the success in practice of VO methods—particularly RVO—depends on subtler factors, and treating RVO as a purely geometric method makes it more difficult to leverage and maximize the effectiveness of these factors. So it is important to view VO methods through multiple lenses: As geometric solvers, as gradient methods, and as utility methods. There is nothing simple about this holistic approach, but collision avoidance is not a simple problem. Understanding both the nuances of the problem space and the complexity of the solution space is the key to developing a system that works for you.

References

van den Berg, J., Guy, S. J., Lin, M., and Manocha, D. 2011. Reciprocal *n*-body collision avoidance. In *Robotics Research*. Berlin, Germany: Springer, pp. 3–19.

van den Berg, J., Lin, M., and Manocha, D. 2008. Reciprocal velocity obstacles for real-time multi-agent navigation. *Proceedings of the IEEE International Conference on Robotics and Automation (ICRA)*, 2008. http://gamma.cs.unc.edu/RVO/icra2008.pdf.

23

Optimization for Smooth Paths

Mark Langerak

23.1 Introduction

Path planning for games and robotics applications typically consists of finding the straight-line shortest path through the environment connecting the start and goal position. However, the straight-line shortest path usually contains abrupt, nonsmooth changes in direction at path apex points, which lead to unnatural agent movement in the path-following phase. Conversely, a smooth path that is free of such sharp kinks greatly improves the realism of agent steering and animation, especially at the path start and goal positions, where the path can be made to align with the agent facing direction.

Generating a smooth path through an environment can be challenging because there are multiple competing constraints of total path length, path curvature, and static obstacle avoidance that must all be satisfied simultaneously. This chapter describes an approach that uses convex optimization to construct a smooth path that optimally balances all these competing constraints. The resulting algorithm is efficient, surprisingly simple, free of special cases, and easily parallelizable. In addition, the techniques used in this chapter serve as an introduction to convex optimization, which has many uses in fields as diverse as AI, computer vision, and image analysis. A source code implementation can be found on the book's website (http://www.gameaipro.com).

23.2 Overview

The corridor map method introduced by Geraerts and Overmars, 2007 is used to construct an initial, nonoptimal path through the static obstacles in the environment. In the

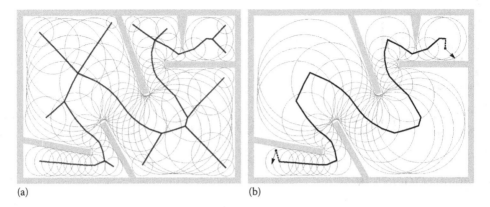

(a)   (b)

Figure 23.1

The corridor map (a) and a path between two points in the corridor map (b).

corridor map method, free space is represented by a graph where the vertices have associated disks. The centers of the disks coincide with the vertex 2D position, and the disk radius is equal to the maximum clearance around that vertex. The disks at neighboring graph vertices overlap, and the union of the disks then represents all of navigable space. See the leftside of Figure 23.1 for an example environment with some static obstacles in light gray and the corresponding corridor map graph.

The corridor map method might be a lesser known representation than the familiar methods of a graph defined over a navigation mesh or over a grid. However, it has several useful properties that make it an excellent choice for the path smoothing algorithm described in this chapter. For one, its graph is compact and low density, so path-planning queries are efficient. Moreover, the corridor map representation makes it straightforward to constrain a path within the bounds of free space, which is crucial for the implementation of the path smoothing algorithm to ensure it does not result in a path that collides with static obstacles.

The rightside of Figure 23.1 shows the result of an A* query on the corridor map graph, which gives the minimal subgraph that connects the vertex whose center is nearest to the start position to the vertex whose center is nearest to the goal. The arrows in the figure denote the agent facing direction at the start position and the desired facing direction at the goal position. The subgraph is prepended and appended with the start and goal positions to construct the initial path connecting the start and the goal. Note that this initial path is highly nonoptimal for the purpose of agent path following since it has greatest clearance from the static obstacles, which implies that its total length is much longer than the shortest straight-line path.

Starting from this initial nonoptimal path state, the iterative algorithm described in this chapter evolves the path over multiple steps by successively moving the waypoints closer to an optimal configuration, that is, the path that satisfies all the competing constraints of smoothness, shortest total length, alignment with the start/goal direction and collision-free agent movement. The result is shown in the left of Figure 23.2.

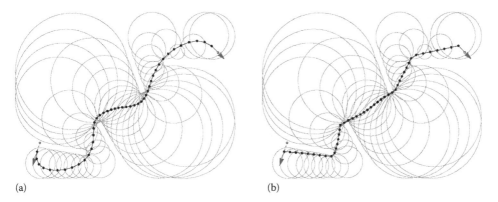

(a)   (b)

Figure 23.2

A smooth (a) and a straight-line path (b).

23.2.1 Definitions

In this section, we will define the mathematical notation used along with a few preliminary definitions. Vectors and scalars are denoted by lowercase letters. Where necessary, vectors use x, y superscripts to refer to the individual elements:

$$a = \begin{pmatrix} a^x \\ a^y \end{pmatrix}$$

The vector dot product is denoted by angle brackets:

$$\langle a, b \rangle = a^x b^x + a^y b^y$$

The definition for the length of a vector uses double vertical bars:

$$\|v\|_2 = \sqrt{\langle v, v \rangle}$$

(The number 2 subscript on the double bars makes it explicit that the vector length is the L^2 norm of a vector.)

A vector space is a rather abstract mathematical construct. In the general sense, it consists of a set, that is, some collection of elements, along with corresponding operators acting on that set. For the path smoothing problem, we need two specific vector space definitions, one for scalar quantities and one for 2D vector quantities. These vector spaces are denoted by uppercase letters U and V, respectively:

$$U = \mathbb{R}^n$$
$$V = \mathbb{R}^{2n}$$

The vector spaces U and V are arrays of length n, with vector space U an array of real (floating point) scalars, and V an array of 2D vectors. Individual elements of a vector space are referenced by an index subscript:

$$a \in V: \ a_i$$

In this particular example, a is an array of 2D vectors, and a_i is the 2D vector at index i in that array. Vector space operators like multiplication, addition, and so on, are defined in the obvious way as the corresponding pair-wise operator over the individual elements. The dot product of vector space V is defined as:

$$a, b \in V: \ \langle a, b \rangle_V = \sum_{i=1}^{n} \langle a_i, b_i \rangle$$

That is, the vector space dot product is the sum of the pair-wise dot products of the 2D vector elements. (The V subscript on the angle brackets distinguishes the vector space dot product from the vector dot product.)

For vector space V, we will make use of the norms:

$$v \in V: \ \|v\|_{V,1} = \sum_{i=1}^{n} \|v_i\|_2$$

$$v \in V: \ \|v\|_{V,2} = \sqrt{\sum_{i=1}^{n} \left(\|v_i\|_2 \right)^2}$$

$$v \in V: \ \|v\|_{V,\infty} = \max_{i=1}^{n} \|v_i\|_2$$

(The V subscript is added to make the distinction between vector and vector space norms clear.) Each of these three vector space norms are constructed similarly: they consist of an inner L^2 norm over the 2D vector elements, followed by an outer L^1, L^2, or L^∞ norm over the resulting scalars, respectively. In the case of the vector space L^2 norm, the outer norm is basically the usual definition of vector length, in this case a vector of length n. The vector space L^1 and L^∞ norms are generalizations of the familiar L^2 norm. The vector space L^1 norm is analogous to the Manhattan distance of a vector, and the L^∞ norm is the so-called max norm, which is simply the absolute max element.

An indicator function is a convenience function for testing set membership. It gives 0 if the element is in the set, otherwise it gives ∞ if the element is not in the set:

$$I_S(x) = \begin{cases} 0 & x \in S \\ \infty & x \notin S \end{cases}$$

The differencing operators give the vector offset between adjacent elements in V:

$$v \in V: \delta^+(v)_i = \begin{cases} (v_{i+1} - v_i)/h & i < n \\ 0 & i = n \end{cases}$$

$$v \in V: \delta^-(v)_i = \begin{cases} v_i/h & i = 1 \\ (v_i - v_{i-1})/h & 1 < i < n \\ -v_{i-1}/h & i = n \end{cases}$$

$$v \in V: \delta^s(v) = -\delta^+(v) + \delta^-(v)$$

The forward differencing operator δ^+ gives the offset from the 2D vector at index i to the next vector at index $i+1$. The boundary condition at index $i=n$ is needed because then there is no "next" vector, and there the offset is set to 0. Similarly, the backward differencing operator δ^- gives the offset from the vector at index i to the previous vector at index $i-1$, with boundary conditions at $i=1$ and $i=n$ to ensure that δ^+ and δ^- are adjoint. The sum-differencing operator δ^s is the vector addition of the vector offsets δ^+ and δ^-. The scalar h is a normalization constant to enforce scale invariance. It depends on the scale of the 2D coordinate space used, and its value should be set to the average distance between neighboring graph vertices.

23.3 Path Smoothing Energy Function

An optimization problem consists of two parts: an energy (aka cost) function and an optimization algorithm for minimizing that energy function. In this section, we will define the energy function; in the following sections, we will derive the optimization algorithm.

The path smoothing energy function gives a score to a particular configuration of the path waypoints. This score is a positive number, where large values mean the path is "bad," and small values mean the path is "good." The goal then is to find the path configuration for which the energy function is minimal. The choice of energy function is crucial. Since it effectively will be evaluated many times in the execution of the optimization algorithm, it needs to be simple and fast, while still accurately assigning high energy to nonsmooth paths and low energy to smooth paths.

As described in the introduction section, the fundamental goal of the path smoothing problem is to find the optimal balance between path smoothness and total path length under the constraint that the resulting path must be collision free. Intuitively, expressing this goal as an energy function leads to a sum of three terms: a term that penalizes (i.e., assigns high energy) to waypoints where the path has sharp kinks, a term that penalizes greater total path length, and a term that enforces the collision-free constraint. In addition, the energy function should include a scaling factor to enable a user-controlled tradeoff between overall path smoothness and total path length. The energy function for the path smoothing problem is then as follows:

$$
w \in U, v \in V : E(v) = \frac{1}{2}\left(\left\|w\delta^s(v)\right\|_{V,2}\right)^2 + \left\|\delta^+(v)\right\|_{V,2} + I_C(v)
$$
$$
C = \left\{v, c \in V, r \in U : \left\|(v-c)/r\right\|_{V,\infty} \le 1\right\}
$$

(23.1)

Here, v are the path waypoint positions, and w are per waypoint weights. Set C represents the maximal clearance disk at each waypoint, where c are the disk centers, and r are the radii. (Note that this path smoothing energy function is convex, so there are no local minima that can trap the optimization in a nonoptimal state, and the algorithm is therefore guaranteed to converge on a globally minimal energy.)

The first term in the energy function gives a high score to nonsmooth paths by penalizing waypoints where the path locally deviates from a straight line. See Figure 23.3 for a visual representation, where the offsets δ^s, δ^+, and δ^- for waypoint 3 are drawn with arrows. The dark arrow shows offset vector δ^s, and it can be seen from the left and

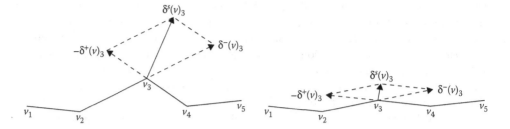

Figure 23.3

A visual representation of the model.

the right Figure 23.3 that its length is relative to how much waypoint v_3 deviates from the straight line connecting v_2 and v_4. The offset vector δ^s length is squared to penalize sharp kinks progressively more than shallow ones, which forces the optimization algorithm to spread out sharp kinks over adjacent waypoints, leading to an overall smoother path.

The second term in the energy function gives a higher score to greater total path length by summing the lengths of the δ^+ vectors. It effectively forces path waypoints to be closer together, resulting in a path that has a shorter total length and which is thus more similar to the straight-line shortest path connecting the start and goal.

Set C acts as a constraint on the optimization problem to ensure the path is collision free. Due to the max norm in the definition, the indicator function I_C gives infinity when one or more waypoints are outside their corresponding maximal clearance disk, otherwise it gives zero. A path that has waypoints that are outside their corresponding maximal clearance disk will have infinite energy therefore, and thus can obviously never be the minimal energy state path.

The required agent facing directions at the start and goal positions are handled by extending the path at both ends with a dummy additional waypoint, which are shown by the small circles in Figure 23.2. The position of the additional waypoints is determined by subtracting or adding the facing direction vector to the start and goal positions. These dummy additional waypoints as well as the path start and goal position are assigned a zero radius clearance disk. This constrains the start/goal positions from shifting around during optimization and similarly prevents the start/goal-facing direction from changing during optimization.

The per waypoint weights w allow a user-controlled tradeoff between path smoothness and overall path length, where lower weights favor short paths and higher weights favor smooth paths. In the limit, when all the weights are set to zero, the energy function only penalizes total path length, and then the path optimization will result in the shortest straight-line path as shown in the right of Figure 23.2. In practice, the weights near the start and goal are boosted to improve alignment of the path with the required agent facing direction. This is done using a bathtub-shaped power curve:

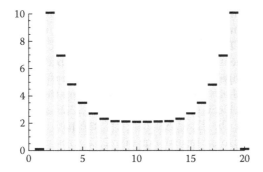

Figure 23.4

A waypoint weight curve.

$$w_i = \begin{cases} w_m + (w_s - w_m)\left(\dfrac{-2(i-2)}{n-3}+1\right)^4 & 2 \le i \le \dfrac{n}{2} \\[3mm] w_m + (w_e - w_m)\left(\dfrac{2(i-2)}{n-3}-1\right)^4 & \dfrac{n}{2} < i \le n-1 \\[3mm] 0 & \text{otherwise} \end{cases}$$

The scalars w_s and w_e are the values of the weight for the start and goal position waypoints, respectively. The end position weights taper off with a power curve to weight w_m at the middle of the path. Index $i=1$ and $i=n$ are the dummy waypoints for the agent facing direction, and there the weights are zero. Figure 23.4 shows a plot for an example weight curve with $w_s = w_e = 10$, $w_m = 2$, and $n = 20$.

23.4 Optimization Algorithm

Minimizing the energy function (Equation 23.1) is a challenging optimization problem due to the discontinuous derivative of the vector space norms and the hard constraints imposed by the maximal clearance disks. In this context, the path smoothing problem is similar to optimization problems found in many computer vision applications, which likewise consist of discontinuous derivatives and have hard constraints. Recent advances in the field have resulted in simple and efficient algorithms that can effectively tackle such optimization tasks; in particular, the Chambolle–Pock preconditioned primal-dual algorithm described in Chambolle and Pock 2011, and Pock and Chambolle 2011 has proven very effective in computer vision applications due to its simple formulation and fast convergence. Furthermore, it generalizes and extends several prior known optimization algorithms such as preconditioned ADMM and Douglas–Rachford splitting, leading to a very general and flexible algorithm.

The algorithm requires that the optimization problem has a specific form, given by:

$$\min_{v \in V}\{E_p(v) = F(K \cdot v) + G(v)\} \tag{23.2}$$

That is, it minimizes some variable v for some energy function E_p, which itself consists of a sum of two (convex) functions F and G. The parameter to function F is the product of a matrix K and variable v. The purpose of matrix K is to encode all the operations on v that depend on adjacent elements. This results in a F and G function that are simple, which is necessary to make the implementation of the algorithm feasible. In addition, matrix K is used to compute a bound on the step sizes, which ensures the algorithm is stable.

The optimization problem defined by Equation 23.2 is rather abstract and completely generic. To make the algorithm concrete, the path smoothing energy function (Equation 23.1) is adapted to the form of Equation 23.2 in multiple steps. First, we define the functions F_1, F_2, and G to represent the three terms in the path smoothing energy function:

$$F_1(v) = \frac{1}{2}\left(\|v\|_{V,2}\right)^2, \quad F_2(v) = \|v\|_{V,2}, \quad G(v) = I_C(v)$$

In the path smoothing energy function (Equation 23.1), the operators $w\,\delta^s$ and δ^+ act on adjacent elements in v, so these are the operators that must be encoded as matrix K. As an intermediate step, we first define the two submatrices $K_1 = w\,\delta^s$ and $K_2 = \delta^+$. We can then state the equivalence:

$$K_1 \cdot v = w\,\delta^s(v), \quad K_2 \cdot v = \delta^+(v)$$

Substituting these as the parameters to functions F_1 and F_2 results in:

$$F_1(K_1 \cdot v) = \frac{1}{2}\left(\left\|w\,\delta^s(v)\right\|_{V,2}\right)^2, \quad F_2(K_2 \cdot v) = \left\|\delta^+(v)\right\|_{V,2}$$

which leads to the minimization problem:

$$\min_{v \in V}\left\{E_p(v) = F_1(K_1 \cdot v) + F_2(K_2 \cdot v) + G(v)\right\}$$

This is already largely similar to the form of Equation 23.2, but instead of one matrix K and one function F, we have two matrices K_1 and K_2, and two functions F_1 and F_2. By "stacking" these matrices and functions, we can combine them into a single definition to make the path smoothing problem compatible with Equation 23.2:

$$K = \begin{pmatrix} K_1 \\ K_2 \end{pmatrix}, \quad F(K \cdot v) = \begin{pmatrix} F_1(K_1 \cdot v) \\ F_2(K_2 \cdot v) \end{pmatrix}$$

Next, matrix K is defined to complete the derivation of the path smoothing problem. For the matrix-vector product $K \cdot v$, it is necessary to first "flatten" v into a column vector $\left(v_1^x, v_1^y, v_2^x, v_2^y, \cdots, v_n^x, v_n^y\right)^T$. Then K is a $4n \times 2n$-dimensional matrix where rows 1 to $2n$ encode the $w\delta^s$ operator, and rows $2n+1$ to $4n$ encode δ^+. See Figure 23.5 for an example with $n = 4$. From Figure 23.5, it is easy to see that applying $K \cdot v$ is the same operation as $w\delta^s(v)$ and $\delta^+(v)$.

Note that in practice, the definition of matrix K is only needed to analyze the optimization algorithm mathematically; it is not used in the final implementation. The matrix

$$
\begin{pmatrix}
\dfrac{2\omega_1}{h} & 0 & -\dfrac{\omega_1}{h} & 0 & 0 & 0 & 0 & 0 \\[4pt]
0 & \dfrac{2\omega_1}{h} & 0 & -\dfrac{\omega_1}{h} & 0 & 0 & 0 & 0 \\[4pt]
-\dfrac{\omega_2}{h} & 0 & \dfrac{2\omega_2}{h} & 0 & -\dfrac{\omega_2}{h} & 0 & 0 & 0 \\[4pt]
0 & -\dfrac{\omega_2}{h} & 0 & \dfrac{2\omega_2}{h} & 0 & -\dfrac{\omega_2}{h} & 0 & 0 \\[4pt]
0 & 0 & -\dfrac{\omega_3}{h} & 0 & \dfrac{2\omega_3}{h} & 0 & -\dfrac{\omega_3}{h} & 0 \\[4pt]
0 & 0 & 0 & -\dfrac{\omega_3}{h} & 0 & \dfrac{2\omega_3}{h} & 0 & -\dfrac{\omega_3}{h} \\[4pt]
0 & 0 & 0 & 0 & -\dfrac{\omega_4}{h} & 0 & 0 & 0 \\[4pt]
0 & 0 & 0 & 0 & 0 & -\dfrac{\omega_4}{h} & 0 & 0 \\[4pt]
-\dfrac{1}{h} & 0 & \dfrac{1}{h} & 0 & 0 & 0 & 0 & 0 \\[4pt]
0 & -\dfrac{1}{h} & 0 & \dfrac{1}{h} & 0 & 0 & 0 & 0 \\[4pt]
0 & 0 & -\dfrac{1}{h} & 0 & \dfrac{1}{h} & 0 & 0 & 0 \\[4pt]
0 & 0 & 0 & -\dfrac{1}{h} & 0 & \dfrac{1}{h} & 0 & 0 \\[4pt]
0 & 0 & 0 & 0 & -\dfrac{1}{h} & 0 & \dfrac{1}{h} & 0 \\[4pt]
0 & 0 & 0 & 0 & 0 & -\dfrac{1}{h} & 0 & \dfrac{1}{h} \\[4pt]
0 & 0 & 0 & 0 & 0 & 0 & 0 & 0 \\[4pt]
0 & 0 & 0 & 0 & 0 & 0 & 0 & 0
\end{pmatrix}
\begin{pmatrix}
v_1^x \\ v_1^y \\ v_2^x \\ v_2^y \\ v_3^x \\ v_3^y \\ v_4^x \\ v_4^y
\end{pmatrix}
=
\begin{pmatrix}
\omega_1\delta^s(v)_1^x \\ \omega_1\delta^s(v)_1^y \\ \omega_2\delta^s(v)_2^x \\ \omega_2\delta^s(v)_2^y \\ \omega_3\delta^s(v)_3^x \\ \omega_3\delta^s(v)_3^y \\ \omega_4\delta^s(v)_4^x \\ \omega_4\delta^s(v)_4^y \\ \delta^+(v)_1^x \\ \delta^+(v)_1^y \\ \delta^+(v)_2^x \\ \delta^+(v)_2^y \\ \delta^+(v)_3^x \\ \delta^+(v)_3^y \\ \delta^+(v)_4^x \\ \delta^+(v)_4^y
\end{pmatrix}
$$

Figure 23.5

Matrix K for $n = 4$.

is very large and sparse, so it is obviously much more efficient to simply use the operators $w\,\delta^s$ and δ^+ in the implementation instead of the actual matrix-vector product $K \cdot v$.

Instead of solving the minimization problem (Equation 23.2) directly, the Chambolle–Pock algorithm solves the related min–max problem:

$$\min_{v \in V} \max_{p \in V} \left\{ E_{pd}(v) = \langle K \cdot v, p \rangle_V + G(v) - F^*(p) \right\} \tag{23.3}$$

The optimization problems Equations 23.2 and 23.3 are equivalent: minimizing Equation 23.2 or solving the min–max problem (Equation 23.3) will result in the same v. The original optimization problem (Equation 23.2) is called the "primal," and Equation 23.3 is called the "primal-dual" problem. Similarly, v is referred to as the primal variable, and the additional variable p is called the dual variable.

The concept of duality and the meaning of the star superscript on F^* are explained further in the next section, but at first glance it may seem that Equation 23.3 is a more complicated problem to solve than Equation 23.2, as there is an additional variable p, and we are now dealing with a coupled min–max problem instead of a pure minimization. However, the additional variable enables the algorithm, on each iteration, to handle p separately while holding v constant and to handle v separately while holding p constant. This results in two smaller subproblems, so the system as a whole is simpler.

In the case of the path smoothing problem, we have two functions F_1 and F_2, so we need one more dual variable q, resulting in the min–max problem:

$$\min_{v \in V} \max_{p,q \in V} \left\{ E_{pd}(v) = \left\langle K \cdot v, \begin{pmatrix} p \\ q \end{pmatrix} \right\rangle_V + G(v) - F_1^*(p) - F_2^*(q) \right\}$$

Note that, similar to what was done to combine matrices K_1 and K_2, the variables p and q are stacked to combine them into a single definition $(p,q)^T$.

23.4.1 Legendre-Fenchel Transform

The Legendre–Fenchel (LF) transform takes a function f and puts in a different form. The transformed function is denoted with a star superscript, f^*, and is referred to as the dual of the original function f. Using the dual of a function can make certain kinds of analysis or operations much more efficient. For example, the well-known Fourier transform takes a time domain signal and transforms (dualizes) it into a frequency domain signal, where convolution and frequency analysis are much more efficient. In the case of the LF transform, the dualization takes the form of a maximization:

$$f^*(k) = \max_{x \in \mathbb{R}^n} \left\{ \langle k, x \rangle - f(x) \right\} \tag{23.4}$$

The LF transform has an interesting geometric interpretation, which is unfortunately out of scope for this chapter. For more information, see Touchette 2005, which gives an excellent explanation of the LF transform. Here we will restrict ourselves to simply deriving the LF transform for the functions F_1 and F_2 by means of the definition given by Equation 23.4.

23.4.1.1 Legendre-Fenchel Transform of F_1

Substituting the definition of F_1 for f in Equation 23.4 results in:

$$p \in V : \quad F_1^*(p) = \max_{x \in V} \left\{ \langle p, x \rangle_V - \frac{1}{2} \langle x, x \rangle_V \right\} \tag{23.5}$$

The maximum occurs where the derivative w.r.t. x is 0:

$$\frac{\partial}{\partial x} \left(\langle p, x \rangle_V - \frac{1}{2} \langle x, x \rangle_V \right) = 0 \Rightarrow p - x = 0$$

So the maximum of F_1 is found where $x = p$. Substituting this back into Equation 23.5 gives:

$$F_1^*(p) = \frac{1}{2} \langle p, p \rangle_V$$

23.4.1.2 Legendre-Fenchel Transform of F_2

Substituting the definition of F_2 for f in Equation 23.4 gives:

$$q \in V : \quad F_2^*(q) = \max_{x \in V} \left\{ \langle q, x \rangle_V - \|x\|_{V,2} \right\} \tag{23.6}$$

The $\langle q, x \rangle_V$ term can be (loosely) seen as the geometric dot product of q and x. This is maximized when q and x are "geometrically coincident," that is, they are a scalar multiple of each other. When q and x are coincident, then by the definition of the dot product $\langle q, x \rangle_V = \|q\|_{V,2} \|x\|_{V,2}$ holds. Substituting this back into Equation 23.6 gives:

$$F_2^*(q) = \max_{x \in V} \left\{ \|q\|_{V,2} \|x\|_{V,2} - \|x\|_{V,2} \right\}$$

This makes it obvious that when $\|q\|_{V,2} \leq 1$, the maximum that can be attained for Equation 23.6 is 0; otherwise when $\|q\|_{V,2} > 1$, the maximum goes to ∞. This is conveniently expressed as the indicator function of an additional set Q:

$$F_2^*(q) = I_Q(q), \quad Q = \left\{ q \in V : \|q\|_{V,2} \leq 1 \right\}$$

23.4.2 Proximity Operator

In the previous section, we derived the dual functions F_1^* and F_2^*. Before we can define the path smoothing algorithm, we also need to derive the so-called proximity operator for functions F_1^*, F_2^*, and G. The proximity operator bounds a function from below with a quadratic in order to smooth out discontinuities in the derivative. This ensures the optimization converges on the minimum without getting trapped in an oscillation around the minimum. See Figure 23.6 for a simple example where the solid line is the original function with a discontinuous derivative, and the dotted lines are quadratic relaxations of that function. The general definition of the proximity operator is given by the minimization:

$$prox_{f,\tau}(x) = \arg\min_{y \in \mathbb{R}^n} \left\{ f(y) + \frac{1}{2\tau} \left(\|y - x\|_2 \right)^2 \right\} \tag{23.7}$$

where the parameter τ controls the amount of relaxation due to the quadratic.

23.4.2.1 Proximity Operator of F_1^*

Substituting F_1^* into Equation 23.7 gives:

$$p \in V : prox_{F_1^*, \sigma}(p)_i = \arg\min_{y \in \mathbb{R}^2} \left\{ \frac{\langle y, y \rangle}{2} + \frac{1}{2\sigma} \left(\|y - p_i\|_2 \right)^2 \right\}$$

$\tau = 0.075$

$\tau = 0.15$

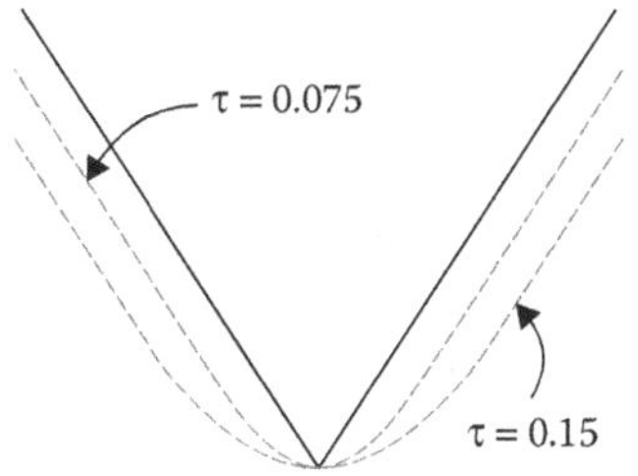

Figure 23.6

Quadratic relaxation.

Note that the proximity operator F_1^* is point-wise separable, meaning that it can be defined in terms of the individual elements p_i. The point-wise separation is possible due to the fact that the operations that depend on adjacent elements of v are encoded in matrix K, and as a consequence, there similarly is no mutual dependence between adjacent elements of p here. This simplifies the derivation of the proximity operator greatly. (In fact, without point-wise separation, the derivation of the proximity operator would not be feasible.) The minimum occurs where the derivative w.r.t. y is 0:

$$\frac{\partial}{\partial y}\left(\frac{\langle y,y \rangle}{2} - \frac{1}{2\sigma}\langle y - p_i, y - p_i \rangle\right) = 0 \Rightarrow y + \frac{y - p_i}{\sigma} = 0$$

Solving this equation for y results in:

$$p \in V : prox_{F_1^*,\sigma}(p)_i = \frac{p_i}{1+\sigma}$$

23.4.2.2 Proximity Operator of F_2^*

Substituting F_2^* into Equation 23.7 gives:

$$q \in V : prox_{F_2^*,\mu}(q) = \underset{y \in V}{\operatorname{argmin}}\left\{I_Q(y) + \frac{1}{2\mu}\left(\|y - q\|_{V,2}\right)^2\right\}$$

The indicator function I_Q completely dominates the minimization—it is 0 when $y \in Q$, otherwise it is ∞ in which case the minimum does not exist. So to attain a minimum, y must be member of Q. Hence, the solution to the proximity operator for F_2^* consists of finding the nearest y to q that is also a member of Q (in convex optimization terms, this is called "projecting" y onto Q.) If y is in Q, this is simply y itself; otherwise y is divided by its L^2 norm, so it satisfies $\|q\|_{V,2} \le 1$. Thus:

$$q \in V : prox_{F_2^*,\mu}(q) = \frac{q}{\max\left(1, \|q\|_{V,2}\right)}$$

23.4.2.3 Proximity Operator of G

Substituting G into Equation 23.7 gives:

$$v \in V : prox_{G,\tau}(v) = \underset{y \in V}{\operatorname{arg\,min}}\left\{I_C(y) + \frac{1}{2\tau}\left(\|y - v\|_{V,2}\right)^2\right\}$$

Similar to the proximity operator of F_2^* above, here the indicator function I_C dominates the minimization, and so the solution consists of finding the nearest y that is in C. The problem is point-wise separable, and the solution is given as the point inside the maximal clearance disk with center c_i and radius r_i that is nearest to v_i:

$$v \in V : prox_{G,\tau}(v)_i = c_i + (v_i - c_i)\frac{r_i}{\max\left(r_i, \|v_i - c_i\|_2\right)}$$

23.4.3 The Chambolle–Pock Primal-Dual Algorithm for Path Smoothing

The general preconditioned Chambolle–Pock algorithm consists of the following steps:

$$p^{k+1} = prox_{F^*, \Sigma}\left(p^k + \Sigma \cdot K \cdot \hat{v}^k\right)$$

$$v^{k+1} = prox_{G,T}\left(v^k - T \cdot K^T \cdot p^{k+1}\right) \qquad (23.8)$$

$$\hat{v}^{k+1} = 2v^{k+1} - v^k$$

These are the calculations for a single iteration of the algorithm, where the superscripts k and $k+1$ refer to the value of the corresponding variable at the current iteration k and the next iteration $k+1$. The implementation of the algorithm repeats the steps (Equation 23.8) multiple times, with successive iterations bringing the values of the variables closer to the optimal solution. In practice, the algorithm runs for some predetermined, fixed number of iterations that brings the state of variable v sufficiently close to the optimal value. Prior to the first iteration $k = 0$, the variables are initialized as $p^0 = q^0 = 0$ and $v^0 = \hat{v}^0 = c$. The diagonal matrices Σ and T are the step sizes for the algorithm, which are defined below.

The general algorithm (Equation 23.8) is adapted to the path smoothing problem by substituting the definitions given in the previous sections: the differencing operators $w\,\delta^s$ and δ^+ are substituted for K, P is substituted with the stacked variable $(p,q)^T$, and $prox_{F^*, \Sigma}$ is substituted with $prox_{F_1^*, \sigma}$ and $prox_{F_2^*, \mu}$. Then the final remaining use of matrix K is eliminated by expanding the product:

$$K^T \cdot \begin{pmatrix} p \\ q \end{pmatrix}^{k+1} \Rightarrow w\,\delta^s\left(p^{k+1}\right) - \delta^-\left(q^{k+1}\right)$$

This results in the path smoothing algorithm:

$$p^{k+1} = prox_{F_1^*, \sigma}\left(p^k + \sigma w\,\delta^s\left(\hat{v}^k\right)\right)$$

$$q^{k+1} = prox_{F_2^*, \mu}\left(q^k + \mu\,\delta^+\left(\hat{v}^k\right)\right)$$

$$v^{k+1} = prox_{G,\tau}\left(v^k - \tau\left(w\,\delta^s\left(p^{k+1}\right) - \delta^-\left(q^{k+1}\right)\right)\right)$$

$$\hat{v}^{k+1} = 2v^{k+1} - v^k$$

By substituting K and K^T with their corresponding differencing operators, the step size matrices Σ and T are no longer applicable. Instead, the step sizes are now represented by the vectors $\sigma, \mu, \tau \in U$, which are the diagonal elements of matrices Σ and T. As proven in Pock and Chambolle 2011, deriving the step-size parameters σ, μ, τ as sums of the rows and columns of matrix K leads to a convergent algorithm:

$$\sigma_i = \frac{1}{\beta \sum_{j=1}^{2n} K_{1_{i,j}}{}^\alpha}, \qquad \mu_i = \frac{1}{\beta \sum_{j=1}^{2n} K_{2_{i,j}}{}^\alpha}, \qquad \tau_i = \frac{\beta}{\sum_{j=1}^{4n} K_{j,i}{}^{2-\alpha}}$$

Expanding the summation gives:

$$\sigma_i = \frac{h^\alpha}{\left(2+2^\alpha\right)\beta w_i^\alpha}, \ \mu_i = \frac{h^\alpha}{2\beta}, \ \tau_i = \frac{\beta h^{2-\alpha}}{2+w_{i-1}^{2-\alpha}+\left(2w_i\right)^{2-\alpha}+w_{i+1}^{2-\alpha}} \tag{23.9}$$

(Note that μ_i is a constant for all i.) The scalar constants $0<\alpha<2$ and $\beta>0$ balance the step sizes to either larger values for σ,μ or larger values for τ. This causes the algorithm to make correspondingly larger steps in either variable p,q or variable v on each iteration, which affects the overall rate of convergence of the algorithm. Well-chosen values for α,β are critical to ensure an optimal rate of convergence. Unfortunately, optimal values for these constants depend on the particular waypoint weights used and the average waypoint separation distance h, so no general best value can be given, and they need to be found by experimentation. Note that the Equations 23.9 are valid only for $2<i<n-1$, that is, they omit the special cases for the step size at $i=1$ and $i=n$. They are omitted because in practice, the algorithm only needs to calculate elements $2<i<n-1$ for p, q, v and $\hat{v}$ on each iteration. This is a consequence of extending the path at either end with two dummy additional waypoints for the agent facing direction. Since these additional waypoints are assigned a zero radius clearance disk, their position remains fixed on each iteration. Their contribution to the path energy is therefore constant and does not need to be calculated. Restricting the algorithm implementation to elements $2<i<n-1$ eliminates all special cases for the boundary conditions of operator $\delta^s, \delta^+, \delta^-$, and the step sizes.

The leftside of Figure 23.7 shows the state of the path as it evolves over 100 iterations of the algorithm. Empirically, the state rapidly converges to a smooth path after only a few initial iterations. Subsequent iterations then pull the waypoints closer together and impose a uniform distribution of waypoints over the length of the path. The rightside of Figure 23.7 is a plot of the value of the energy function (Equation 23.1) at each iteration, which shows that the energy decreases (however not necessarily monotonically) on successive iterations.

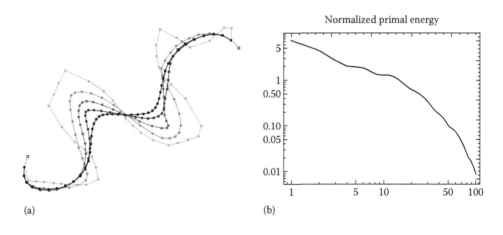

(a)   (b)

Figure 23.7

(a) Path evolution and (b) energy plot.

23. Optimization for Smooth Paths

23.5 Conclusion

In this chapter, we have given a detailed description of an algorithm for path smoothing using iterative minimization. As can be seen from the source code provided with this chapter on the book's website (http://www.gameaipro.com), the implementation only requires a few lines of C++ code. The computation at each iteration consists of simple linear operations, making the method very efficient overall. Moreover, since information exchange for neighboring waypoints only occurs after each iteration, the algorithm inner loops that update the primal and dual variables are essentially entirely data parallel, which makes the algorithm ideally suited to a GPGPU implementation.

Finally, note that this chapter describes just one particular application of the Chambolle–Pock algorithm. However, the algorithm itself is very general and can be adapted to solve a wide variety of optimization problems. The main hurdle in adapting it to new applications is deriving a suitable model, along with its associated Legendre–Fenchel transform(s) and proximity operators. Depending on the problem, this may be more or less challenging. However, once a suitable model is found, the resulting code is invariably simple and efficient.

References

Chambolle, A. and T. Pock. 2011. A first-order primal-dual algorithm for convex problems with applications to imaging. *Journal of Mathematical Imaging and Vision*, 40(1), 120–145.

Geraerts, R. and M. Overmars. 2007. The corridor map method: A general framework for real-time high-quality path planning. *Computer Animation and Virtual Worlds*, 18, 107–119.

Pock, T. and A. Chambolle. 2011. Diagonal preconditioning for first order primal-dual algorithms in convex optimization. *IEEE International Conference on Computer Vision (ICCV)*, Washington, DC, pp. 1762–1769.

Touchette, H. 2005. Legendre-Fenchel transforms in a nutshell. School of Mathematical Sciences, Queen Mary, University of London. http://www.physics.sun.ac.za/~htouchette/archive/notes/lfth2.pdf (accessed May 26, 2016).

24

3D Flight Navigation Using Sparse Voxel Octrees

Daniel Brewer

24.1 Introduction

Navigating two-dimensional spaces is something we are quite familiar with in the game AI field. Regular grids, corridor maps, and navigation meshes (navmeshes) are all very well known and documented problem spaces. However, navigating in full three-dimensional environments where the agents are not constrained to the ground is quite a challenging problem space and is compounded when having to deal with very large, sparsely populated volumes that have clusters of dense, complex regions.

A Sparse Voxel Octree (SVO) is a spatial structure used in graphics rendering, particularly ray-tracing. This structure is optimized for handling large, sparsely populated regions. This chapter will cover how we adapted SVOs for use in 3D flight navigation in *Warframe*, discuss modifications to the A* search algorithm to work on this adaptive grid representation and go into the details of tuning the heuristic to speed up the search by sacrificing optimality.

24.2 Alternative Techniques

Before covering how to use SVOs to represent flight navigation, we will briefly cover a few other alternatives.

A simple approach is to use a connected waypoint graph. Bounding volumes of free space can be manually placed by the level designer. Clear paths between volumes can be marked up as connections in the graph. These annotations work well in small areas or to simply provide occasional extra flight shortcuts above normal ground navigation. But, waypoint graphs in 3D have the same problems as in 2D space. There are a limited number of connections between volumes, which results in unnatural flight-paths as agents deviate to go back to a specific connection. Another limitation of this approach is that the graphs are typically made by hand and are therefore static and cannot easily adapt to changes in the level.

Alternatively, it is possible to extend navmeshes to be used for flight path planning. A series of navmeshes can be created at various heights above the ground. Special flight-links can be used to connect these meshes to allow flying avatars to path up or down through the multiple layers of NavMesh. This technique can work well in confined spaces such as indoors or for creatures restricted to hovering near the ground. In very large volumes, such as a 2 km by 2 km by 2 km cube in an asteroid field, it becomes impossible to decide how many layers of NavMesh will be required to cover the volume adequately.

Regular grids are another option, though the sheer size of the search space is a major drawback. A 3D regular grid covering the aforementioned 2 km cube at 2 m resolution would require a billion grid locations!

Given the issues mentioned with each approach, an adaptive representation of the volume is required. More detail is needed in the dense, cluttered regions and wide the open regions should occupy as little memory as possible. Ideally, this representation can be constructed quickly and dynamically at runtime in order to handle dynamic levels where the collision geometry is not known ahead of time.

24.3 Sparse Voxel Octrees

SVOs are a popular graphics structure used for lighting and ray-tracing. Since they are essentially an octree, they facilitate fast position lookups, as you hierarchically split the volume into eight partitions at each level of the tree. The data structure contains neighbor connectivity information instead of just parent–child links to speed up traversal through the tree for ray-tracing. We can repurpose this connectivity information for path planning. There are several techniques for constructing SVOs, some of which boast interactive frame-rate performance by optimizing and parallelizing the construction algorithm (Schwarz and Seidel 2010). These optimizations are beyond the scope of this chapter, however you can refer to their paper for further information.

One big difference between a typical octree data structure and an SVO is the way the data are stored in memory. In an SVO, the data for each level of the tree are usually compacted together and stored in Morton Code order in memory. The Morton order is a z-shaped space-filling curve that maps three-dimensional coordinates into a one-dimensional sequence (Morton 1966, Haverkort and Freek van Walderveen 2008). It does this by interleaving the bits from each coordinate. For instance, the 2D x/y coordinate (0,3) is represented in binary as (00,11) and encoded as 1010. This method has the advantageous property of keeping neighbors within a quadtree or octree locally coherent. Figure 24.1 shows how Morton Codes fill 2D and 3D space. Storing the nodes in Morton order flattens the entire three-dimensional octree into a linear, one-dimensional array.

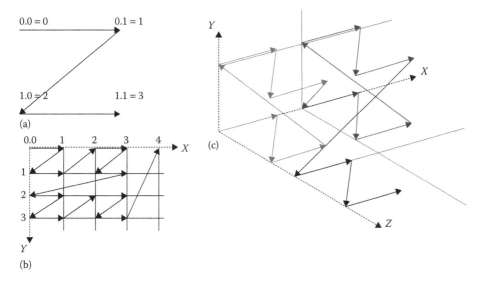

Figure 24.1

Diagrams showing 2D Morton Order (a, b). Note how the two-dimensional coordinates are mapped onto a single-dimensional sequence, shown by the line with arrows. 3D coordinates are mapped onto a single-dimensional sequence of Morton Codes in a similar fashion (c).

Figure 24.2 provides a high-level illustration of how the data in the SVO are arranged. Nodes from each level of the octree are stored in their own array, shown in the upper right of the figure, and the leaf nodes are stored in a separate array of 64-bit values. Following are the details of what is stored each node, and how the leaf nodes differ from other nodes in the SVO.

Each node in the tree requires a position so we know where it is in space. It also needs a link to its lower resolution parent node and a link to the first, higher resolution, child node. All nodes, except leaf nodes, will always have eight children. Since these children are stored contiguously in Morton Code order, we only need a link to the first child, and we can simply offset 0–7 to go to individual child nodes. Additionally, to help in traversal through the tree, each node contains six links to its neighbors through each of its faces.

Leaf nodes are handled differently. Since we are only concerned with collision or free space, our voxel data require only a single bit to store its state. The overhead of storing links with each voxel would be too costly. We can however use a small, compact $4 \times 4 \times 4$ voxel grid for each leaf; this fits nicely into 64 bits.

When dealing with massive environments, every bit of memory is important. Using pointers for links will mean that the data size will vary drastically between 32 bit and 64 bit operating systems. In order to control memory usage, offsets into arrays are used for the links instead of pointers. Links are a general purpose way of referencing both an arbitrary node in the octree and an arbitrary voxel. They are used both within the octree and in the A* search. So, links need to be able to go up and down layers of the octree, not only between neighbors on the same layer. Additionally, the voxels in our leaf nodes are really

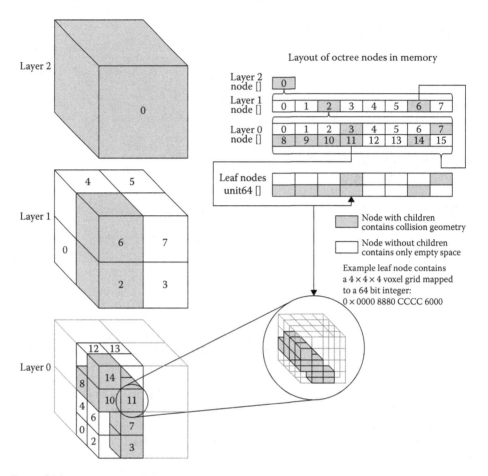

Figure 24.2

Simple illustration of the arrangement of the nodes in a Sparse Voxel Octree. Each occupied node in a layer has eight children in the layer below it. The bottom-most layer maps directly onto the leaf node array. The leaf nodes, however, are not Octree nodes but simply a 64-bit integer representing a 4 × 4 × 4 voxel grid.

compound nodes representing 64 different locations, which we call subnodes. We pack our links into 32 bit integers as follows:

> 4 bits—layer index 0 to 15
> 22 bits—node index 0 to 4,194,303
> 6 bit—subnode index 0 to 63 (only used for indexing voxels inside leaf nodes)

24.4 Creating the SVO

We based our construction of the SVO on the article mentioned in the previous section (Schwarz and Seidel 2010). The tree is constructed from the bottom up, one layer at a time. This is different from the typical octree construction that splits parent nodes from the top down until arriving at the desired resolution of the child node. Doing it one layer at a time keeps each layer coherent in memory and also allows for parallelization to speed up the construction.

The first step is to determine how many leaf nodes are required. To do this, rasterize the collision geometry at a low resolution. If the final resolution is 2 m per voxel, then the leaf nodes in the SVO will be $4 \times 2 = 8$ m cubes. The parent of a leaf node will always have to be split; this means having two leaf nodes next to each other in each direction. The low-resolution rasterization can therefore be performed at a 16 m resolution, which is effectively layer 1 in the octree, where the leaves are in layer 0. Instead of rasterizing into a voxel grid, we simply keep a sorted list of unique Morton Codes of the solid voxels.

Once complete, the number of leaf nodes required can be calculated by counting the number of unique Morton Codes from the low resolution (layer 1) rasterize step. Eight leaf nodes (at layer 0) are required for each Morton Code. Their 3D coordinates can be calculated from the Morton Codes, and the memory for the nodes can be allocated and initialized in a single contiguous block.

The octree structure can now be built up from the lowest to the highest level. Bitwise operations can be used to modify nodes at the current level to get the Morton Code for the parent level. The parent–child links between layers are filled in on the way up; afterward the neighbor links are filled in while traversing back down.

If a node has no neighbor at the same level, then the neighbor link is set to that node's higher level parent's neighbor. This ensures that each node always has a link to a neighbor through each of its faces. Figure 24.3 illustrates how the neighbor links are set up.

Finally, rasterization is performed at the desired resolution into the leaf nodes. Note that unlike a traditional octree, the term leaf node only refers to the occupied, highest resolution nodes in the octree, that is, layer 0 nodes. The SVO only requires leaf nodes where collision geometry exists. A higher layer node that does not contain any collision geometry will not have any child nodes. These nodes are referred to as childless nodes

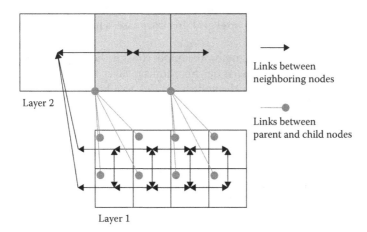

Links between
neighboring nodes

Links between
parent and child nodes

Layer 2

Layer 1

Figure 24.3

Neighbor links in the Sparse Voxel Octree connect to neighbors of the same layer, and if there is no neighbor in the same layer, the neighbor links point to the parent's neighbor.

instead of leaf nodes in traditional octrees. Taking the example SVO in Figure 24.2, node 0 in layer 1 is a childless node and contains only empty space and can be freely traversed. Node 6 in layer 1 however, does have children: layer 0, nodes 8–15. Most leaf nodes, such as node 11 in layer 0, will be partially blocked and have some solid and some empty voxels.

Some leaf nodes will be completely free of collision geometry, such as node 0 in layer 0. The data payload for a leaf is only a 64-bit integer, and an empty leaf will contain the value 0. These nodes can be considered padding for memory alignment. The speed advantage of not culling them outweighs the small additional memory cost. As explained below, during pathfinding, any leaf node with a value of 0 can be skipped over, as it is open space, and any node with a value of –1, or 0xFFFFFFFFFFFFFFFF, will be fully blocked and need not be explored.

24.5 Pathfinding through a SVO

The SVO is now a connected graph representing the free space that agents can traverse. A graph search algorithm can be used to find paths through this space. We initially chose to implement the standard A* search.

The first step is to look up the locations of the start and end points for the desired path and push the start node onto the open list. Next, pop the best node off the open list and mark it as visited. Expand this node by getting the neighboring nodes, scoring them with the A* f-cost, distance traveled plus the estimate of the distance to goal, and then push them onto the open list. This continues until the end point is reached.

Looking up positions is the same in an SVO as in a standard octree. Start at the top of the tree and test whether the point is inside the axis-aligned box of each child. Once the child containing the point has been identified, we repeat the test one layer deeper down the octree. Since octrees subdivide the volume by eight at each layer of the tree, this procedure is very fast. If we arrive at a childless node, then the point is inside a large volume of empty space. If we arrive at a leaf node, then we can calculate which voxel within the leaf contains the point. We refer to this as the subnode index, and it ranges from 0 to 63 as it indexes a specific bit in the 64-bit voxel grid. In either case, a link can be used to represent this location.

To explore nodes in the SVO graph, we simply consult the neighbor links. Referring back to Figure 24.2, layer 1 node 4 has neighbor links to layer 1 node 0, layer 1 node 5, and layer 1 node 6. It is not a problem if a node has a link to a higher level node (e.g., layer 1 linking to layer 2), as this means the search is moving into a larger open space. The search can freely jump between layers of the SVO as necessary.

A minor complication comes when moving from a low-resolution level to a neighbor that has higher resolution children, such as going from layer 1 node 4 to layer 1 node 6 in Figure 24.2. This is solved by pushing the low-resolution node (i.e., layer 1 node 6) to the open list when first encountered. When this node is popped off, instead of processing it as normal, we find the higher resolution children that are neighbors of the previous node and score and push those onto the open list. In our Figure 24.2 example, these new nodes would be layer 0 nodes 8, 9, 12, and 13. The search loop then proceeds as normal. Figure 24.4 shows a 2D example of the order of exploration of nodes jumping from higher level layers through lower level nodes and back up to higher level nodes again.

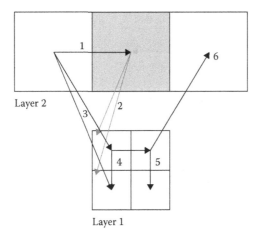

Figure 24.4

Node expansion during A* search. To expand a node that has higher resolution children, add the children neighboring the previous node to the open list and expand each of them in turn through the usual search loop.

Another complication to the search arises when we reach a leaf node. The voxel grid representing each leaf is a 64-bit integer. If this value is 0, it means the leaf node is a empty space, and it is treated like any other node in the tree. If the value is 0×FFFFFFFFFFFFFFFF, or −1, it means the leaf is entirely solid and will block all movement. This node is then marked closed, and the search will continue through the rest of the open nodes. Any other value means the leaf node contains some open space and some solid collision.

Each voxel can be treated as a separate node in the search graph. However, there are no explicit links in these tiny 4 × 4 × 4 voxel grids. Neighbors are calculated implicitly between voxels based on the 3D coordinates within the voxel grid. To avoid confusion between voxels and octree nodes, voxels inside leaf nodes are referred to by the subnode index, which is simply the 6-bit index into the 64-bit integer representing the voxel in the 4 × 4 × 4 grid. Once we reach edge of the tiny voxel grid, the search continues to the neighbor of the leaf node containing the grid.

24.6 Complications and Optimizations

It is easy to forget how big the 3D search space can get. Adding visualizations and statistics to the search will show how much space A* is actually searching. The results can be significantly larger than anticipated (Brewer 2015). The adaptive grid nature of the octree certainly helps the search jump over large tracts of open space. However, the plain A* search is designed to find the optimal path and will often get bogged down exploring all the tiny nodes in the densely populated regions instead of circling around them through larger nodes. Figure 24.5 shows a simple form of this "leap-ahead-and-back-fill" problem.

It is possible to tweak the distances by using center of faces of the cubes instead of node centers and to use Manhattan distance instead of Euclidian distance. This tends to

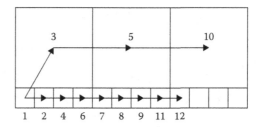

Figure 24.5

Vanilla A* search does not take advantage of exploring larger nodes and instead goes back to explore all the small nodes on a more direct route to the goal.

only help in simple cases and does not provide as much benefit in more complex maps. It is important to experiment on your own maps to see which is better for your specific situation.

Another optimization is to bias the A* toward a greedier search by weighting the score more toward the estimation than the distance traveled. This is not an uncommon A* optimization in games (Rabin and Sturtevant 2013) and adjusts the search to prefer exploring nodes it thinks are closer to the goal. This greedy approach does help significantly, however the search can still push through lots of tiny nodes instead of taking advantage of the larger, open ones.

The heuristic can further be adjusted with a node size compensation factor. In this approach, both the cost and estimation values are adjusted depending on the size of the node. Different compensation amounts are used for each component. The goal is to make it cheaper to go through large nodes and more expensive to go through small ones. This helps dramatically, but one final adjustment is to use a unit cost for distance traveled instead of Euclidian distance. This means that no matter how big the node is, traveling through it has the same cost. This effectively biases the search even more toward exploring through large nodes.

Using a greedy search and node size compensation are always at least an order of magnitude better than straight A* and using unit node costs helps the search use the larger nodes and more often than not, gets an extra order of magnitude speed boost. The resulting path is not an optimal path. Agents will prefer to stay to open-space regions and will tend to avoid dense clusters of collision geometry, unless it is necessary to navigate into them.

The next problem that still hurts the optimized heuristic is an expected A* issue that gets exacerbated in 3D. This is the wave-front exploration pattern as A* tries to search around an obstacle. In 2D, when A* hits a line obstacle, it spreads out to either side in order to try find a way around. In 3D when the search hits an obstacle, it has to explore up and down as well as left and right. This can result in an expanding cone of explored nodes, spreading out behind the surface until a way around is found.

JPS (Harabor and Grastien 2011) is one approach to overcome the A* wave-front expansion shortfall. It should be possible to extend our 3D search in the same way. We attempted this approach and found a great reduction in the number of nodes expanded during the

24. 3D Flight Navigation Using Sparse Voxel Octrees

search, however the time taken for the search was actually an order of magnitude slower than the tweaked heuristic A*. Our initial implementation of 3D JPS was admittedly quite naive and unoptimized, however JPS still visits a lot of nodes in 2D while finding the jump points, and in 3D, this becomes an $O(n^3)$ flood fill instead of $O(n^2)$. This optimization was not pursued further, though a form of jump point expansion may prove to be a useful optimization. Caution must be taken to ensure that it does in fact improve performance instead of hindering it. See (Sturtevant and Rabin 2016) for more discussion of these issues.

Another obvious optimization would be to use a hierarchical search. Since we already have a hierarchical graph structure, this does seem like an obvious choice. This approach would find a path at the lowest resolution and then refine the higher detail levels until a suitably detailed path has been found. However, doing this would require the search to know whether it can traverse from each face to every other face of each node at every level of the tree. Care needs to be taken, so this extra information does not end up bloating memory usage substantially. This is still an option worthy of future exploration, as it may substantially help the search performance.

24.7 Conclusion

As video game environments become more complex and detailed, players are becoming more demanding of new gameplay experiences. Using octrees for 3D navigation is not a particularly novel idea, however if you have never faced this problem, it can be a daunting problem space with many unforeseen traps. The advice provided in this chapter should provide you with a good starting direction.

If you do not take anything else away from this chapter, be sure to add visualizations and statistical reports to your algorithms to fully understand how they are functioning and ensure they are functioning as intended.

References

Brewer, D. 2015. Getting off the NavMesh: Navigating in Fully 3D Environments. GDC 2015. San Francisco, CA: AAAI Press. Slides http://www.gdcvault.com/play/1022017/Getting-off-the-NavMesh-Navigating, Video http://www.gdcvault.com/play/1022016/Getting-off-the-NavMesh-Navigating.

Harabor, D., and Grastien, A. 2011. Online graph pruning for pathfinding on grid maps. In *Proceedings of the 25th National Conference on Artificial Intelligence (AAAI)*. San Francisco, CA. https://users.cecs.anu.edu.au/~dharabor/data/papers/harabor-grastien-aaai11.pdf.

Haverkort, H., and van Walderveen, F. 2008. Space-filling curves for spatial data structures. TU Eindhoven. http://www.win.tue.nl/~hermanh/stack/dagstuhl08-talk.pdf.

Morton, G. M. 1966. *A Computer Oriented Geodetic Data Base and a New Technique in File Sequencing. Technical Report.* Ottawa, Canada: IBM Ltd.

Rabin, S., and Sturtevant, N. R. 2013. Pathfinding architecture optimizations. In *Game AI Pro*, ed. S. Rabin. Boca Raton, FL: CRC Press, pp. 241–252. http://www.gameaipro.com/GameAIPro/GameAIPro_Chapter17_Pathfinding_Architecture_Optimizations.pdf.

Schwarz, M., and Seidel, H. P. 2010. Fast Parallel Surface and Solid Voxelization on GPUs. *ACM Transactions on Graphics, 29, 6 (Proceedings of SIGGRAPH Asia 2010), Article 179*. New York, NY: ACM. http://research.michael-schwarz.com/publ/files/vox-siga10.pdf.

Sturtevant, N. R., and Rabin, S. 2016. Canonical orderings on grids. In *International Joint Conference on Artificial Intelligence*. New York: IJCAI, pp. 683–689. http://web.cs.du.edu/~sturtevant/papers/SturtevantRabin16.pdf.

25

Faster A* with Goal Bounding

Steve Rabin and Nathan R. Sturtevant

25.1 Introduction

Goal bounding is a pathfinding optimization technique that can speed up A* by roughly eight times on a grid (Rabin and Sturtevant 2016), however, it is applicable to any graph search space, including waypoint graphs or navmeshes (navigation meshes). Goal bounding is not a search algorithm itself, but rather a method to *prune* the search space, thus radically reducing the number of nodes that need to be considered to find the goal. This is accomplished by preprocessing the search space offline and using the precomputed data to avoid exploring many nodes that do not lead to the goal.

This chapter will introduce the goal-bounding concept, walk through the runtime code, and then show the necessary preprocessing steps. We will then discuss experimental data that shows the effective speed-up to a standard A* implementation.

25.1.1 Goal-Bounding Constraints

Goal bounding has three constraints that limit whether it is appropriate to use in your game:

1. *Map constraint:* The map must be static and cannot change during gameplay. Nodes and edges cannot be added or deleted.

2. *Memory constraint:* For each node in the map, there is a requirement of four values per node edge in memory during runtime. Grid nodes have eight edges, and navmesh nodes have three edges. Typically, each value is 2 bytes.

3. *Precomputation constraint:* The precomputation is $O(n^2)$ in the number of nodes. This is a costly computation and can take from 5 minutes to several hours per map. This is performed offline before the game ships.

The most important constraint is that your game maps must be static. That is to say that the nodes and edges in your search space must not change during gameplay, and the cost to go from one node to another must also not change. The reason is that connection data must be precomputed. Changing a single node, edge, or cost would invalidate all of the precomputed data. Because the precomputed data takes so long to create, it is not feasible to dynamically rerun the computation if the map changes.

The other primary constraint is that goal bounding requires extra memory at runtime for the precomputed data. For every node, there has to be four values per edge leading to another node. On a grid, each node has eight edges (or connections) to other nodes, so the necessary data for a grid search space are 32 values per node. On a navmesh, typically each poly node has three edges, so the necessary data for a navmesh search space are 12 values per poly node. Typically, these values will need to be 2 bytes each, but for smaller maps, 1 byte each might suffice (e.g., a grid map with a height and width less than 256).

Lastly, a minor constraint is that each map must be precomputed offline, which takes time. The precomputation algorithm is $O(n^2)$ in the number of total nodes on the map. For example, a very large 1000×1000 grid map would have 1 million nodes, requiring $1,000,000^2$ or 1 trillion operations during precomputation for that map. Depending on the map size, this can take between 5 minutes and several hours per map. It is computationally demanding enough that you could not precompute the data at runtime. However, there are optimizations to Dijkstra for uniform cost grids, such as Canonical Dijkstra that can make this computation much faster (Sturtevant and Rabin 2017).

Fortunately, there are many things that are not constraints for goal bounding. For example, the following aspects are very flexible:

1. Goal-bounding works on *any* graph search space, including grids, waypoint graphs, quadtrees, octrees, and navmeshes, as long as the points in these graphs are associated with coordinates in space.

2. Goal bounding can be applied to *any* search algorithm (A*, Dijkstra, JPS+, etc.). Typically, A* is best for games, but goal bounding can work with Dijkstra and works extremely well with JPS+ (a variant of A* only for uniform cost grids).

3. The map can have nonuniform costs between nodes, meaning the cost to go from one node to another node can vary as long as it does not change during the game. Some algorithms like JPS+ have restrictions such that they only work on uniform cost grids, where the cost between grid squares must be consistent.

25.2 Concept

The name *goal bounding* comes from the core concept. For each edge adjacent to a node, we precompute a bounding box (4 values) that contains all goals that can be optimally reached by exploring this edge. At runtime, we only explore this node's edge if the goal of the search lies in the bounding box. Reread those last two sentences again, because this is the entire runtime algorithm.

In Figure 25.1, consider the node marked with a circle. The gray nodes in the left map can all be reached *optimally* by exploring the left edge of the circle node (we will discuss later how this is computed). The gray *bounding box* in the right map contains all of the gray nodes from the left map and represents what needs to be precomputed (4 values that define a bounding box: left, right, top, and bottom). This precomputed bounding box is stored in the left edge of the circle node. At runtime, if we are at the circle node and considering exploring the left edge, we would check to see if the goal lies in the bounding box. If it does, we explore this edge as is normally done in the A* algorithm. If the goal does not lie in the bounding box, we skip this edge (the edge is pruned from the search).

Goal bounding can be similarly applied to navmeshes. Consider the black node in the navmesh in Figure 25.2. The dark gray nodes can be reached optimally through the bottom right edge of the black node. Figure 25.3 shows a bounding box around these nodes. This is the identical concept as shown on the grid in Figure 25.1.

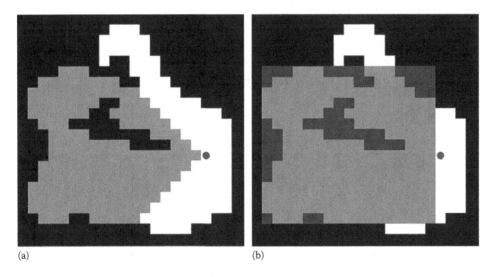

(a) (b)

Figure 25.1

The map in (a) shows all of the nodes (in gray) that can be reached optimally by exploring the left edge of the circle node. The map in (b) shows a bounding box of the nodes in the left image. This bounding box is stored in the left edge of the circle node.

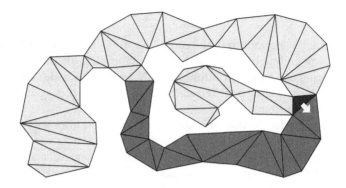

Figure 25.2

Nodes marked in dark gray can be reached optimally from exploring the bottom right edge of the black node. All other nodes in the map can only be reached optimally by exploring either the top edge or the left edge of the black node.

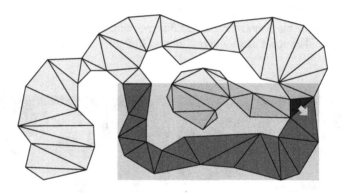

Figure 25.3

The bounding box containing all nodes that can be reached optimally from the bottom right edge of the black node. In goal bounding, this bounding box is stored in the bottom right edge of the black node.

25.3 Runtime

For A* with goal bounding to work, it is assumed that every node edge has a precomputed bounding box containing all nodes that can be reached optimally through that edge. With this data, the only addition to the runtime is a simple check, as shown in bold in Listing 25.1.

The goal-bounding check in Listing 25.1 tests whether we really want to explore a neighboring node, through the parent node's edge. If the check succeeds (the goal of the search is within the bounding box), then the search algorithm proceeds as normal through this edge. If the check fails, the edge is *pruned* by simply skipping it. This has the dramatic effect of not exploring that edge *and all of the subsequent edges*, thus pruning huge swaths of the search space. This accounts for goal bounding's dramatic speed improvement

Listing 25.1. A* algorithm with the goal bounding check added (in bold).

```
procedure AStarSearch(start, goal)
{
    Push (start, openlist)
    while (openlist is not empty)
    {
        n = PopLowestCost(openlist)

        if (n is goal)
            return success

        foreach (neighbor d in n)
        {
            if (WithinBoundingBox(n, d, goal))
            {
                // Process d in the standard A* manner
            }
        }

        Push (n, closedlist)
    }
    return failure
}
```

(Rabin and Sturtevant 2016). Note that this goal-bounding check can be inserted into any search algorithm at the point the algorithm is considering a neighboring node.

25.4 Precomputation

Precomputation consists of computing a bounding box for every edge of every node. If we can design an algorithm that computes this information for a single node, then it is just a matter of iterating that algorithm over every node in the map. In fact, the problem is *embarrassingly parallel* in which we can kick off one thread per node in the map, since each node's bounding boxes are independent of all other node's bounding boxes. With enough cores running the threads, the precomputation time can be greatly minimized.

To compute the bounding boxes for all edges of a single node, we need to use a slightly enhanced Dijkstra search algorithm. Recall that Dijkstra is the same as A*, but the heuristic cost is zero. This causes the search to spread out evenly, in cost, away from the starting point. For our purposes, we will start the Dijkstra search at our single node and give it no destination, causing it to search all nodes in the map, as if it was performing a floodfill.

Using Dijkstra to floodfill, the map has the effect of marking every node with the *optimal* "next step" to optimally get back to the start node. This next step is simply the parent pointer that is recorded during the search. However, the crucial piece of information that we really want to know for a given node is not the next step to take, but which starting node edge was required to eventually get to that node. Think of every node in the map as being marked with the starting node's edge that is on the optimal path back to the starting node, as shown in Figure 25.4.

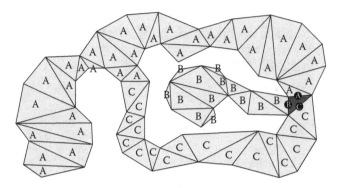

Figure 25.4

The result of a Dijkstra floodfill starting from the black node. Each node during the Dijkstra search is marked with the starting edge on the optimal path back to the starting node.

In a Dijkstra search, this starting node edge is normally not recorded, but now we need to store this information. Every node's data structure needs to contain a new value representing this starting node edge. During the Dijkstra search, when the neighbors of a node are explored, the starting node edge is passed down to the neighboring nodes as they are placed on the open list. This transfers the starting node edge information from node to node during the search.

Once the Dijkstra floodfill has completed, every node is marked with a starting node edge. In the case of Figure 25.4, each node is marked with either an A, B, or C. The final task is to iterate through all nodes in the map and build up the bounding boxes that contain each starting node edge, as shown in Figure 25.5. Once complete, each bounding box (4 values representing left, right, top, and bottom) is stored on the appropriate starting node's edge. This is the data that are used during runtime to prune the search during the goal-bounding check.

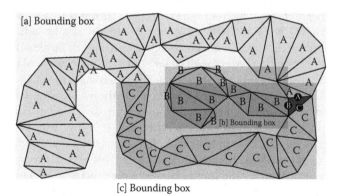

Figure 25.5

All nodes are iterated through to determine each bounding box for each starting edge.

25.5 Empirical Results

In order to evaluate the effectiveness of goal bounding, we applied the algorithm to a similar setup as the Grid-Based Path Planning Competition (Sturtevant 2014), a competition that has run since 2012 for the purpose of comparing different approaches to grid-based path planning. All experiments were performed on maps from the GPPC competition and the Moving AI map repository (Sturtevant 2012). This includes maps from *StarCraft*, *Warcraft III*, and *Dragon Age*. We ran our code on a 2.4 GHz Intel Xeon E5620 with 12 GB of RAM.

Table 25.1 shows the comparison between a highly optimized A* solution, the same A* solution with goal bounding, JPS+, and JPS+ with goal bounding. The A* solution with goal bounding was 8.2 times faster than A* by itself. The JPS+ solution with goal bounding was 7.2 times faster than JPS+.

25.5.1 Applying Goal Bounding to JPS+

As shown in Table 25.1, JPS+ is an algorithm that can dramatically speed up pathfinding compared with A*, however it only works on uniform cost grids (where the cost between nodes must be consistent). JPS+ is a variant of A* that achieves its speed from pruning nodes from the search space, similar to goal bounding. However, JPS+ and goal bounding work in complementary ways so that combined effect is to speed up pathfinding by ~1500 times over A*. Although it is outside the scope of this chapter to explain JPS+ with goal bounding, there are two good resources if you wish to implement it (Rabin 2015, Rabin and Sturtevant 2016).

25.6 Similarities to Previous Algorithms

At its core, goal bounding is an *approximation* of the Floyd–Warshall all-pairs shortest paths algorithm. In Floyd–Warshall, the path between every single pair of nodes is precomputed and stored in a look-up table. Using Floyd–Warshall at runtime, no search algorithm is run, because the optimal path is simply looked up. This requires an enormous amount of data, which is $O(n^2)$ in the number of nodes. This amount of data is impractical for most games. For example, a *StarCraft* map of roughly 1000×1000 nodes would require about four terabytes.

As goal bounding is an approximation of Floyd–Warshall, it does not require nearly as much data. However, as mentioned previously in Section 25.1.1, it does require 32 values per node on a grid search space and 12 values per node on a navmesh search space (assuming triangular nodes). A *StarCraft* map of roughly 1000×1000 nodes would

Table 25.1 Comparison of Search Algorithm Speeds

Algorithm	Time (ms)	A* Factor
A*	15.492	1.0
A* with goal bounding	1.888	8.2
JPS+	0.072	215.2
JPS+ with goal bounding	0.010	1549.2

require about 60 MB of goal bounding data. Luckily, modern games using a navmesh might only have about 4000 total nodes for a level, which would require less than 100 KB of goal-bounding data.

The goal-bounding algorithm was first introduced as an optimization to Dijkstra on road networks in 2005 and at the time was called geometric containers (Wagner et al. 2005). In 2014, Rabin independently reinvented geometric containers for use with A* and JPS+, introducing it as goal bounding to a GDC audience (Rabin 2015). Due to this history, it would be appropriate to refer to the algorithm as either geometric containers (Wagner et al. 2005), goal bounding (Rabin 2015), or simply as bounding boxes (Rabin and Sturtevant 2016).

25.7 Conclusion

For games that meet the constraints, goal bounding can speed up pathfinding dramatically—by nearly an order of magnitude. Not only can goal bounding be applied to any search algorithm on any type of search space, it can also be applied with other optimizations, such as hierarchical pathfinding, overestimating the heuristic, or open list optimizations (Rabin and Sturtevant 2013).

References

Rabin, S. 2015. JPS+ now with Goal Bounding: Over 1000 × Faster than A*, GDC 2015. http://www.gameaipro.com/Rabin_AISummitGDC2015_JPSPlusGoalBounding.zip (accessed February 12, 2017).

Rabin, S., and Sturtevant, N. R. 2013. Pathfinding optimizations. In *Game AI Pro*, ed. S. Rabin. Boca Raton, FL: CRC Press.

Rabin, S., and Sturtevant, N. R. 2016. Combining Bounding Boxes and JPS to Prune Grid Pathfinding, *AAAI'16 Proceedings of the Thirtieth AAAI Conference on Artificial Intelligence*. Phoenix, AZ: AAAI.

Sturtevant, N. R. 2012. Benchmarks for grid-based pathfinding. *Transactions on Computational Intelligence and AI in Games*, 4(2), 144–148.

Sturtevant, N. R. 2014. The grid-based path-planning competition. *AI Magazine*, 35(3), 66–68.

Sturtevant, N. R., and Rabin, S. 2017. Faster Dijkstra search on uniform cost grids. In *Game AI Pro 3*, ed. S. Rabin. Boca Raton, FL: CRC Press.

Wagner, D., Willhalm, T., and Zaroliagis, C. D. 2005. Geometric containers for efficient shortest-path computation. *ACM Journal of Experimental Algorithmics*, 10.

26

Faster Dijkstra Search on Uniform Cost Grids

Nathan R. Sturtevant and Steve Rabin

26.1 Introduction

Dijkstra search is commonly used for single-source shortest path computations, which can provide valuable information about distances between states for many purposes in games, such as heuristics (Rabin and Sturtevant 2013), influence maps, or other analysis. In this chapter, we describe how we borrowed recent ideas from Jump Point Search (JPS) (Harabor and Grastien 2011) to significantly speed up Dijkstra search on uniform cost grids. We call this new algorithm Canonical Dijkstra. Although the algorithm has been described before (Sturtevant and Rabin 2016), this chapter provides more detail and examples of how the algorithms work in practice. This is just one example of how the ideas of JPS can be applied more broadly; we hope this will become a valuable part of your library of approaches. Note that the chapter does assume that the reader is familiar with how A* works.

26.2 Decomposing Jump Point Search

As Canonical Dijkstra builds on the ideas of JPS, we will describe the key ideas from JPS first. JPS has been described elsewhere in this book series (Rabin and Silva 2015). We describe it here in a slightly different manner (following Sturtevant and Rabin 2016) that will greatly simplify our presentation of Canonical Dijkstra.

26.2.1 Canonical Ordering of Paths

One of the problems with search on grids is that there are many duplicate paths between states. While A* will find these duplicates and avoid putting duplicates on the open list, it is costly to do so, because we still generate all of these states during the search and must look them up to detect that they are duplicates. It would be better if we could never generate the duplicates in the first place.

We can do this in two steps. In the first step, we generate a basic canonical ordering. A canonical ordering is a way of choosing which optimal path we prefer among all possible optimal paths. In Figure 26.1, we show a small map that has three possible optimal paths between the start and the goal. We define the canonical path as the path that has all diagonal moves before cardinal moves. It is more efficient to only generate the canonical path(s) and never generate any other paths.

We can generate states according to the canonical ordering directly (without comparing optimal paths) by limiting the successors of each state according to the parent. If the current state was reached by a diagonal action, then we allow three legal moves from the child: (1) the same diagonal action that was used to reach the state and (2 and 3) the two cardinal components of the same diagonal action. If a cardinal action (N/S/E/W) was used to reach a state, the only legal move is to move in the same direction. In the canonical ordering, we always take diagonal actions before cardinal actions, so once a cardinal action is part of a path, all remaining actions must also be cardinal actions.

We illustrate this in part (a) on the left of Figure 26.2, where the start state is marked with an "S" and lines label the canonical paths. Each state that is reached is reached optimally by a single path, and no duplicates will be generated. But, we also notice that not all states in the map are reached. In particular, there are obstacles that block some canonical paths. Luckily, we can fix this problem when generating the canonical ordering.

Suppose the search is currently moving north. Normally the search would continue north until an obstacle was reached and then would stop. But now, we need to do one additional check. If the search passes on obstacle to the east, which then ends, it knows that the basic canonical ordering will not reach this state. So, we need to reset the canonical ordering to allow it to reach states that are blocked by obstacles. We illustrate this in part (b) on the right of Figure 26.2. The black dots are the places where the canonical ordering was restarted (once again allowing diagonal moves) after passing obstacles. These dots are called *jump points*.

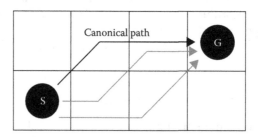

Figure 26.1

The canonical path (top) has diagonal actions before cardinal actions, unlike the noncanonical paths (in gray).

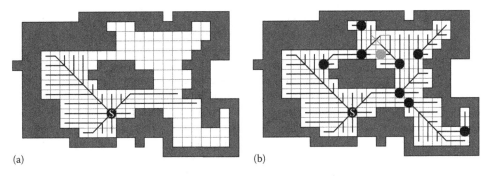

(a)   (b)

Figure 26.2

(a) The basic canonical ordering starting from the state marked S. (b) The full canonical ordering, including jump points (black circles).

Using jump points guarantees that every state in the map will be reached. While the number of duplicate paths is greatly reduced, because we only generate successors along the black lines, there still can be duplicates such as the one jump point in gray. This jump point can be reached from two different directions. Search is needed to resolve the optimal path lengths in this region of the map.

26.2.2 JPS and Canonical Orderings

We can now describe JPS in terms of the canonical ordering. The basic version of JPS does no preprocessing on the map before search. At runtime, it starts at the start state and generates a basic canonical ordering. All states visited when generating the canonical ordering are immediately discarded with the exception of jump points and the goal state, which are placed in the open list. It then chooses the best state from the open list to expand next. If this state is the goal, it terminates. Otherwise, it generates the canonical ordering from this new state, putting any new jump points or the goal into the open list. This process continues until the goal is found. It is possible that a jump point can be reached from two different directions, which is why jump points need to be placed in the open list. This ensures that a jump point is not expanded until it is reached with the optimal path.

JPS can be seen as searching on an abstract graph defined by the jump points and the goal in the graph. These are the only states that are put into the open list. But, because it has not preprocessed the map, it still has to scan the map to find the jump points and the goal. Scanning the map is far faster than putting all of these states into the open list, so JPS is usually faster than a regular A* search. Note, however, that JPS might scan more of the map than is necessary. So, in large, wide open spaces JPS can have a significant overhead. Given this understanding of JPS, we can now describe Canonical Dijkstra.

26.3 Canonical Dijkstra

Canonical Dijkstra is, in many ways, similar to JPS. It uses the canonical ordering to generate states and searches over jump points. But, while JPS only puts jump points and the goal into the open and closed lists, Canonical Dijkstra needs to record the distance to every state in the state space in the closed list. Thus, Canonical Dijkstra must write the g-cost of every state that it visits (not just the jump points) into the closed list. This is where Canonical Dijkstra saves over a regular Dijkstra search—Dijkstra's algorithm would put all of these states into the open list before expanding them and writing their costs to the closed list. Canonical Dijkstra writes these values directly to the closed list.

We show the first step of Canonical Dijkstra in Figure 26.3, but now we label the g-cost of each state as it is filled in by the search. In this example, diagonals have cost 1.5. To begin (part (a) on the left), the start is in open with cost 0.0. When the start state is expanded (part (b) on the right), the canonical ordering is generated, and the g-cost of every state visited is filled in a single step. Three jump points are reached, which are added to the open list; these states are marked with circles. This process continues until all states are reached by the search.

The most interesting step is shown in Figure 26.4. Here we see what happens when the search reaches the same state from different directions. The next state to be expanded

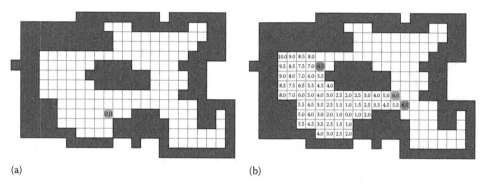

(a)   (b)

Figure 26.3

The first step of Canonical Dijkstra. Initially, (a) the start state is in the open list with cost 0. After the first expansion step, (b) the canonical ordering is followed until jump points are reached, and all visited states are labeled with their g-costs.

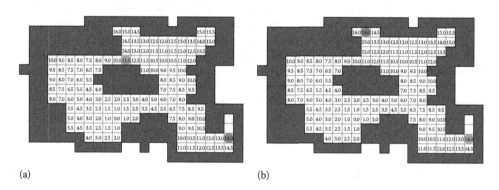

(a)   (b)

Figure 26.4

(a) In this step, Canonical Dijkstra expands the state at the top, finding a shorter path to several states nearby that have already been visited. (b) The search also finds a state that was not previously a jump point, but when reached from the new path is now a jump point.

(part (a) on the left) has cost 11.0 and is found at the top of the map. This state can reach its N, NE, and E neighbors with shorter path cost than they were previously reached. So, the g-costs are updated (part (b) on the right) after the node is expanded. One of these states (with g-cost 14.0 in the top side of the figure) was not previously a jump point. But, when reached from this direction, this state is a jump point. So, the state must be removed from the closed list and put onto the open list for further expansion.

Pseudocode for the Canonical Dijkstra algorithm can be found in Listing 26.1. The main procedure is a best-first search that repeatedly removes the best state from the open list. The canonical ordering code is the meat of the algorithm. While generating the canonical ordering, it keeps track of the current g-cost. As long as the canonical ordering finds a shorter cost path to a given state, the g-costs for that state are written directly into the closed list. When the canonical ordering generates a state with equal or larger g-cost than the copy in the open list, the process stops. When the canonical ordering finds a jump point, it adds that jump point to the open list. Since there is no goal, we do not have to check for the goal.

Listing 26.1. Canonical Dijkstra pseudocode.

```
CanonicalDijkstra(start)
{
    initialize all states to be in closed with cost ∞
    place start in open with cost 0
    while (open not empty)
        remove best from open
        CanonicalOrdering(best, parent of best, 0)
}

CanonicalOrdering(child, parent, cost)
{
    if (child in closed)
        if (cost of child in closed > cost)
            update cost of child in closed
        else
            return
    if (child is jump point)
        if on closed, remove from closed
        update parent // for canonical ordering
        add child to open with cost
    else if (action from parent to child is diagonal d)
        next = Apply(d, child)
        CanonicalOrdering(next, child, cost + diagonal)
        next = Apply(first cardinal in d, child)
        CanonicalOrdering(next, child, cost + cardinal)
        next = Apply(second cardinal in d, child)
        CanonicalOrdering(next, child, cost + cardinal)
    else if (action from parent to child is cardinal c)
        next = Apply(c, child)
        CanonicalOrdering(next, child, cost + cardinal)
}
```

26.3.1 Performance

The performance of Canonical Dijkstra depends on the type of map used. In random maps, there are many jump points, so the savings are lesser than on maps with larger open areas, where many g-costs can be written very quickly, bypassing the open list. We found 2.5× speedup on random maps and a 4.0× speedup on maps from *StarCraft*. These savings were independent of whether the base implementation was standard or high performance.

26.4 Conclusion

This chapter shows that JPS is using a canonical ordering to avoid duplicates during search. It borrows the idea of the canonical ordering to build an improved version of Dijkstra search that can perform single-source shortest path computations more efficiently by avoiding putting too many states into the open list.

References

Harabor, D. and Grastien, A. 2011. Online graph pruning for pathfinding on grid maps. In *Proceedings of the Twenty-Fifth {AAAI} Conference on Artificial Intelligence*. San Francisco, CA, pp. 1114–1119.

Rabin, S. and Sturtevant, N. R. 2013. Pathfinding architecture optimizations. In *Game AI Pro*, ed S. Rabin. Boca Raton, FL: CRC Press, pp. 241–252. http://www.gameaipro.com/GameAIPro/GameAIPro_Chapter17_Pathfinding_Architecture_Optimizations.pdf.

Rabin, S. and Silva, F. 2015. JPS+: An extreme A* speed optimization for static uniform cost grids. In *Game AI Pro 2*, ed. S. Rabin. Boca Raton, FL: CRC Press, pp. 131–143.

Sturtevant, N. R. and Rabin, S. 2016. Canonical Orderings on Grids, *International Joint Conference on Artificial Intelligence (IJCAI)*, pp. 683–689. http://web.cs.du.edu/~sturtevant/papers/SturtevantRabin16.pdf.

Printed in the United States
by Baker & Taylor Publisher Services